AN APPROACH TO QUALITY IMPROVEMENT THAT WORKS

SECOND EDITION

To Lea, Todd, and Mark
with love and gratitude.

AN APPROACH TO QUALITY IMPROVEMENT THAT WORKS

SECOND EDITION

A. DONALD STRATTON

ASQC QUALITY PRESS

AN APPROACH TO QUALITY IMPROVEMENT THAT WORKS, SECOND EDITION

A. Donald Stratton

Library of Congress Cataloging-in-Publication Data

Stratton, A. Donald.
   An approach to quality improvement that works / A.
Donald Stratton. — 2nd ed.
      p. cm.
   Includes bibliographical references (p.) and index.
   ISBN 0-87389-090-6
   1. Quality control. 2 Production management — Quality
   control.
   I. Title.
   TS156.S78 1991
   658.5'62—dc20   90-26339
                                                                  CIP

10987654321

ISBN 0-87389-090-6

Acquisitions Editor: Jeanine L. Lau
Production Editor: Tammy Griffin
Set in Century Schoolbook by DanTon Typographers. Cover design by Artistic
License. Printed and bound by Port City Press.

Printed in the United States of America

ASQC Quality Press
310 West Wisconsin Avenue
Milwaukee, Wisconsin 53203

CONTENTS

FOREWORD

Don Stratton joined StorageTek in August of 1988 shortly after the first edition of his book, *An Approach to Quality Improvement that Works,* appeared in print. Don's passion is to help implement quality improvement throughout our entire organization. We see this as a vital necessity in the decade of the nineties and beyond. Our competition is on this path; our customers demand it, and we are becoming a leader in it.

Don worked with 42 small groups throughout the StorageTek world in his first year. He used the Phase I, II, III approach with heavy emphasis in using the cause and effect/force field analysis (CE/FFA) techniques in Phase II. We saw, over time, improvement in communication, morale, participative management, and time discipline. Over the longer pull we expect to see decided improvement in results across all organizations. We are beginning to see this already.

Don, like other quality professionals, stresses dedication, patience, and time that I am now beginning to understand. There is "no instant pudding" as Dr. Deming has said and we are in the game for the long pull. I have counseled with some of my counterparts, studied the subject of quality improvement, and attended the workshops. I now chair our top level Quality Council that meets regularly to lead the quality effort at StorageTek. I can share this with you:

- The CEO must lead the effort and be the champion.
- Quality cannot be delegated.
- It is a painstakingly slow process.
- Key business processes must be defined and owners determined.
- A specific cross-functional group needs to be the catalyst and guide the effort. This group needs to steer the effort and advise the highest council.
- The quality effort must be pervasive and cover the entire organization.
- Do not put up with the cry for more budget. This is the way we should be doing our jobs in the first place.
- Potential savings are enormous. These start to accrue the minute you start down the quality improvement path.

I feel this book, which is heavily oriented to a technique that has proved successful, will give executives, managers, and quality practitioners the ammunition and perspective to fully implement quality improvement in the 90s. Don's technique is very powerful in capturing the energy, skill, and knowledge of those closest to the work and in a timely manner. This is a key factor in moving organizations forward in this decade.

Ryal Poppa
CEO, Chairman, President
StorageTek

PREFACE

This work would not be possible without the contribution of hundreds of Quality Action Team members. These fine people come from many varied organizations throughout AT&T, Storage Technology Corporation (StorageTek), the Florida Motor Vehicle Agency, the Forestry Division of the Florida Agriculture Department and South Central Bell.

I have been greatly influenced by Dr. W. Edwards Deming's work. I attended his four-day course in October 1983, and took 30 pages of notes to which I still refer to this day. I have read and reread his book, *Quality, Productivity, and Competitive Position,* as well as its successor, *Out of the Crisis.* We owe a lot to NBC for its White Paper entitled "If Japan Can, Why Can't We" for helping discover Dr. Deming in the United States.

The study of Dr. Deming's work combined with over 30 years of experience provided a unique view of what could be done to implement Dr. Deming's philosophies in a meaningful and efficient way.

I have been using force field analysis successfully since 1970 in various projects. When combined with cause and effect studies we have a very powerful tool to develop solutions to problems. It was Dr. Kurt Lewin who developed force field analysis and Dr. Kaoru Ishikawa who developed cause and effect.

I also have had the opportunity to work with a great number of good people who have provided help and encouragement along the way. These include Herman Hasselbauer and Jack Pursel, who were 20 years ahead of their time in management style, Ryal Poppa who continues to encourage and inspire, and fine associates such as Billy Terrell, Darrell Storholt, Len Widra, Carl Perry, Glen Kirk, Susan Anderson, and Jeff Armstrong. My work with the quality advisory group at StorageTek over the last two years has been fruitful. Lillian Simpson of Florida Motor Vehicle and Patrick Fennimore of the Florida Division of Forestry are making a difference.

My association with Dr. Bikramjit S. Garcha and Ken Charon of Georgia State University, as well as Warren Nickel, formerly of IBM, has been helpful. I am indebted to Bill Scherkenbach for his work, support, and book, *The Deming Route to Quality and Productivity,* and also to Masaaki Imai, author of *Kaizen.*

Two secretaries have been outstanding in their efforts to understand poor handwriting and in listening to endless tapes; they are Betty Turner of Atlanta and Barb Kelley of Denver.

But most of all, the main reason for this book is Dr. Deming. A spark was ignited back in 1983 that still burns brightly. He, too, would be one to light a candle rather than curse the darkness. His encouragement through correspondence has caused articles to be published, many talks and seminars to be given, and now this second edition of my book.

INTRODUCTION

Japan now owns a major interest in Rockefeller Center and major real estate all over the U.S. What more do we need to see and hear to wake up. Some areas of American management became serious about quality improvement in the eighties, but I think we have a long way to go in the nineties. Some evidence of this is that very few American companies have won the prestigious Malcolm Baldrige (quality improvement) award. Unfortunately most American industry is still giving lip service to quality improvement. Production cost cutting, meeting schedules, and managing defects come first—not quality. This must change dramatically in the nineties.

Some reasons for our apparent slowness to put quality in the forefront may be:

- Many of our business leaders still come from the days of the fifties and sixties when meeting production and schedules were the only major concerns. Consumers in those days just bought — bought — bought. Producers just produced — produced — produced. When it broke we bought another one.

- The specter of international competition was not a threat. Yes, we had some focus on such competition, but this did not become a substantial threat until the seventies. The automobile industry perhaps felt this the most and took the most dramatic action to turn things around. (Have you driven a Ford lately?)

- True quality improvement takes time. The quality gurus say that if you start now doing all the right things it may take five to eight years to begin to see solid, meaningful results and perhaps a decade to see this perpetrated in all aspects of the company. The Malcolm Baldrige award recognizes this by its reward criteria which examine "how long" a company has been on a true quality improvement path.

- Measurement systems are definitely short term. Quarterly dividends, stock prices, margins, profits, annual budgets, appraisals and reviews are not in sync with a five-year or, even worse, 10-year plan. Can anyone show me a 10-year plan?

- Our penchant for short-term results has also led to a short-term management style. This takes form in two ways. (1) The rapid movement of managers up the line. Two years is thought of as max-time on any one assignment. (2) The exceptionally talented move from industry to industry in pursuit of ever-increasing responsibility. The long-term view is not even in the picture—let alone cared about in the way it should be to achieve meaningful progress.

Although discussing why we are where we are at present is necessary, this is all you will hear of it from me. All too often we read books, and go to lectures, and come away with a major dose of information about what is wrong and find very little about how to improve it. The rest of this book will concentrate on *implementation*. Just as the three most important words in real estate are location, location, location; the three most important words in quality improvement are *implement, implement, implement.*

Two things drive me in this regard. One is the notion that those closest to the work really have an enormous amount of skill, energy, and knowledge that needs to be tapped. Those words are really a combination of thoughts that came to me from great contemporary business leaders whom I quoted in my first book. These include Donald Petersen, CEO of Ford; the late James Olson when he was CEO of AT&T; Michael MacCoby, author of *The Leader*; Robert Waterman and Tom Peters, co-authors of *In Search of Excellence*; and John Naisbitt, co-author of *Reinventing the Corporation.*

I have personally worked with over 100 small groups of people as facilitator. Most of these groups are fine people from AT&T where I worked with pride and a good sense of accomplishment for 31 years, and also Storage Technology Corporation where I now work. In all of this work and experience, I can report with a great deal of confidence that, in fact, those closest to the work do have an enormous amount of skill, energy, and knowledge that needs to be tapped. In my talks throughout the world I remind my audiences of Tom Peters' words in *Thriving on Chaos*:[1]

> Indeed, the chief reason for our failure in world-class competition is our failure to tap our work force's potential.

I ask the audience to remember the words "tap our work force's potential." I tell them, "I know how to do this," and I say the same thing to you. Read this book carefully and learn how to do this, and also learn how to get management's attention and active involvement in this process.

I mentioned earlier that there are two things that drive me. The second is the theory of variability. Dr. W. Edwards Deming first taught me of this in his four-day lecture and it was later reinforced by reading his work *Out of the Crisis*.[2]

Dr. Deming reminds us that the theory of variability was given to us by Dr. Walter Shewhart of Bell Telephone Laboratories in the 1920s. When Dr. Deming opened the 40th Anniversary Congress of the American Society for Quality Control in Anaheim, California, he told an interesting story. He said that Dr. Shewhart went to the Hawthorne Works of the Western Electric plant and tried to explain the theory of variability to the management team in 1924. He said, "They didn't understand it then and they can still make that claim!"

Those of us in the AT&T delegation to that conference felt somewhat embarrassed. Dr. Deming has a way of jolting people with facts that tend to help them over the long pull. As those of us from AT&T discussed Dr. Deming's comment defensively, we began to realize that the truth was that none of us had been taught the Shewhart theory of variability that had been around since 1924. Some of us vowed to not let that happen again—perhaps I was at the forefront of this effort. I discuss this theory in every talk I give, have written about it in several publications, and will discuss it again in this book.

One other idea will be discussed at length that relates directly to implementing the two aforementioned theories. Dr. Deming tells us that it is necessary to base action on theory, and that although the actions resulting from this theory may not be perfect, they can be improved upon over time. The theory in this book is to combine the two disciplines of cause and effect (CE) (Ishikawa)[3] and force field analysis (FFA) (Lewin).[4] When we do this we end up with an extremely powerful implementation tool. When this tool is used with quality action teams (small groups), quality resolution teams (implementation groups), and quality review teams (higher level review) we end up with improved quality and productivity.

This approach, although successful anywhere, is particularly appropriate in the white-collar areas. Leaving out accounting, billing, marketing, customer service, field service, information systems, legal, engineering, and R&D is a fatal error. We must stop looking only to production for productivity and look to the entire corporation. I heard a lecture in which the speaker reported an estimated future loss of $47 billion in information system failures in the U.S. This is 8 percent of GNP. This appears ridiculous when compared to the amount we spend on education which is about 7 percent of GNP.

Some say the way to do it is to reorganize, to put people together who need to work together in the earlier stage of a project, to "give them the resources and get out of their way," to not use mass inspection, to not build up massive inventories, etc. The quality gurus would say this is the way it should have been in the first place. Break down barriers to getting the job done, drive out fear, be extremely careful of wrong use of measurements, keep inventories at a minimum, establish long-term relationships with suppliers. This *is* the way it should have been in the first place.

So, this is an implementation book. From this point on, throughout all the chapters you will learn not what's wrong, but how to implement. Some of my contemporaries agree that it is not important which theory(ies) or approaches you go with. It is important to *implement* to have success with one theory. The rest will follow. If statistical methods are needed they will follow, if design of experiments are needed they will follow, if cost of quality is needed it will emerge, if small group activity is required it will happen. Quality consultants are emerging who will help groups use the right tools. There is only one thing that will not happen automatically. That is top management understanding, knowledge of what needs to be done, and active involvement to make it happen. This needs to be worked at and driven from the very top.

The following questions need to be asked and will be answered in this book:

- How do you get management's attention to act decisively in helping workers do a better job to break down the barriers that prevent quality excellence?
- How do you get workers to participate more in managerial decisions?
- How do you get out there and ask questions to get the workers' ideas crystallized?
- How do you, as manager, unleash the workers' creative ideas to solve problems?
- And finally, how does management set in motion a way to implement these ideas so that the work can be done better?

Here is a way, here is a method, here is a procedure that will launch you into meaningful quality improvement. It has had a successful seven-year track record in more than one industry. It is ready to be implemented in *many* other industries including the government, the military, hospitals, and schools at all levels. Some of my "students" have used this method in churches, in real estate business, and in their personal relationships just as I have.

PART 1

THE STEPS

I have developed a lecture that is built around the question which has been asked the most over the last seven years. The question is, "OK, I've heard all the comments, I've read all the books now 'How do I get started?' After every talk people always ask for copies of the slides. I have never fully complied with this request. Here is the essence of the talk which has grown to a two-day seminar given in Perth, Australia; Sao Paulo, Brazil; throughout AT&T and StorageTek (worldwide); Oklahoma State University, Denver University to a group of Chinese business people; and other specific companies.

There are five elements to the answer to the question, "How do I get started?" They are:

(1) Educate yourself.
(2) Find a friend.
(3) Implement quality improvement in the friend's organization.
(4) Record and tell about successes.
(5) Wait for the phone to ring.

Let's examine each of these in turn.

Educate Yourself

In a talk to about 300 people at Oklahoma State University I asked, "How many of you have a degree in quality improvement?" To no one's surprise no one raised their hand. Most were engineers with CEs, MEs, and EEs. Herein lies the problem. Most business leaders today are strong in engineering, business, and finance, but few know about the importance of quality improvement. We must therefore educate ourselves about the subject. Attendance at one Deming seminar will impress you with the fact that what is needed is not just a course or two in basic statistics, but a "transformation of the American style of management."[5]

It will take a lot more than the alphabet soup approach to get through quality improvement. We have SPC, QC, QA, JIT, MBO, GD, DOE, OA, TEI, CTR, BM, STC, SQC, PMP, SQA, SQE, EDI, and STSM. Yet there is still little meaningful progress. Why? Let me submit that we are extremely willing to let the consultants and the programs do it for us. I recently heard Mr. Bill Scherkenbach say, "five years ago everyone asked about control charts, two years ago they asked about Taguchi experiments and now they are asking about goal deployment."

Management thinks the programs will do it and most are extremely reluctant to become actively involved themselves. The companies whose chief executive officers are, by example, getting actively involved in quality improvement are those that are excelling. Donald Petersen, CEO of Ford Motor Company, was recognized by his peers as the top CEO in the U.S. He earned this special honor, rightfully, for turning his company completely around. He has said, "I'm proud to be counted as a disciple of Dr. W. Edwards Deming."[6] The same can be said about Kearns of Xerox, Houghton of Corning Glass Works, Stemple of GM, Danforth formerly of Westinghouse, Melohn of North American Tool and Die, and Garvin of Motorola.

Yes, Dr. Deming is a statistician. He claims he is an apprentice statistician. Some say Dr. Deming is preaching use of statistics as the salvation of American industry. I say he is preaching for the *transformation* of the *American style* of *management*. This goes *far beyond* the alphabet soup way of managing mentioned above. Study Dr. Deming's 14 points. How many relate directly or indirectly to statistics? My answer is "one." One of 14, with the rest aimed squarely at what management needs to do to accomplish the transformation.

These are the gems of wisdom one discovers when traveling down the path of true quality improvement. What are some others? Michael MacCoby, who wrote *The Leader*,[7] said:

> 84 percent of the workers believe they would work harder if they could participate more in management decisions.

Robert Waterman, who was co-author of *In Search of Excellence,*[8] said (paraphrased):

> Management must develop the ability, humility and will to get out there and listen to the workers.

John Naisbitt, author of *Megatrends* and *Re-Inventing the Corporation,*[9] said (all paraphrased):

> McGregor, who gave us the X-Y theory of management, was 25 years ahead of his time.

> The job of the manager of the nineties is to coach, teach, nurture.

> Later on Naisbitt adds the attribute "to facilitate."

As mentioned in the Introduction, Tom Peters said (paraphrased):

> We have failed to tap our work force's potential.

As previously mentioned, Donald Petersen of Ford said (paraphrased):

> We must learn to capture the enormous skill, energy, and knowledge of the work force. Management must develop systems to enhance this, not stifle it.

The late James Olson, former CEO of AT&T, said:

> We want, need and will *act on* the best thoughts of our employees on how the work they do can be done better.

Six giants in their fields—six quotes that if studied carefully, all say the same thing. I have found that when the major contributors *all* start saying the same thing, we indeed have some direction to follow that's worthwhile.

Let's look further at what the quality gurus are saying.

Dr. Deming's advice is, "We need a transformation of the American style of management." His often used quote, "American Industry has just gotten used to burning toast and scraping it!"

Dr. Juran reminds us of the American managers' strength in knowledge of engineering and finance, but weakness in quality improvement.

Armand Feigenbaum has reminded us that there is probably more to be gained in the white-collar area than any other area.

Philip Crosby asks, "Why spend all this time finding, fixing and fighting when you could have *prevented* the problem in the first place?"

Four more thoughts that are *all* on target. Different ideas, but all aimed at similar targets.

- Transformation of the American style of management.
- Education on quality improvement for American management.
- The grand opportunity of white-collar productivity.
- Spend meaningful time on prevention activity.

I strongly feel that a combination of the 10 previous ideas makes for a direction in the nineties that is powerful, meaningful, and focused; a *direction* that will ensure American industry regains the number one position. We have all the resources—all we need is the will, the willpower, and the profound knowledge of how to constantly improve.

The Deming Formula

Dr. Deming starts his four-day lecture with a formula. He writes the year 1950 on the board or Vugraph paper and states: "This is what I told the Japanese in 1950." If you improve your quality you improve your productivity automatically—it's a chain reaction. You do this by lowering waste, lowering restarts, lowering rework. When this finally happens you then can capture markets with higher quality, lower cost of goods and services. This will allow you to stay in business and provide more jobs. Deming then goes on to say, "So simple."

We in American industry do not find that lowering waste, restarts, and rework is simple at all. We have found a way to not eliminate waste, restarts, and rework. The way is called "workaround." Workaround occurs when the process or system is so messed up we work around it.

You discover this by drawing a flow diagram of the process. Whenever you find a loop away from the mainstream of the process question it. It could be a workaround. Work to eliminate workaround whenever possible. At times this will reap benefits such as reducing cycle time, using all resources more efficiently, and cutting costs substantially.

The 85/15 Rule

At one time Dr. Deming attributed 85 percent of the reason for variability to the process and 15 percent of the reason to people, machines, and tools. In his most recent book *Out of the Crisis*, he changed that statistic to 94/6. I really think he was trying to get our attention with that change. In my work with over 100 small groups I have tracked the data over seven years and found that 82 percent of the time it was the process and 18 percent of the time it was people, machines, or tools. The main point of this is not whether it's 82 or 80 or even 94 percent; it is that management must become actively involved to fix, change, or improve the process which they control. The people do not control the process they work in, but they do have good knowledge about how to fix it.

William Scherkenbach, who wrote *The Deming Route to Quality and Productivity*,[10] reminds us that management is responsible for the entire pie—not just the 85 percent aimed at improving the process. Since when, Scherkenbach asks, isn't management responsible for the people they hire and train or don't train, the machines and tools they buy or don't buy, and maintain or don't maintain? Management is 100 percent responsible for taking action to improve the process as well as assure that the issues of people, machines, and tools are constantly monitored and improved.

The people closest to the problem, job, or area needing improvement can help a great deal with their knowledge and skill. This is a what to do book. I'll discuss how to do this with concrete examples later in this text.

Find a Friend

The second element of getting started is to find a friend. This sounds somewhat simplistic, but it is important to understand. You cannot implement quality improvement in a hostile environment. A true quality improvement professional should not waste his/her time in hostile environments where the leader and/or the staff is not at least neutral.

I have worked in areas where the top person was supportive and the immediate reports were skeptical. This is almost a normal situation. Skepticism, however, is much different than outright noncooperation. The best environment is when the entire management team is supportive. This takes form in allowing maximum time to the improvement effort, selecting good people to work in Phase II, volunteering to chair quality resolution teams in Phase III, and following through to implement improvement on an ongoing basis.

It is far best to be invited in to implement quality improvement than to force your way in. I have used this tactic in my new company StorageTek, and found it very effective. It took me three months to gain credibility. Because of my level I could have forced my way in earlier, but clearly this would have been a mistake. Good work was accomplished in our printer operations, software, calibration, information systems, field service, accounting, account management, and

Puerto Rico operations, all in the fourth to sixth month.

I did several things to help the "invitation" come sooner. I sent to *all* management levels regular mailings on quality improvement which also included an offer from me to help out where needed. I became very close to the editor of our monthly newspaper and as a result had five consecutive stories published on quality improvement. I spoke both internally and externally and made sure the word got out concerning good feedback. Private one-on-one discussions also took place on a regular basis.

The result of this work was an invitation to work with the aforementioned organizations. This has mushroomed into a massive effort involving every major organization in the company worldwide. Some examples of this work will be cited later.

Implement Quality Improvement in the Friend's Organization

It really doesn't matter what method, of the many that exist, is used to improve quality. What does matter is that the implementor believes in the method and that it works. The implementor needs to follow through to assure success. There are many companies that never pass the awareness level. They go to the courses, conferences, and quality colleges, get excited about the need for change, but come back without any earthly idea, as they say in the south, about how to implement a meaningful quality improvement plan.

One method used a few years back was to find and recognize quality improvement champions. This is dangerous because it allows the rest of the management team to say, "Let the champion worry about quality." I recall a discussion with a project manager who was bargaining with me to provide a full-time quality professional to his project. He said he wanted someone to "eat, drink, and sleep quality in his organization 24 hours a day, seven days a week." He didn't say, but it was certainly implied, that he didn't want to worry about quality; he wanted to delegate quality to someone else.

This is no different than delegating responsibility. Management 101 says you cannot delegate responsibility; you can delegate authority only. Far too many managers are still delegating quality to the quality control department or to the quality professional, or even worse to the consultant. I do not allow this. It is sometimes an uphill battle, but it must be done. One must help management understand that they own the process and therefore they must improve it. No one else can do this. What will happen with some success, in implementing quality improvement, is that although you start with one successful method, other methods will slowly evolve and also be used. This happens because of a turned-on educated management team that looks for many ways to improve the process. Statistical methods is one of these ways, as are participative management, cost of quality, quality circles, quality councils, root cause analysis, design of experiments, goal deployment, and control charts. This list will grow as we move into the nineties.

My method has worked in six different companies that I know of and possibly more through use of the written material I have provided since 1986. Some view my method as a technique of combining the discipline of cause and effect and force field analysis (CE/FFA). This is a valuable contribution to the world of quality improvement, but the more important contribution is getting management actively involved in listening to and responding appropriately to the ideas of those closest to the work. In this book you will read about how we get management involved in Phase I, and then again in Phase III, and then again in the implementation phase.

Record and Tell About Successes

This is the fun part. My best success story involves an organization that literally survived being eliminated because of the work they did over a three-year period in improving the quality of their operation. Five organizations were being consolidated to two. The director who won told me it was the result of what his organization had done over a three-year period to improve quality. He had specific examples of quality improvement, his peers didn't. This saved 500 jobs and added 1,000 more.

Most examples of success are not as dramatic, but they are important and have amounted to millions of dollars that went directly to the bottom line. I recall an accounting group that improved on time payments by 2 percent. This resulted in satisfying over 1,000 clients. I recall an engineering and installation organization that improved quality measures tenfold over a four-year period. I recall a customer service group that improved open item count from 50,000 to less than 7,000 in less than one year. The same group improved on time delivery of specs to the factories from 30 percent to 91 percent in less than one year. A metrology group decreased inventory of expensive test sets from 325 to 50 and increased turnaround time of calibrated test sets from 24.7 to 3.4 days, saving over a half million dollars. As rework is reduced, the amount of production per employee increases, which is pure improvement of productivity—the ultimate reward.

In all of the work the most important improvements cannot be measured. Improvements in morale, opening up lines of communication, improving participative management, time management, and improved discipline cannot be measured. As Masaaki Imai tells us in *Kaizen*,[11] these things are of vast importance in our daily efforts to improve the process. He calls these things process criteria as opposed to the results criteria with which we are all familiar.

I am usually asked "What kind of matrix would one look at, both in white-collar and production areas?" The list is as follows:

MEASUREMENT MATRIX

Mission	Statistic "Hard Numbers"
Reduce cost of installation	• Burden rate • Installation cost • Sustaining cost per unit • Purchase price per PC/WS
Reduce flow time	• Working days/order by order type • Customer order prep time per order • Percent on time payments • Turnaround time of test sets from calibration
Reduce variability	• Installation date versus completion date • Customer need date versus install date
Makes process easier for the user	• Number of contacts for users per transaction
Improved customer service	• Percent open items per period
Reduce incidence of ordering the wrong product	• Follow-on orders within 60 days of original installation • Trouble calls • Returns of software to warehouse
Reduce incidence of incorrect product delivered	• Percent installs (trouble tickets)
Spec to factories	• Percent on-time spec delivery to factories

There is always a payoff in the area of process criteria. I recall an installation manager making a report at a staff meeting. His quality results had shown dramatic improvement over a one-year period. His boss asked for an explanation of how he did it. He said, "I assigned an installer to go throughout the entire state and implement the cause and effect/force field analysis process." The manager attributed improved quality to the improved morale and communication that took place in the CE/FFA sessions.

The subject of success stories usually relates to the hard numbers we use as measurement. It is very important to understand the concepts taught to us by Dr. Masaaki Imai in his book about *Kaizen*.[11] Kaizen means improvement. Imai tells us that his improvement occurs in the East every day. This refers to improvement of the processes from A to B to C, and finally to the end result D in a typical process flow. He suggests that Western management usually starts at D, the end result, or bottom line as we call it. He suggests that Japanese management starts at A to slowly but surely improve the process every day. This work is constantly supported and stimulated, not necessarily by money, but by recognition in the form of a thank you, a handshake, a pat on the back, a lunch. They have been at it for over 30 years and have racked up some impressive results as everyone knows. It can be done in the U.S.—it must be done if we are to succeed in the nineties.

So why share success stories? To brag? To get a raise? No, share success stories to get others involved. It is amazing what one article will do to get others asking the question, "Can I make the same kind of improvements in my organization?" There are many ways to get the word out:

- Articles in company news media.
- TV tapes of speeches and small group activity.
- Commendation at a staff meeting.
- Letters to key people.
- Word of mouth.
- Recognition of quality teams.
- Magazine articles.
- Talks at conferences (internal and external).
- Being published in technical journals and writing books.

I have used every one of these mediums with good success. The common denominator is knowing, understanding, and believing what you are talking about. The most important point to understand is that no matter how knowledgeable you are, you cannot get meaningful results by pushing your way in. An invitation is a must. You can create the atmosphere to get the invitation as mentioned, but as stated earlier you cannot reach the plateau of meaningful improvement in a hostile environment. An even worse case is when the environment is not hostile, everything seems to be in order, but the top guy in an organization is really faking it. Again, the top is not the CEO, but the middle manager in charge of a large responsibility. If that person is faking or giving lip service, his team knows it and nothing will happen—absolutely nothing. I have seen this happen time after time.

I aim this discussion at the thousands of quality improvement practitioners who are out there fighting, against all odds, to do what is right and don't get the support. This book would be a fairy tale if I didn't recognize the good work that seems to get nowhere because of an uninformed or, even worse, an ignorant management team. My advice is don't give up. Analyze that organization and find a key person who will cooperate. You can make progress with that person's organization in spite of uninformed leadership from above that person. Keep at it, record your success stories, and wait for the phone to ring.

If you're extremely lucky, as I am, you will report to a CEO who is a believer in quality improvement. He will chair the highest level quality council and ask you to vice-chair it with him. He will act by word and deed as the true champion of quality improvement and will tell his subordinates to become actively involved in the quality improvement effort and will follow to assure they do. He will also communicate a constant and believable message to the entire employee body. I have such a boss, his name is Ryal Poppa— CEO, chairman and president of StorageTek. He wrote the Foreword to this book.

Wait for the Phone to Ring

I guarantee that as you record and tell about successes the phone will literally ring off the hook. In my case calls have come from others in the organization, from universities inviting me to serve on productivity boards or give seminars, from foreign countries wanting to learn more about quality improvement, from other companies asking for advice and help, and from companies asking for guidance.

I have worked with over 100 small groups, delivered talks at major seminars throughout the United States and Brazil, have implemented my three-phase program in many parts of the world. All of this came by way of invitation—the phone is literally ringing off the hook! Throughout all of this I have tried to respond in a positive way. It's good to be part of a movement that will result in the U.S. regaining economic power and strength.

Summary

By far, the education process of learning about quality improvement is the most important segment of getting started. This goes for the quality practitioner as well as for the management team, and the entire work force. Management must replace old, worn-out authoritarian nonsense with leadership. This leadership must include the wisdom of Douglas McGregor in using participative management and understanding and implementing the Y theory of management.

When this is in place, the use of statistical techniques will work; use of quality teams will work; implementation of new ideas will work; morale and communication will improve; processes will improve immensely; waste, restarts, rework, and workaround will diminish substantially; and yes, the bottom line will show remarkable improvement.

After the education process, use of the tactics of finding a friend, implementing quality improvement in the friend's organization, and sharing success stories, will indeed help the phone ring off the hook. This will *all* occur because we will put the customer first. When this happens, when customers are so delighted they are literally knocking the door down to do business with you—then and only then will we be on the right track.

PART 2

THE PROCESS

Those interested in reading source documents on cause and effect can refer to Kaoru Ishikawa's book, *Guide to Quality Control.*[3] Force field analysis is documented in *Field Theory and Social Science* by Kurt Lewin.[4] The CE/FFA (cause and effect/force field analysis) technique allows those closest to the issues to identify problems, their causes, and the forces affecting improvement. It produces straightforward information so management can solve these problems and follow through on areas affected by people, machines, or tools.

Implementation of the CE/FFA approach has evolved into a four-phase process.

Phase I

This involves an intensive session with management teams that are interested in implementing the quality improvement approach. Again, it is advantageous to work with groups that express interest rather than to force-feed groups with little interest.

The purpose of this session is to help the management team understand its role in implementing and supporting quality improvement. We discuss what management experts say about how to manage, as well as what quality experts (i.e., Deming, J. M. Juran, Philip B. Crosby, Armand V. Feigenbaum) say about how to improve quality. When both expert groups say the same thing, management, indeed, has something to listen to and act upon. Many of Deming's points fit this category. For instance, management expert Douglas McGregor[12] gave us the X-Y theory of management 25 years ago which Deming discusses, but in a different way. The end result, however, is the same—trust your employees, believe in them, avoid over-management, and drive out fear. Naisbitt stated in his book, *Re-inventing the Corporation,*[9] that McGregor was 25 years ahead of his time.

Dr. Juran puts it another way:

> An obstacle to participation by upper managers is their limited experiences and training in managing for quality. As discussed, they have extensive experience in management of the business and finance but not managing for quality.[14]

We discuss the importance of management forming quality resolution teams (QRT) to act on employee or management group ideas generated by the quality action teams (QAT).

We examine the CE/FFA studies performed by many different groups. We use examples to emphasize that it is the process that needs fixing, and that relatively lower levels of supervision can put these improvements into effect. We don't lose sight of the fact that higher management should get involved in 10 percent of the cases; employees can help in 15 percent of the cases; and middle and lower management levels can act on the remaining 75 percent. This is what I have found in over 100 cases of working with small groups in five different companies.

When time permits, we use videotapes to support these points. Deming's videotapes, the NBC White Paper, and Juran's tapes give a good idea of what American industry needs to do. Even though it is nine years old and addresses only the blue-collar areas, it is still a good tape to gain understanding. We produced our own tapes which define the CE/FFA purpose and show a live session with a group of employees using the CE/FFA process.

In summary, the purpose of Phase I is to get management's commitment to initiate QATs and QRTs, and to help them understand the discipline of CE/FFA. This ensures their active involvement. Sessions with the management team usually go well if the head person is open-minded and willing to lead the team in a new direction. This is so important that I strongly recommend spending time only with groups that have such a leader. Put those who need prodding on the bottom of your priority list; this cannot be overemphasized. If an organization's top person is not totally committed to quality improvement, nothing will happen. I differ from most people on this point—by "top" I do not mean the CEO or president. You can be successful only if the top person is a "location head"; you must have his or her total support for improvement to occur. Usually location heads function independently and have the power to get things done. One thing that will not happen unless you have the CEO's full understanding, support and active involvement is turning an entire company around. All the gurus agree with this and I can now better understand this in my work at StorageTek. As I mentioned, we do have a CEO who knows how to manage in this new economic age and has put quality improvement in the forefront.

Phase II

In Phase II, I work with a small group (six to 10 people) and use the CE/FFA technique to explore a problem. First we go over the basics of the Deming formula and the 85/15 rule. The formula is well-known, but few, I find, really understand it. Deming tells us that if quality is improved, productivity is automatically improved. This is done by lowering waste, restarts, and rework. In my work with hundreds of people, I find that everyone, regardless of his or her job, experiences some degree of waste, restarts, or rework. These are the elements that need to be vigorously attacked to improve quality and productivity. Deming says that once this happens higher quality and lower cost goods and services can be provided, enabling you to stay in business and provide more jobs. The next step is to explain the 85/15 rule.

In a recent lecture Deming stated that the common cause/special cause idea originally came from Walter A. Shewhart of the former Bell Telephone Laboratories. Shewhart is renowned for his development of the statistical control chart depicting an in-control or out-of-control process. It is interesting that he, too, gave us the rule of variability.

The numbers are not important. Deming now says it is 94/6; Juran says it is 80/20; in my work with over 100 small groups it comes out to be 82/18.

The theory states that defects or problem areas are divided into two distinct parts. The first part is common causes—systems or process problems. These systems or processes can be in production lines or accounting organizations. They are owned and controlled 100 percent by management. Management buys the raw material, schedules the people, machines, or robots to work the material, and determines the precise method and use of every element in the process through customer delivery. Only management can change, fix, or alter the process.

The second part of a defect or problem area is known as special causes. These special causes can be attributed to people, machines, or tools and occur approximately 15 percent of the time.

In my 30 years of business experience, when a defect occurred we usually looked for "who" did it, and we usually found someone to take the blame even though that person may have been working in an inefficient process. Management has the absurd need to pin the blame on someone and to be on record as disciplining him or her to ensure that it won't happen again.

Yes, people do make mistakes; and, yes, something must be done about this. If the problem is the process 82 percent of the time—and since management owns the process—then management needs to change the process to obtain continuous improvement. Management should not blame, coerce, or cajole the person on the job.

Deming demonstrates this succinctly in his red and white bead experiment. I didn't comprehend the experiment until months after I saw it, but the bead exercise inferred that management must remove the red beads from the system—blaming the employee, or cajoling as Deming does very well in his experiment, doesn't accomplish anything.

William W. Scherkenbach explains the 85/15 rule well in his book, *The Deming Route to Quality and Productivity.*[10] He makes a valid point. As we discussed, it is wrong for management to give the employee the impression that he or she is responsible only for 15 percent of the problems. The employee may have a good idea of how to fix the process (which is in the 85 percent category) and management should encourage systems to get employee input. This is what CE/FFA does. In the words of one of our customers who asked me to help improve quality in his organization, "CE/FFA is a well-disciplined, powerful, well-organized process for problem solving."

The next step in working with the small group is to have it define the type of quality defects or quality problems it is encountering. It may be that management specifies the problem area to be studied by the small group. This is fine. If the problem is not specified by management, then it becomes the responsibility of a small group of experts. I prefer the latter course. Usually the people closest to the work can come up with an impressive list of problem areas that need exploration.

Once the problems are defined, the facilitator asks the small group to pick the most important one to solve. This whole selection process could take up to an hour.

We call the selected problem the effect; we draw a cause and effect diagram and do a cause and effect study. This process is documented in Ishikawa's book, *Guide to Quality Control.*[3] We stop after each cause is determined, and we explode each cause into its restraining and driving forces, which will be discussed later.

The causes are then ranked in order of importance. This is helpful input for management's consideration. Why tackle cause 10 before causes one through nine are considered? There is one exception to this question. If cause 10 takes one day to implement, and cause one takes four months, then, by all means, tackle cause 10 first and get it out of the way. The prioritization gives management the input to muster the necessary resources for attacking each cause.

We don't stop here, however. It is very important to go to management with suggested solutions—not just problems. This is not new. Every management book states it, but few people practice it. How many times have you, as manager, heard, "We can't do this because. . ." instead of, "We can do this and here's how. . . ." One QAT member, after an 11-hour session, stated, "It was refreshing to focus on solutions rather than just problems as is done in many of these kinds of exercises."

The small group's next step is to do a force field analysis of each cause. This, in essence, is an exercise that helps the small group determine why the cause exists in the first place. This must be known before what to do about it can be determined.

This session usually takes from six to 10 hours, based on the complexity of the problem and accomplishes two objectives: (1) each member becomes trained as a facilitator, and (2) a list of recommendations is formed for action by management.

During facilitator training, the entire six to 10 hour session allows the leader to get to know each participant in terms of potential as a future facilitator. This is shared with management. Specific training takes place during the session in two ways. I tell the group I'm wearing two hats—a teacher's hat and a facilitator's hat. As a teacher, I relate experiences; as a facilitator, I "do" the CE/FFA then ask each member to do the same.

During the teaching part I share my experiences with the participants which helps move the sessions along. For example: *How to Handle the Introduction.* I show an 18-minute tape produced at AT&T that gives a brief introduction to CE/FFA and shows a live group using the process with appropriate verbal instruction. After the tape, I describe the Deming formula and discuss it in relation to the 85/15 rule. Two purposes are accomplished in this introduction: (1) the group loosens up, and (2) I gain credibility. The group begins to realize this is not another witch hunt. One conferee's comment sticks in my mind: "I thought this was just going to be another quality meeting where someone gets beat over the head. Instead I became convinced management really wanted to know how to make things better."

Tools to Use. I like to use the 18-minute videotape entitled *Cause and Effect/Force Field Analysis,* a television and a videocassette player to show the tape, and a booklet entitled *Quality Teams—How Do They Work.* The booklet is helpful for management and participants of QATs and QRTs and can be examined prior to a CE/FFA session. A 54-inch by 48-inch-wide easel or two small easels put together and a roll of masking tape are also needed.

How to Set Up the Room. For the CE/FFA session I like a room big enough for six to 10 participants to sit in a semicircle around the easel. Tables are not necessary and, in fact, hinder good discussion. However, we place enough tables behind the semicircle to accommodate six observers. Allowing observers works provided the facilitator enforces strict rules of nonparticipation. Their questions can be handled at break or during lunch.

Minimum/Maximum Number of Participants. Much has been written about the ideal size of a small group. I find that less than six people or more than 10 people tends to be ineffective. In the group of six or less there is usually not enough experience; however, I have worked with groups as small as five and as large as 14 and everything worked out—but I'm sure luck was on my side.

How to Memorize Names of Participants. During the CE/FFA videotape I pass around a sign-up sheet that reads "First—Last—Name." It's surprising how many people use initials if you don't specify this. While the tape is playing, I memorize the names of each group member. This may be a bit manipulative, but I find people really appreciate being called by name. I do admit to them later how I did it so they may also use this technique.

How to Handle the Verbose or Quiet Participant. In both situations the group usually curbs too much participation or bolsters someone who may not feel good about participating. As facilitator, one must break in if the verbose participant is off on a tangent or out of control; I believe the quiet participant should be left alone. Generally the group will take care of this, although I have seen some people not say one word during their entire time together. This could be due to inexperience or some other unknown problem. However, I do check with management to assure the session will not place undue pressure on any individual.

How to Handle Disagreement. Healthy disagreement sometimes leads to a breakthrough in understanding a particular problem. Compromise can develop to strengthen the situation. The key word here is "healthy." This is generally the case; the basis for disagreement is usually someone's lack of knowledge or understanding about a particular situation. It is good to try to discuss as many views as possible, and reach some kind of consensus.

The Cause and Effect Basics. This is easy to explain by using the cause and effect diagram (see page 45). I recently was reminded of the process by a friend while we discussed cholesterol. Cholesterol is the effect. The doctor helps the patient understand the causes, inappropriate diet usually being the number one cause. In some people, however, chemical imbalance is the primary cause, not diet. In this case the exact cause must be determined before an appropriate "fix" can be made. There may be many causes in business-related examples—improper grounding, late payments, or inaccurate office records. I have seen as few as five causes and as many as 12 causes developed by small groups.

The Force Field Analysis Basics. The use of the force field diagram is the best way to explain this process (see page 48). Let's discuss an example. Suppose one of the causes is lack of training. First, we write the words *The level of* on top of the easel pad and then use words to finish the sentence as best as possible. This may then read *The level of training is too low.* Another example could be *The level of absenteeism is too high.* The idea is to define the cause in terms of the level being too high or too low.

After the *cause* is defined in terms of level (too high or too low), draw a horizontal line across the middle of the page. Ask the group to picture the level of training being at the level of the horizontal line. Then say if the level of training is too low, something is keeping that horizontal line where it is—we call this *restraining forces.*

Write the words *restraining forces* on the top of the easel paper. The group then defines the restraining forces. Examples in this case could be: *too much on-the-job training by inexperienced people, lack of manuals, lack of dedicated training space,* and *lack of trainers.* When all known restraining forces are listed across the page, we go to the bottom of the page and ask what can be done about each restraining force and write down the answers. We call these *driving forces* and write these words on the bottom of the page. Draw an arrow to the horizontal lines to the corresponding restraining force. (Refer to the example on page 48.) The whole idea of force field will become more apparent as you read through the examples in *Part Four, Examples of Drawing Cause and Effect and Force Field Analysis Diagrams.*

The Importance of Defining Solutions. As mentioned in the Introduction, it is important to present management with suggested solutions rather than just problems. Employees closest to the work often have very good ideas about what these solutions are and can make solid recommendations. If we stop at the problem definition as presented in the classic cause and effect, we miss the opportunity for needed input.

Why It Is Important for Each Participant to "Do" a Force Field Analysis. The prime facilitator, trained and certified in CE/FFA, does the introduction, the cause and effect analysis, and the first force field analysis. The facilitator then "passes the crayon" to the work-group member sitting in the first chair on either side of the semicircle. The reasons for this are:

- The group tries to understand the process, knowing they will have to do it.
- This is the best way to learn the process.
- It gives the facilitator a good idea of who can excel at this; this is shared with management.
- It guarantees high-level group involvement.
- It helps avoid facilitator burnout during the six- to 10-hour period.

These reasons answer a question that often comes up: "You're so good at this, why don't you do it all?" Through extensive experience with this, I can report that something very positive happens when a group member gets up and participates—the entire group benefits. I highly recommend this method.

The Role of the Facilitator While the Group Member Does the FFA. The facilitator sits in the chair of the group member doing the FFA and participates in the roles of gatekeeper, encourager, harmonizer, consensus seeker, feedback seeker, standard setter, and processor. Let's examine each role. (Further information may be obtained by reading *Making Meetings Work* by Leland P. Bradford.[13])

- *Gatekeeper*—Keeps the "door open" for timid, less talkative members to contribute.
- *Encourager*—Shows in a caring way how members of the group can help one another.
- *Harmonizer*—Helps in a conflict situation; gets heavily involved when the group polarizes and cannot reach a consensus.
- *Consensus seeker*—Gets members to reach agreement on what is best for all; keeps discussion on target.
- *Feedback seeker*—Gives individual and group feedback on progress. Feedback may be appropriate during the session, break, lunch, or dinner.
- *Standard setter*—Presents the image of being ready for work, on time, interested in the group's progress, and participating where appropriate during an intense six to 10 hours. The best compliment is the group wanting to work harder than the facilitator,

opting to work late or come in early once they are comfortable with the process.

- *Processor*—Keeps track of using the CE/FFA process.

The presentation time frame is usually as follows:

- *Introduction*—30 minutes, including the 18-minute videotape.
- *Cause and effect*—45 minutes to 1½ hours.
- *The first four force fields*—30 to 60 minutes each.
- *Remaining force fields*—20 to 30 minutes each.
- *Summary*—30 minutes.

With these time frames in mind the facilitator can closely monitor the process time length.

Monitoring the content of the process is quite different and has already been mentioned.

The Importance of Rank Ordering Causes. It is important to prioritize causes for management to understand what employees view as important problems. We recommend tackling the most difficult problems first. As mentioned, if one cause would take hours to solve and another months, eliminate the lesser problem first.

How to Summarize. When all force fields are completed the facilitator again takes over. We tape up and display the original cause and effect analysis and all the force field analyses. The facilitator starts with cause number one and asks the group whether the first driving force is the responsibility of management or the worker to implement. When all driving forces are tallied this gives a rough estimate of how many are management or process problems and how many are worker, machine, or tool problems (see Phase III discussion on page 23).

The facilitator also asks group members what level of supervision, in their view, should be responsible for implementing each driving force. These data are recorded and summarized.

How to Organize the Management Presentation. It is recommended that the senior-level manager open this session and set the tone. He or she should restate the session's purpose and thank the QAT.

The facilitator then reviews the basic Deming theory and the 85/15 rule. Next, the tally sheet showing the number of management- or worker-controlled driving forces is discussed.

At this point the facilitator introduces the group member who will explain the cause and effect analysis. You will recall that the work group started to actually "do" force field analysis number two. The facilitator did the cause and effect and the first force field analysis. Prior to the Phase III session, the facilitator asks for volunteers to explain the cause and effect and first force field analysis, excluding those who already have a force field to explain. This usually works smoothly and gives almost everyone a chance to participate in the Phase III session.

Lately, we have worked it out so everyone makes a presentation. One person can be assigned restraining forces and another driving forces of the same force field. This gives everyone a voice and makes for a better session.

At the end of the Phase III session the facilitator sums up by going to the board and writing the words *What's next?* The suggestion is made to form a QRT made up of supervisors, with representation from the QAT. Two representatives are sufficient to provide the continuity necessary for understanding the analysis. A chairman should be appointed at this stage. At the very end it is good for the facilitator to recognize the hard work of the QAT. This can be done by verbal praise and by presenting a certificate to each participant.

How to Condition Management for Phase III. It is important to condition management prior to the Phase III session. Recommendations are going to be made that may challenge or embarrass some of the attendees, e.g., "Why didn't I think of that?" or "Why didn't this get fixed five years ago!" The conditioning should aim at eliminating management's defensiveness or brow-beating.

When opening the Phase III session it is a good idea for the facilitator to announce that it is an input session, *not* an action determination session. This will happen later in the QRT.

How to Track Results. The best way for a QRT to track results is to *not* issue minutes. It is difficult, at best, to find any action items in most sets of minutes. Volumes are often written, but seldom does one find concise descriptions of the action item, the responsible person, or the target dates—much less anything about estimated annual cost savings.

I recommend, therefore, using a simple spread sheet with the following headings typed across the page:

- *Action item* (called driving force).
- *Person responsible.*
- *Target date.*
- *Actual date.*
- *Comments.*
- *Estimated annual cost savings.*

This document should become known as the action register list of each QRT and each quality review team. It should be used to track progress and determine if higher management levels should get involved.

How to Have Fun Doing the CE/FFA. Six to 10 hours may not seem like a long time. Use of CE/FFA demands a high level of group attention and participation. When levity can be utilized, it is certainly encouraged. This relieves tension and stress and often aids the group along the way. The form of levity should be relating group experiences, not by telling jokes. It is amazing how a group member's comment or action can lead to such humor.

The best way facilitators learn is by *doing* it. This is why we give as many people as possible the opportunity to actually lead the force field analysis session.

We found that it is also possible to include a small group of observers. These people are separated from the work group by space or tables and are not allowed to participate in the actual work group session. They are asked to write down their questions and discuss them with the experienced facilitator during break or in a special session.

The first reaction of most people is to reject the idea of observers. My experience indicates it can work if the facilitator strictly enforces the above criteria. The workers and observers both respond beautifully when they know the rules!

We call these small groups QATs.

Phase III

This is a most exciting event. The workers get a chance to share their findings with the management team—and I have seen six management levels together at the same time. Good quality presentations result in spite of lack of extensive preparation or written reports.

The QAT actually uses the same easel charts it used in the work session. As we discussed, at least one participant always writes everything down in the same format on 8-inch by 11-inch paper, so this can be reproduced and handed out at the session with management.

During a particular Phase III session, a manager leaned over during the middle of an employee presentation and whispered to me, "It took me six months at 'charm school' to learn how to talk with such authority. How did you do this in 10 hours?"

It's not teaching people how to talk—it's giving them a tool that allows them to express information they know better than anyone else. I have seen hundreds of people do this with a zero percent failure rate—and this covers a wide spectrum of talent, from labor grades in installation to software developers with PhDs. The common thread is their individual job expertise. Yes, this is perhaps the most underutilized resource in industry today. All we have to do is turn it on. As Tom Melohn, president of North American Tool and Die, said, "They're out there, guys—go out and find 'em."

At this point it is good for the facilitator to recognize the good work of the small group. Very often these people have never made a presentation to their own supervisor let alone four levels of management. This recognition can be verbal praise and the presentation of certificates to each group member.

After the employee presentations and while the entire group, workers, and management are still present, it is important for the facilitator to emphasize the summary results. This could be done at the very beginning of the session, depending on the situation as the facilitator sees it.

Results to the following data:

- 63 Driving forces (solutions).
- 82 percent—Common causes (management-owned process problems).
- 18 percent—Special causes (people, machines, and tools).

Of the 82 percent management-controlled problems:
- 60 percent—Can be implemented at lower levels of management.
- 30 percent—Can be implemented by middle management.
- 10 percent—Can be implemented by higher management.

This next part is designed to address Deming's concern about management's lack of support for employee groups. I actually get management's commitment to "do something"; as mentioned in the Phase I discussion, we pin down management's responsibility.

I ask management to form a QRT that will address each driving force. As mentioned before, I ask them to use a spread sheet to track progress and send it to me. The spread sheet is nothing new but, used in this context, becomes a powerful communication tool with the original QAT.

I also recommend to the highest level person that he or she chair a quality review team that will meet at least once every other month to review progress. The department heads then chair their own QRT; these heads make up the review team.

Phase IV

In this phase we take a micro view of the process. Every job, whether it's production or white collar, is part of a process. The purpose of this examination is to pinpoint measurable areas of the process, build a data base in these measurements, identify potential or real problem areas, and take action to correct and prevent future problems.

Flow charts are a good method to use for identifying the overall process and pinpointing the areas requiring specific measurement. It is possible to use any one of the statistical tools to understand the data, but we recommend the use of control charts. AT&T's *Statistical Quality Control Handbook*[14] is an excellent source document that explains the various statistical methods.

As discussed in the handbook, we encourage using the triangle concept of a supervisor, a statistical analyst, and a key person in the group being analyzed. This small group (1) meets periodically to go over the data, (2) determines its meaning, (3) decides on action to be taken as a result of the data, or (4) seeks more data.

It is now important to understand that this entire four-phase approach is as appropriate for white-collar jobs as it is for production-oriented jobs. In fact, it is critical to immediately implement these phases in the white-collar areas.

___PART 3___
THE FACILITATOR

Let's now go back to the Phase II area and discuss the facilitator's role—organization, problem selection, and cause and effect and force field analysis. The CE/FFA technique uses small groups drawn from either manufacturing or service and administrative operations. The team works with a trained, experienced facilitator knowledgeable about both cause and effect and force field analysis.

All the reading and looking at videotapes, however, cannot replace firsthand experience. We have found that the only way to train facilitators is to put them in a "learn by doing" environment. It reminds me of a Chinese proverb used by many training organizations to illustrate the importance of *doing*:

> "I hear, I forget
> I see, I remember
> I do, I understand."

This is extremely appropriate regarding facilitator training. When they do it, they understand it!

Learning by doing training takes from six to 10 hours. Trainees are part of a small group (six to 10 people) assigned to work on a specific quality problem using the CE/FFA technique. They observe an experienced facilitator develop the problem area to be explored using group consensus, perform a modified cause and effect study on the major problem selected, and initiate a force field analysis on the first cause.

Under the careful eye of an experienced facilitator, the facilitator trainees then initiate a force field analysis on the remaining causes. In addition to this hands-on experience, we provide new facilitators with the following ongoing support:

- *Access to an experienced facilitator*–Helps the new person by answering questions prior to working with the first group and provides ongoing support.
- *Observation of working groups*–Works well as long as the observers are separated from the group and are not allowed to participate in discussions. Questions are written down and answered by an experienced facilitator during break, after the completed CE/FFA session, or in a post-session facilitator role and observer discussion.
- *Workbook describing facilitator role and CE/FFA process*–Pamphlet-size booklets describing the process with illustrations; this is aimed primarily at the work force but is also a good summary for the facilitator.
- *An 18-minute videotape*–Shows a live group using the CE/FFA process.
- *Direct contact with the process initiator*–Includes private sessions prior to the actual small group session or consultation during a small group session.
- *Periodic facilitator seminars*–Reviews the basics of how to get started and what the cause and effect and force field analysis is; discusses unique problems the facilitators have encountered since the last session. New ideas are also introduced.

The facilitator becomes the key person to provide solid communication between workers and management—defining what needs to be done for process improvement.

Let's examine the facilitator's role more closely.

Facilitator Responsibilities

The facilitator must create an atmosphere that allows free and open group discussions. The facilitator must avoid the temptation to make speeches, direct the discussion, or squelch ideas inappropriate to the topic at hand. Sometimes this may mean letting one to two participants ramble on rather than risk losing credibility for the discussion openness. There is a time, however, when "war stories" must be labeled as such and limited. You can use the cause and effect and force field analysis structure to your advantage in leading group discussion and keeping on track.

All discussions should be free of any type of facilitator censorship. Without understanding this at the beginning, some of the best ideas could be lost before they are even mentioned. This does not mean that the process becomes a gripe session or free-for-all. Rather, the facilitator has to keep the group on track without stifling the contributions of its members.

As facilitator, your opinions are not appropriate; you are seeking the group's ideas. On the other hand, your job is to help clarify some of the group's thoughts. Do this by suggesting examples to reduce confusion. It is also appropriate to suggest combining similar thoughts or ideas, with the permission of those who raised them. And when the group seems to meander, you must get them back on track.

You also have the responsibility to record on paper as accurately and concisely as possible the group's thoughts.

Exercising some of these responsibilities requires practice. Leadership talent is important; in fact, one of the reasons a facilitator is selected is because of his or her ability to lead small group discussions.

Organizing the Quality Action Team

The group applying these techniques should include six to 10 people who share common work problems. Although any group can use these techniques, it is best to involve employees closest to the problems who are capable of identifying what actually happens on the job.

Each location and organization uses QATs in its own special way, but may give it different names. You should be able to adapt these techniques to the objectives of your version of the QAT.

Formal quality improvement groups operate as part of a larger quality program undertaken by the location or organization. They usually meet at regular intervals and have follow-up responsibilities for pursuing problems to positive resolutions. These techniques can help groups better identify problems and pinpoint action to be taken.

Ad hoc groups are usually organized by supervisors trying to come to grips with a specific problem. These groups continue to function until the specific need has been satisfied. Although *ad hoc* groups can try to immediately tackle their problem, they should consider more than just the problem at hand to take full advantage of these techniques.

These techniques have been used successfully with workers at all levels as well as with many levels of management. They have been used successfully combining workers and supervisors in a group.

The group should schedule six to 10 hours to complete one exercise. This time can be broken into smaller units, but to be productive we recommend meeting for at least two consecutive hours. Management approval is obviously necessary, if only to authorize the time and to provide the meeting place.

The ideal situation allows the group to meet for two sessions in two days. The first day would require six consecutive hours of work; the second day would require two to six more hours, depending on the problem. In this way, the group stays intact and on target.

However, this ideal situation is not always attainable. We have seen groups meet once weekly for one-hour sessions and still get the job done. A strong facilitator is required especially in these situations.

Key Advice to Facilitators

At the conclusion of a recent session the top executive, who observed all three phases, made this statement:

> You obviously have acquired some good facilitator skills. Can you share with us what you feel contributes to being a good facilitator?

My answer was:

> There is one thing that stands out as being the most important. You must sincerely believe that the group you are working with truly knows more about the problem than you do. When you believe this the rest falls into place.

All that you have read, so far, about the facilitator skills is important. The answer above is the key advice that will carry any facilitator through. If you truly believe that the small group's collective knowledge is far superior to any one person's knowledge— including your own—then you will succeed by using your own common sense to get that knowledge out and be able to capitalize on it.

You just do not say to yourself that now is the time to act as gatekeeper, or harmonizer, etc. All of this should fall into place naturally. It is somewhat similar to an athlete. He or she practices on the elements profusely, but during the game what one learned in practice must flow naturally. Your work as a facilitator works the same way.

Another bit of advice is that it's really best if you, as facilitator, are not an expert on the problem being explored. I recall working with another company in the area of accounting. I was not an expert in accounting or familiar with the company. A group member made quite a plea that he should only work with groups in accounting. He went on for 10 minutes building his case. When he finished I made the following comment:

> Bill, I don't know anything about accounting or this company for that matter. How am I doing as facilitator?

The group laughed, Bill smiled, and we carried on.

Let's look specifically at the facilitator's role in each of these three areas. Since the first edition of this book was written, I have found a better way to work with groups to discover the "effect" or the problem area to be explored. I have found that on some occasions the effect is very specific and in other cases it is very generic. Let me explain.

As mentioned, there are two ways to determine what the effect is that the group will explore. One is by management definition, the other is to allow the small group to determine the effect (or problem area). I find the latter more appropriate. The reason is that the group closest to the work has a very good idea of what the problems and the solutions are.

I recall receiving a call from a director who insisted the small group work on the problem of "availability." I told him I would do this if the small group agreed that "availability" was the problem. The director asked if he and his staff could sit in on the Phase II session as observers.

I asked if he felt his presence would impede conversation of the QAT. He said he didn't think so because the group did not report directly to him and came from all over the U.S. So, picture the QAT sitting in 10 chairs in an arc around the easel with tables in the back of the room with about six observers, including the director.

I started by setting the ground rules. The front row (QAT) does the talking, the back row does the listening. I remind the observers that I will answer any questions concerning the process at breaks or lunch.

After this is clear to everyone, I then ask the QAT "What kinds of problems are you encountering in getting your job done?" The group, using a brainstorming type session developed about 20 problem areas. "Availability" was one of them. In refining the list of 20 problem areas in the cause and effect analysis, including rank ordering of causes, the group refined the 20 down to 10 major causes. "Availability" in the rank order became number 4. Three other causes ranked higher in priority than availability. The director and his staff were astonished yet pleased to find this out and to see it happen.

This is an example of letting the group decide the effect. There is a transition that takes place in going from the brainstorming list of 20 to the cause and effect diagram. That transition takes place by the facilitator asking the question:

> Because all these things exist what effect does this have on your organization?

The answer is readily apparent and before long someone will say words to the effect that:

> Our organization is not as effective as it could be.

This, then, becomes the effect in the cause and effect diagram. At times the group will zero in on a specific defect or problem as mentioned earlier. Examples are grounding (see Part V), late payments, mean time failure of the activator, connecting, and cabling.

Sub-Drawing the Cause and Effect Diagram

Usually the problem definition as described above and the definition of specific root causes, takes anywhere from one to two hours. The facilitator writes in the effect as previously described on the right side of the easel pad, draws a dashed line vertically down the right side of the pad and then a horizontal line across the middle of the pad stopping at the dashed line (see examples in Part Four). After the diagram is written the facilitator asks:

> OK, using the brainstorming list as a guide, tell me what are the major causes of (whatever the effect is).

What happens here is another refining and distillation of the brainstorming list. I have never, in over 100 sessions, seen less than five or more than 12 causes developed. I do not know the significance of this. Facilitators can use this as a guide. Even I became nervous recently when a particular QAT insisted they had 18 causes. They stuck with this through the rank ordering process, but then changed the 18 to 10 as they performed the force field analysis. This is another example of the self-correcting nature of this process which will be described later.

After all the causes are written down I then instruct the group, "Please rank order the causes."

This becomes a very interesting exercise. Groups usually debate vigorously about the rank order of the first, second, and third causes.

The remainder do not get as much debate which confirms they are probably not in the same league as this particular QAT.

During the rank ordering another refinement takes place and this is the real reason I do it. I have seen 15 causes become eight, 10 become six, nine become five, and so on. The reason for this is what looks like something different on a brainstorm list can sometimes fit into a major cause either as part of it or other times as an example of how the major cause manifests itself.

After the rank ordering the facilitator is ready for the first force field analysis. Place the cause and effect analysis on a wall or just under the pad so all can see it.

Sub-Drawing the Force Field Analysis

It is important that the facilitator draw the first force field. He/she shows by example, how to do it. Even though it is a rather simple process, it is amazing how confused some people get when you ask them to do it.

Start by drawing a horizontal line across the middle of the pad. Then tell the group to think of this line as "the level of" line. An employee named Phil in Atlanta said this once in his explanations to a group and I never forgot it. I taught Phil the process, but he was the first I know of to use this phrase in describing the line. This is helpful because you are trying to picture the cause you are working on at a particular level.

We used the examples of training and absenteeism previously. These are good examples for the facilitator to keep in mind at this point. If training was the cause, the facilitator would say, "Picture the level of training being at the level of the line on this easel." The level is too low, something is causing it to be that low and we call this restraining forces. Write the words *restraining forces* on top of the page just under the words *The level of training is too low.* Then write the words *driving forces* in the middle or the bottom of the pad.

Ask the group to then define the restraining forces. For some reason there is less debate about these restraining forces. It is important for the facilitator to write these down almost as they are stated provided there is no debate. The first force field usually will contain six to 12 restraining forces. It also is common for the remaining force fields to have fewer and fewer restraining forces. This is a good way to validate the rank ordering of the causes.

Let's say you have eight force fields. Number one has eight or 10 restraining forces, number two has six, number three has six, number four has five, and number five has 10. At this point it is good to question whether number five is ranked properly. In most cases the group will decide to give it a higher ranking. The facilitator moves this along by asking, "Is number five of higher significance than number one, number two," etc. (until the new slot is agreed upon). This is another example of the self-correcting nature of the process.

After the last restraining force is agreed upon, the facilitator arbitrarily numbers the restraining forces. You'll appreciate why we do this in a minute. After the restraining forces are numbered the facilitator asks, "OK, what do you recommend we do about each restraining force? Let's start with number one."

After a driving force is defined, the facilitator asks the group if that particular action would affect restraining forces on top of the chart by number. It is much easier to call off the numbers at this point than read all the words in each restraining force. In some cases we reach as many as 94 driving forces against 60 or 70 restraining forces. Use the numbers, it's much more efficient.

When the first force field is finished the facilitator tears the sheet off the pad and tapes it on a wall so the group can see it. At times a solution offered in a prior force field can be applied as a solution to other restraining forces. A note is made "see force field number ———."

At this point the facilitator hands the marker to the QAT member sitting on the right or left side of the arc. This usually comes as a great surprise to everyone. I have already discussed the reason for doing this. Participants really get interested at this moment. They now understand at this moment that they, in fact, are going to "learn by doing."

Let's talk for a moment about the QAT participation in the Phase III management presentation. The facilitator has completed the cause and effect analysis and the first force field. This means these two elements need to be assigned to two of the QAT members. Since these are the very first to be presented it is important to pick two people who can do it effectively. The facilitator can get a very good idea of who these people are from their participation in the first hour of the procedure. Once you have these two cited choose those who will do force fields two through the end accordingly. Sometimes it is necessary to have the folks share a force field; one does the restraining force, the other does the driving force.

It is important to understand why we go to such extremes to have everyone participate. After six to 10 intensive hours of work on a subject that is very important to the group, it is most important that everyone get a chance to participate in front of their own management team. In most cases all want to participate regardless of how they protest that they don't want to. On very rare occasions you may get an outright refusal. In those cases honor the refusal. In the one instance this happened, the person later "volunteered" to take part. Her name was Ana—she did a great job and really captured the support and admiration of her QAT coworkers.

As soon as the facilitator hands the marker to the first QAT member to "do" force field number two, he/she actually sits in the chair of the QAT member. The facilitator continues to do this throughout the entire procedure until the last force field is complete. Many ask why; some even suggest leaving the room at this point. This would be a drastic mistake. A rapport has been built between the facilitator and QAT participants which is very constructive and it must continue. The facilitator uses all the approaches mentioned earlier in a natural way. The QAT members need this kind of participation.

In a recent experience I had worked on a Friday from 8 A.M. to 5 P.M. In this case we needed another three or four hours to complete the presentation. I was scheduled to travel for the next two weeks so I suggested that the group carry on without me. The group unanimously requested and agreed that we meet on Sunday to finish up. This is an example of the real discipline that occurs during these sessions.

Facilitator Tips on How to Summarize

After the last force field is complete the facilitator then takes active control again. The purpose is to summarize the work so far completed in terms of categorizing driving forces by common and special causes, as well as helping determine what levels of management and/or worker need to get involved in the implementation process. This sounds like quite a talk, but it's quite simple. This can be completed in a half hour for 30 to 50 driving forces. Ninety-four driving forces took one hour.

I write the following words on the pad and ask someone to help tally the numbers:

Management

Worker

Management Levels:
1
2
3
4
5
6

The QAT member selected stays at the easel and I go around the room and address each driving force. I ask the question "Who can implement this driving force, management or worker?"

If the answer is worker I write the letter "W" on top of the driving force. If the answer is management I write the letter "M" and then ask the question, "What level?" Sometimes it is one specific level such as 1 or 2, other times it is a combination of levels such as 2, 3, and 4, and other times it applies to all levels.

When the above questions have been answered for all driving forces we end up with data that tells us what percent is management, what percent worker, and of the management what percent can be implemented at what levels.

Usually we come pretty close to Deming's original 85/15 management/worker ratio. My data of over 100 groups shows it as 82/18, remarkably close. The facilitator should be ready, however, for remarkably different data at times, and know what to do with it.

I can recall a case where the data was 100/0. This came from a group of installation supervisors in southern Florida. This was a remarkable occasion because during the Phase I discussion this particular group wanted to throw me out of the place when I discussed the 85/15 rule. They felt it was all the workers' fault and management had no responsibility at all. Needless to say, their own conclusions at the end of Phase II startled them. One even said, "Don, I apologize. I understand better now what you were trying to explain to us yesterday. Our management team really needs to get their act together."

On another occasion I recall the data coming out 60/40. This was a group of very highly paid scientists in a research and development organization. As I thought about the 40 percent it became obvious that this caliber "worker" would have more impact in that particular work environment. As we continue to work with employees of this sophistication, my guess would be the 85 percent will be pulled down and the 15 percent will be pushed up.

Sub-Management Levels

Now let's discuss the management data from the facilitator's standpoint. I have found that a normal finding, as mentioned earlier, is that 60 percent of the time lower management can solve the problem, 30 percent of the time middle management can solve the problem, and in only 10 percent of the cases does it go to higher management. Again, you will find exceptions. I recall a case when lower management was 20 percent, middle 25 percent, and higher 55 percent. This means real trouble because the higher you go the more serious the problem and the longer it takes to get things done.

I ask my management friends, however, "Isn't it good to know the data? To know what levels need to do to make things better?" It's much better than rocking along thinking that the lower levels can do it all—they can't.

Lillian Simpson of the Florida Motor Vehicle Division of License developed the following guidelines for facilitators in her division. I endorse this guideline fully. It breaks down each step and specifically defines the materials needed and how to use them—down to the color of the markers! Black and red are the marker colors I usually use—you can use any two colors you wish!

This step-by-step description of the procedure is accurate and can be used by facilitators getting ready for their mission voyage in using the CE/FFA technique.

Florida Motor Vehicle Division of License

For Facilitation of Concept of Publication
by
A. Donald Stratton
An Approach to Quality Improvement That Works

Both the *Deming and Stratton* concept have had a powerful impact on our division. As a result, management feels that employee knowledge is important to the process of getting the job done. They believe those doing the job are the experts and are highly qualified to give suggestions/recommendations to improve their work process. Therefore, management has implemented the Service Improvement Program to help tap the resources our experts have to offer. This program is designed to encourage ideas and creativity by providing time and resources to enable groups of employees to meet, identify problems and solutions, and present their solutions to management. Employees who know that management will listen to these problems and will implement suggested solutions, where possible, are encouraged to participate.

Management then sets in motion a program to implement the solutions these experts offer so the work can be done better. Improve the process and you, in turn, improve productivity and service.

James H. Cox, director, Division of Driver Licenses, is quoted as saying:

> "The Service Improvement Program for our division is already rendering success stories, our people now hear the message that we want, need, and value their contributions. The courage and intelligence of our people truly impress me! Stratton and Deming have certainly given us tools to improve service."

The objective of the facilitator, as discussed in Stratton's book, will be outlined in this module. The facilitator's major role is to keep the group on track and to assist the group in avoiding gripe sessions. Remember, we are here to solve problems. The facilitator should create an atmosphere that allows free and open discussion. Although it is sometimes difficult, it is important to be patient and allow the team to form their own ideas; avoid offering solutions to their problems. A facilitator does not need to be knowledgeable of the problems discussed. His or her job is to let the ideas flow and to give encouragement when discussion becomes slow.

Remember, this program is a "help tool" for management and will open the lines of communication between worker and management. *All levels* of management should be active *participants* for maximum success. Those who need to know, will know, and those empowered to make or assist in making decisions or changes will also be involved. This also assures the worker that management is committed to the program and will support and encourage all workers. This should be a very positive and productive, non-threatening process.

Read the complete module prior to beginning the process. Study reference material, give ample notice to participants and management, make preparations, and have your equipment and room set up. Be Prepared!

The entire process has 4 phases. Major emphasis in this module will be placed on Phase II and III.

Phase I   Management meets, reviews programs, and commits to the program. (This has been done in our division. Top level management has committed to this program.)

Phase II   Working with a small group on problem areas.

Phase III Presenting management with solutions to the problem.

Phase IV   Resolution of problems identified and Review Process is chaired by the division director to assure proper implementation of resolutions.

PHASE II

Specifically the trainee will:

- Learn to identify a theme or problem to work on.
- Learn to identify solutions to problems.
- Learn the technique of doing cause and effect.
- Learn the technique of Force Field Analyses.
- Learn to analyze problem using cause and effect/force field analysis.
- Learn to prepare recommendations for implementing a solution.
- Learn by participation how to make presentation to management.
- Learn to define management levels/responsibilities.

- Learn how to be a facilitator of the complete process by hands-on involvement and participation.

Room set-up and facility: Room which will seat 15 to 20 people and is large enough to place the six to 10 experts (Action Team) in a semi-circle around the facilitator. More space will be necessary when management is involved or observers are invited. Avoid allowing management who supervise experts to attend during Phase II.

Equipment: The room will need a monitor and VCR (7-1/2″ VHS), two easels (equal in size to place side by side), two full easel pads, markers (black and red), masking tape (used to post sheets from the flip chart so they will remain visible throughout the process, and a hand calculator.

Reference material: *An Approach to Quality Improvement That Works*, by A. Donald Stratton, *Red Q (Quality Teams)* book.

Stratton/Cause and Effect/18 mm video.
Channel 6—Stratton Video.
Cox—Division Director Video.

Optional references: *Out of the Crisis* by Dr. Deming
The Deming Management Method by Walton

Time frames: Allow six to 10 hours for Phase II, Action Team and Phase III, and presentation of recommendations to management.
- Introduction—1/2 hour including video (18 min.).
- Cause and effect—45 minutes to 1-1/2 hours.
- First force field—45 minutes to one hour.
- Remaining force fields—20 to 30 minutes each.
- Summary—1/2 hour.
- Presentation to management—two hours.

NOTES/REFERENCES   PHASE II ACTION TEAM

I. Make Preparations.

A. Read pages one through 26 of *An Approach to Quality Improvement That Works.*

Management - chief and assistant chief assign teams with input from "next level supervisors" through immediate supervisors or as designated.

B. Management assigns six to 10 employees who perform work of the same type (homogeneous job duties) or cross functional group to serve as experts on the Quality Action Team.

C. Notify all employees chosen to be experts on the Quality Action Team.
1. Prepare and disseminate schedules. Include a list of experts, dates, times, and any other necessary instructions.
2. Schedule Phase II and III* for eight to 10 hours. *See time frames.

Room set-up and facility

D. Set up room - (previously explained).

II. Begin Phase II.

A. Management starts Quality Action Team. Gives commitment and support to action teams.

1. Explain Deming concept and how it relates to quality service.
2. Explain theory of variability.

Stratton cause and effect video (18 minutes)

3. Show 18 minute video entitled "Cause and Effect Force Field Analysis."

B. Quality Action Team identifies and lists problems/defects.

Reference page 17 &
18 *An Approach to
Quality Improvement
That Works*

C. Do cause and effect: (CE)

cause = problem
effect = the effect the "causes"
or problems have on our organization not being as effective as
it should be.
• Facilitator does cause and effect
and one force field analysis as
instruction to the group.
1. Use problems already listed (in
step I) as reference.
2. Group selects only the major or
primary causes to place in
bubbles and uses those left as
bullets or explanation when
they relate to, or explain the
problem. (refer to diagrams
referenced)
3. Number in rank or priority
order those causes identified by
the Quality Action Team.

Reference Page 9 *Red
Q book*

D. Do force field analysis on *each* of
the major causes identified.

Reference Page 20 *An
Approach to Quality
Improvement That
Works*

1. Study concept and formation of
the force field.

Reference Page 6 *An
Approach to Quality
Improvement That
Works* Diagram Page

2. Determine level of the problem
or cause. Is it too high or too
low? List and number in upper
left-hand corner. Example:

#1 Level of morale is too low.

NOTE: Restraining force = problem or
cause.
Driving force = solutions suggested to solve problems.

Reference Diagrams
Page 21, 22, 23 *An Approach to Quality Improvement That Works*

3. Label restraining and driving forces:

    Example: if level is too low—you would want to drive it up or if level is too high drive it down.

E. After you have completed the cause and effect force field analysis (FFA), to explain the process begin letting the "experts" do the FFA.

    Remember:
    "I hear, I forget
    I see, I remember
    I do, I understand."

    1. Guide each expert through an FFA process.
    *Remember the experts are training to become facilitators.

F. Explain management levels: who and what levels are responsible for which problems.

    1. Draw a chart to show six levels of management. Example:
    1. TBA
    2. TBA
    3. Assistant Chief
    4. Chief
    5. Assistant Director
    6. *Director*
    _____
    W = Worker

    2. On each cause of your force field analysis place the appropriate number(s) of which level(s) of management or worker are responsible for correcting that problem.

3. Then the group should count and tally how many of each level are responsible. Calculate the percentages of responsibilities for each level of management or worker.

Reference Page 8 *An Approach to Quality Improvement That Works*

4. Do summary, list percentages of responsibility; i.e., management, worker.

NOTES/REFERENCES PHASE III

Reference Page 9 and 10 *An Approach to Quality Improvement That Works*

G. Presentation to management.

1. Appoint an expert to give the introduction to management, then assign each expert a cause or effect to present to management. (Include everyone.) This process is very difficult and group support is essential. Be there when you are needed and remind the group to work together and help each other during their presentations.

2. Facilitator opens to announce that this is an input session.

3. Facilitator reviews and explains tally sheet and the 85/15 rule to management.

4. Facilitator ends by writing "What's Next" on the board. QRT members are selected.

5. Praise group.

What's Next?

Resolution team members should be identified by management. This should include the appropriate members of the management staff and two or three of the experts. The experts selected for the resolution team should be appointed by the facilitator; however, the management levels involved should be appointed by the chairman of the resolution team, the assistant division director.

Summary

I have expanded this chapter substantially from the first edition's version. This is mainly due to the many questions I have been asked by facilitators all over the country. The overriding thing to carry with you is the notion that those closest to the work do have great ideas which need to be tapped. This process allows you to do this rapidly and with a high degree of discipline. If we were in the business of idea production, distillation of those ideas and then implementing those possible, this would be the most efficient method. It includes the attribute of group memory by the writing down, in a very understandable form, the group's thoughts. Because of my schedule I have had Phase II sessions stop and then continue three weeks later. The participants, after a very brief review of the "sheets," knew exactly where they were and continued on without difficulty. Without the "sheets" some groups would almost start from scratch and discuss the same issues again.

___PART 4___

EXAMPLES OF DRAWING CAUSE AND EFFECT AND FORCE FIELD ANALYSIS DIAGRAMS

In the last chapter we discussed how to find the effect in a generic (organizational efficiency) and specific (defect known) situation. Let's look at how to draw a cause and effect diagram.

Start by drawing a broken vertical line that separates the major causes from the effect in the Ishikawa chart (Figure 1). Write the effect on the right and the causes on the left.

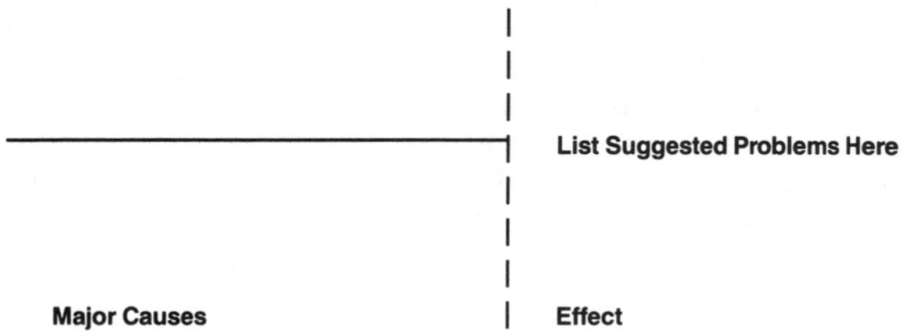

Major Causes   **Effect**

FIGURE 1

Effects are those quality problems or defects that occur on the specific job to which each group is assigned. In a production environment these could be the kinds of defects for which the individual workers or work unit might be written up in a quality audit. In white-collar groups you will find that groups often define causes when asked to define effects. (See *The Visit—Phase II,* page 58.)

One of the difficulties in getting started is distinguishing between the effects and the major causes. Often participants will want to suggest problems that occurred earlier in the work flow, before reaching them, such as receiving wrong or faulty components. Although that may be a serious problem, the group should focus on the results of having to work with those kinds of situations—results for which they are likely to be criticized.

Note each of these effects on the diagram. When several suggestions are similar, ask the individuals if they might be talking about the same thing. Don't make assumptions. It's important to let the group members clarify for themselves what they really mean.

After a reasonable time—approximately 30 to 45 minutes—or when the suggestions seem exhausted, have the group reach a consensus on the *one effect* that is the most significant problem affecting quality.

Start by letting group members volunteer their choices and reasons for these choices. If the consensus does not appear to be forthcoming, poll the group. Work on what appears to be a clear majority of opinion, even if you have to poll the group several times to narrow the selection. It's important that all group members own the problem.

There are times when management may wish to specify the quality effect being examined. This may be the result of negative trends, quality audits, or anticipation of quality-type problems in specific areas. The key here is to put the correct group of people together to examine that problem.

After the group determines the number one quality problem, the facilitator draws a cause and effect diagram on the pad and asks them to suggest its major causes. The facilitator diagrams those causes, shown in Figure 2. Right now the group looks for causes only; the process calls for identifying solutions later, during the force field analysis. If someone does volunteer a solution, the facilitator should ask that person to write it down so that it won't be forgotten; the group then keeps looking for major causes of the effect.

At this point, the group must organize the causes into order of importance. Figure 3 shows a completed cause and effect study. This particular group started with 10 possible causes; by setting priorities and reorganizing, they narrowed the list to six.

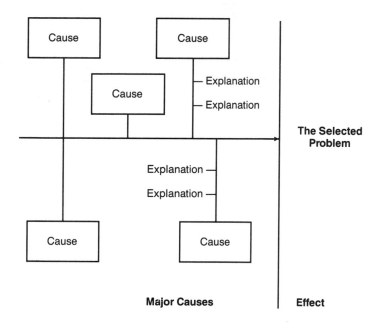

FIGURE 2   Cause and Effect Study

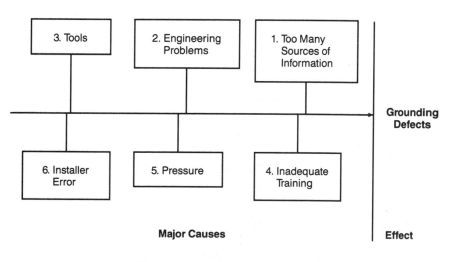

FIGURE 3   Grounding Defects

Force Field Analysis

This concept states that any problem or situation is a result of forces acting upon it. Restraining forces keep the problem situation at its current level. Driving forces push the situation toward improvement. Restraining forces are the causes of problems; driving forces are the solutions.

In a force field analysis, a horizontal line is used to represent the current problem level (Figure 4). We described the current force field situation by stating whether the level of the problem is too high or too low. In this case, for example, the level of information (cause 1) is too high.

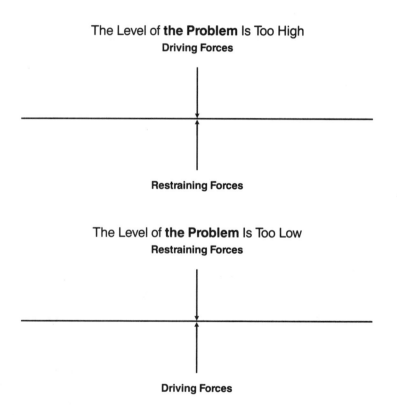

FIGURE 4

Figure 4 shows how a problem is diagrammed in a force field analysis. If the problem situation is too high, restraining forces are shown as pushing it up while driving forces drive it down toward improvement. If the problem situation is too low, restraining forces push it down, and driving forces push it up toward improvement.

The force field analysis process begins by the group examining the most important cause identified in the cause and effect study and states whether its level is too high or too low. The group then identifies the restraining forces—the situations and events that keep the problem situation at its current level. In the group we have been referring to, the first analysis was "the level of information is too high." This group of installers and supervisors determined that too many sources of information was the number one cause of grounding nonconformances before verification and correction.

They saw the following restraining forces contributing to that problem level:

- Different grounding requirements for each type of equipment.
- Changes in requirements and timely notification.
- Different interpretations of grounding requirements.
- Workers' inability to absorb too many information sources, compounded by the need for additional clerical support and the need to distribute information over a wide geographic area.

Each of these restraining forces is diagrammed in Figure 5. For forces that compound the restraining force, the vectors are connected to the restraining force itself.

The Level of **Information** Is Too High

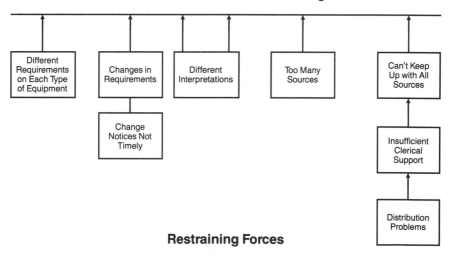

Restraining Forces

FIGURE 5

As the group identifies restraining forces, someone is likely to offer solutions. Just as when solutions were offered during the cause and effect study, the facilitator should acknowledge the value of the idea, remind the group that it is looking for restraining forces only at this time, and ask the person to make a note of the solution.

After the group identifies a significant number of restraining forces, it starts looking for driving forces to counter each specific restraining force (Figure 6). In this case, the group identified "clarify information" and "make it simple" as driving forces to counter "different interpretations."

The Level of **Information** Is Too High

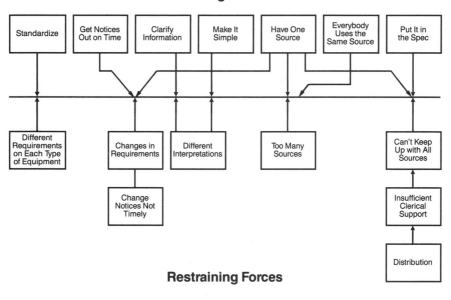

Driving Forces

Restraining Forces

FIGURE 6

In some cases, more than one driving force will be found for a specific restraining force. The diagram shows this by pointing the arrows from both driving forces toward the opposing restraining forces.

Often, one driving force will counter more than one restraining force. Again, arrows from that driving force are shown in opposition to all the restraining forces it can counter. The example has "have one source of information" as a driving force countering "changes in requirements," "too many sources," and "can't keep up with all sources."

Once the group identifies all the restraining forces and their opposing driving forces for a specific major cause of a quality problem, it has completed a force field analysis. The diagram presents a specific problem along with a prescription for its solution. To complete

the process, the group goes through each major cause identified in the cause and effect study and performs the same kind of force field analysis.

It should be noted that this process is self-correcting. In this case, the group initially identified six causes, as shown in Figure 5. As the group was pursuing the force field analysis, however, it discovered a seventh cause, poor motivation. This cause was then ranked third in order of importance.

The analysis of low motivation shows how the cause and effect study/force field analysis process is self-correcting. Low motivation was first suggested as a possible restraining force that kept the level of information too high (i.e., as a contributing factor to one of the six original causes). The person suggesting low motivation was hesitant to raise the issue, but the group's openness eventually created an atmosphere in which he felt free to address it. Once the issue was out in the open, it quickly became apparent to the group that low motivation did not really contribute to the level of information being too high. They saw that it belonged with the major causes of grounding problems.

Cause and Effect/Force Field Analysis in a White-Collar Organization

Let's look at another example of CE/FFA in action—this time in a service setting attempting to reduce late payments. This group started with a list of 12 possible causes, then narrowed the list down to eight major causes, as shown in Figure 7. These white-collar workers selected "inadequate training" as the number one cause of late payments in their organization; that is, the group determined that "the level of training is too low."

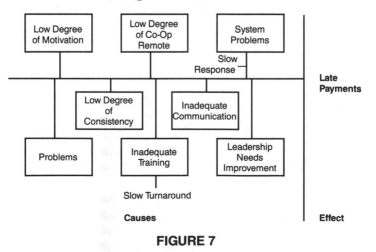

FIGURE 7

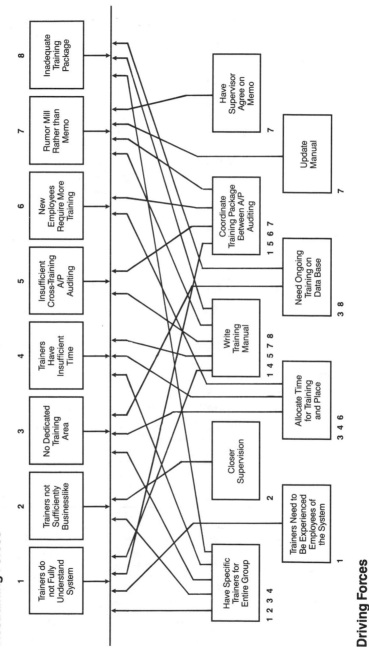

The Level of Training Is Too Low

Restraining Forces

1	2	3	4	5	6	7	8
Trainers do not Fully Understand System	Trainers not Sufficiently Businesslike	No Dedicated Training Area	Trainers Have Insufficient Time	Insufficient Cross-Training A/P Auditing	New Employees Require More Training	Rumor Mill Rather than Memo	Inadequate Training Package

Have Specific Trainers for Entire Group — 1 2 3 4

Trainers Need to Be Experienced Employees of the System — 2

Closer Supervision

Allocate Time for Training and Place — 3 4 6

Write Training Manual — 1 4 5 7 8

Coordinate Training Package Between A/P Auditing — 1 5 6 7

Need Ongoing Training on Data Base — 3 8

Have Supervisor Agree on Memo — 7

Update Manual — 7

Driving Forces

FIGURE 8

The group identified the following restraining forces:

- Trainers were not sufficiently businesslike.
- There was no specific training area.
- Trainers had insufficient time.
- There was insufficient cross-training of accounts payable and auditing personnel.
- New employees required more training.
- Information was communicated through rumor rather than memorandum.
- The training package was inadequate.

The resulting CE/FFA diagram is shown in Figure 8.

The arrow crossings can make the CE/FFA analysis results difficult to understand at first, especially if the arrows are all the same color. To make the results clearer, the restraining forces can be numbered, and the driving forces assigned numbers according to the restraining force they affect, as was done in Figure 8. The numbers can be used to help understand which driving forces affect which restraining forces.

Proving the 85/15 Rule

The completed force field analysis diagram provides a significant list of positive suggestions to solving quality problems. To determine ownership of the problems, the group writes "M" for management or "W" for worker on each driving force. (When you add up the totals, you will find that management owns close to 85 percent of the driving forces, just as Deming and Juran suggest.) Next, the facilitator asks the group to specify the supervision level necessary to act on each driving force, and writes these levels next to each "M." This is the group's best guess, of course, but experience shows these groups are usually quite accurate in their assessment. As mentioned, we have surprisingly found that a great number of solutions can be put in place by lower levels—60 percent can be resolved at first and second levels of management.

The same process is repeated for worker-related solutions. Communicating these ideas to workers becomes the responsibility of both group and management.

The group's findings should be documented. This means copying the developed diagrams as part of the cause and effect study and each force field analysis. Documentation should also include notes and pertinent observations. In preparing these documents, time is of the essence and elegance does not matter. This documentation can be shared with all managers who attend the Phase III session; it can also be used by the QRT.

Long-Term Commitment

Some of the issues identified by the groups are products of years—perhaps even decades—of doing things one way. Changing traditional patterns is always difficult. In fact, Deming suggests that such basic changes happen slowly, over a period of years. Quality is both a start and commitment. The quality resolution team will require reasonable time to pursue these issues to appropriate resolutions for improvement to result.

Summary

In the first phase we discuss the following with the management team location head:

- Get active involvement in a quality improvement program.
- Explain the factors of a good quality improvement program.
- Explain the Deming philosophy and key points of other quality philosophies.
- Discuss what other companies are doing.
- Explain CE/FFA.

In Phase II we actually conduct a CE/FFA session with six to 10 people. The purpose is twofold:

- Develop recommendations to make the process better, using the CE/FFA technique.
- Train participants and observers to be facilitators, using the CE/FFA technique.

In Phase III the small group makes a presentation to management on their findings. This purpose is also twofold:

- Help management understand employees' views of what needs to be done to help them do their work better.
- Get management commitment to establish QRTs to address and resolve problems.

In actual work with over 100 QATs and the resulting QRTs, we find this process to work, provided management is 100 percent supportive.

Phase IV is primarily aimed at white-collar groups where in-process checks are instituted to ensure quality. Flow charts depicting specific areas to be measured are introduced and data are gathered at these checkpoints. The data are analyzed to determine if the process is in control and how it can be continuously improved.

PART 5
ANATOMY OF A SUCCESSFUL FIELD TRIP

The initial contact:

"Hello, Don, this is Jim. Can you come and help us improve the quality of our operation? I've been working with a group in the planning area and, as you know, I'm the quality coordinator for our organization."

"Sure, Jim. I'd be glad to help. Our only problem will be getting it on the calendar. What do you have in mind?"

"Well, we are familiar with your four-phase approach and believe that the first three phases are appropriate right now. In fact the manager volunteered his group at our last staff meeting. Both heard you talk and want CE/FFA implemented in our organization."

"Are you saying you want the entire three-phase approach?"

"Yes."

"Who will Phase I be directed at?"

"The entire manager's organization."

"I'll give the Phase I discussion to the entire group, then I will ask the management team to leave, and I'll work with the small group using the CE/FFA technique. How much time would you like to have for the Phase I session? What do you want to accomplish?"

"Well, many of these people have already heard about your work but they haven't seen you face-to-face. So, we would really like you to give them a basic appreciation of your philosophy, whatever results you can share, and, of course, your CE/FFA approach and how that works."

"To accomplish this, I can do anything from one hour to four hours, based on the time you have. How about a two-hour session with the entire group? Would you want me to include the 18-minute videotape on CE/FFA showing a live group using the disciplines?"

"Absolutely. Let's plan on the two-hour session including the tape."

"Sounds to me like we'll need two days. First I'll give the Phase I talk, then the supervisors can leave, and I'll begin work with the QAT. This will take from six to 10 hours and, as you know, we refer to this as Phase II. Then we will begin Phase III, which will last from one to two hours."

"Sounds good. What will you need?"

"For Phase I, a 35 mm carousel projector with a remote control that reaches the screen. I'll also need a videocassette player and an easel to write on—any size. For Phase II, the most important thing is a 54-inch by 48-inch easel. If you can't find one you can put two small easels together. We won't need any other equipment for Phase III."

"Thanks, Don. We're all looking forward to this."

The Visit—Phase I

I arrived at the site of the Phase I session at 8:30 A.M. The room was magnificent. It was a small, plush theater-style room with a stage, large screen, and all kinds of front screen audiovisual equipment.

The audience was also impressive. It was obvious they were high level, technically oriented people who knew what they were about.

The talk went well. No talk is ever exactly the same. Many times I find myself reacting to even a positive or negative gesture and inserting a comment that wasn't thought of previously. In this particular talk it appeared the group was seeking more definitions of Deming's "drive out fear" point.

I shared with them an experience I encountered at the Juran Institute Impro Program. I was a speaker and arranged a professional quality display. I believe it was the first for AT&T. After my presentation, I went to the display area where many conferees were gathered.

One of the visuals in the display was a list of principles we developed, one of which concentrated on driving out fear. A comment was made by a young conferee: "Why would anyone include the idea that fear even exists in our company?" I tried to explain to her that fear manifests itself in many different ways. I told her about a QAT I worked with that constantly referred to its boss's office as "never-never land." All 10 QAT members were unanimous in their opinion that the boss's office was not a place to be seen or heard. It was a place to be avoided, at all costs. I asked the conferee how long she worked for her company. She replied, "Two years." I just said, "Keep your eyes open; you'll find fear. It's still there unfortunately."

Because they seemed tuned in to this particular point I shared with this group the ideas of William W. Scherkenbach of Ford Motor Company on this subject.[10]

Scherkenbach refers to the thousands of hours of research that can result from a CEO's raised eyebrow at a meeting. My experience says the raised eyebrow can come from someone at a level a lot lower than the CEO. How many hours of work are wasted chasing rainbows, finding answers to questions that aren't ever asked—because of fear?

Scherkenbach also refers to the wasted hours putting together black books for people who go to meetings so they'll know all the answers. The reason people can't go to meetings without all the answers is fear. We ought to be able to say, "I'll find out in 24 hours," rather than lose three man-weeks putting the bogus black book together. I agree.

The other Deming point that many people challenge is the elimination of numerical goals and work standards. This group was no exception. Some say, "You only get what you measure." I say, "And that's all you get!" Time and time again I have talked to people in many companies who could do more than they were asked to do. This, of course, is after experience sets in—not during the initial stages that require maximum training. I always ask this question of the measurement advocates: "If you're so enamored with measuring people why don't you tell them you'll let them go home when they meet their bogie?" Most people would be home by 2:00 P.M. in a normal workday. You see—and here is the enormous waste—we certainly wouldn't let them go home when they meet their bogie, so they really are doing what management asks: five hours of work in eight hours. What a waste.

The other idea stressed by Deming is how we use numbers to manage people. He strongly advocates the elimination of slogans, exhortations, and acclamation aimed at the worker to shape up. We had a situation where someone had the idea of motivating engineers to do a better job by drawing cartoons of engineers making mistakes. When management began to understand that the *process* the engineers were working on was the problem, not the engineers, the cartoons disappeared almost overnight.

The best example of the negative effect numbers can have on the work force is an experience with an accounting group. In working with the QAT, one cause of late payments was low morale in the group. A fairly low level employee was at the easel doing the force field analysis on low morale. One of the group members said, "Let's face it. What causes low morale in our group are the charts."

This was a group of 140 employees divided into four sections. The group was measured by four critical measures each month. The head supervisor ranked each section and hung four large charts each month so everyone would know who was first, second, third, and fourth. God help the group that came in last! They were ostracized and supervisors fought verbally in full view of the work force. Group 1 would not eat lunch with groups 2, 3, and 4, etc.

Then came the Phase III session with management. The head supervisor was a 240-pound crewcut type, with a manufacturing background. He wanted to tear me apart during the Phase I discussion on eliminating work standards. During the Phase II session, though, he was remarkably interested, sensitive, and attentive while hearing his own people discuss how to make things better.

When the young employee got up to discuss why morale was low, the entire QAT group gasped at the thought of little Nancy announcing to the management team the idea of taking down the charts. When she did, Mr. Boss just wrote it down. After the meeting he went out on the floor and took the charts down himself. He became an overnight hero; his results improved remarkably. In six months, late payments rose from 95 percent to 97 percent on time. Sounds like a small improvement. When looking at this improvement from the customer's viewpoint, however, there were about 1,000 more satisfied customers at the 97 percent level than at the 95 percent level. This is a remarkable improvement in results.

It's not that management should throw away all data. They need data to know what's going on. The important thing to gain from this experience is how to use the data when involving employees.

The group seemed to appreciate the Phase I discussion. They were supportive during the talk and made good comments afterward. I felt like this was going to be a worthwhile trip.

The Visit—Phase II

The QAT was made up of 12 people. All were experts in area planning. The employee length of service ranged from three to 30 years. This was an energetic, extremely intelligent group. They appeared eager to get started, though somewhat apprehensive. This is usually the case.

The first step in Phase II is to ask the group to list the kind of problem areas they face in getting their job done. In about one-half hour, the group developed this list:

- Using obsolete methods.
- Insufficient teamwork.
- Group coordination.
- Changing product environment.
- Unclear direction/responsibilities.
- Lack of training.
- Lack of management support.
- Unclear job description.
- Unclear interfacing between organizations.
- Lack of communication and commitment.
- Lack of understanding customers' needs.
- Low or confused acceptance by the technical group.
- Multiple product lines' overcommitment.
- Control span.

In analyzing this list, you'll find that it contains more causes than anything else. The key question is, how are these causes manifested? What is the *effect* related to these causes? The answer in this case was that organization is not as effective as it could be.

Whenever you ask a white-collar group what kind of problems it is having, the group usually answers with the causes, as was the case here. When you ask what the result is the group defines the effect in the cause and effect analysis.

This is the key difference to using cause and effect other than in the classic way, when the effect is known. Ishikawa's well-known example of a known effect is the wobble of a machine. In the white-collar world, the effect is not as apparent. You must work with a group to define it. Once it is defined, it becomes quite apparent and understood by the group.

Some white-collar effects are:

- Late payments.
- Wrong terms and conditions.
- Unknown customers' needs.
- Disorganized work process.
- Inaccurate office records.
- Too much unbilled.
- Ineffective customer contact.
- Inadequate customer service.

The group does a cause and effect analysis once the effect is defined. The group defines each cause and uses the original brainstorming list as a guide. Sometimes all items are used; most times the original list is refined. When all the causes are defined, the group ranks them in order of importance for management. The rank order for this group is as follows:

(1)   No clear direction and responsibility.
(2)   Low or confused acceptance.
(3)   Insufficient teamwork.
(4)   Lack of leverage over supporting organizations.
(5)   Lack of involvement in the commitment process.
(6)   Lack of training.
(7)   Confusion among levels of management.
(8)   Too much reactive behavior.
(9)   Insufficient resources.
(10) Different goals among organizations.

The self-correcting feature of the exercise came about during the force field analysis session when the group realized that numbers seven and 10 were being addressed throughout the entire exercise and did not need to be handled separately. This analysis ended up with just eight defined causes.

The group developed eight force field analyses covering each of the causes listed. These are diagrammed in Figures 9 to 17.

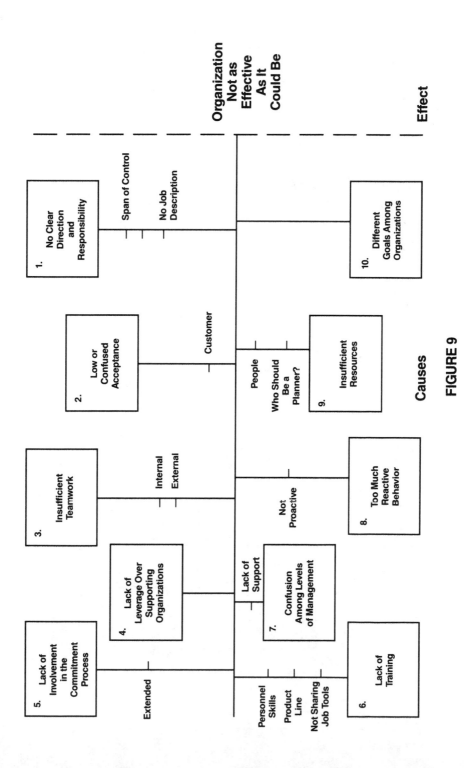

Organization Not as Effective As It Could Be

Effect

1. No Clear Direction and Responsibility
— Span of Control
— No Job Description

2. Low or Confused Acceptance
— Customer

3. Insufficient Teamwork
— Internal
— External

4. Lack of Leverage Over Supporting Organizations

5. Lack of Involvement in the Commitment Process
— Extended

6. Lack of Training
— Personnel Skills
— Product Line
— Not Sharing Job Tools

7. Confusion Among Levels of Management
— Lack of Support

8. Too Much Reactive Behavior
— Not Proactive

9. Insufficient Resources
— People Who Should Be a Planner?

10. Different Goals Among Organizations

Causes

FIGURE 9

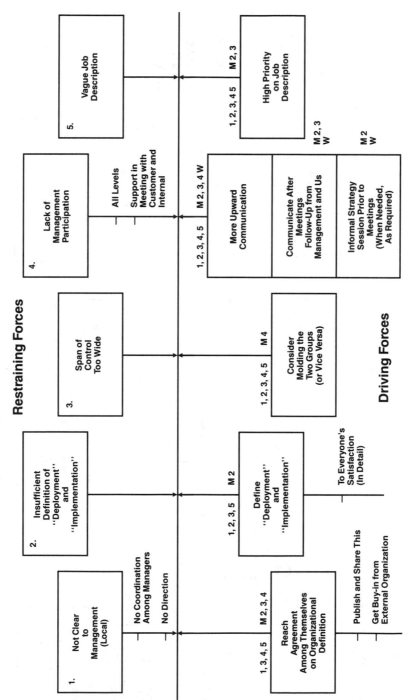

1 — Level of Clear Direction and Responsibility Is Too Low

Restraining Forces

Driving Forces

FIGURE 10

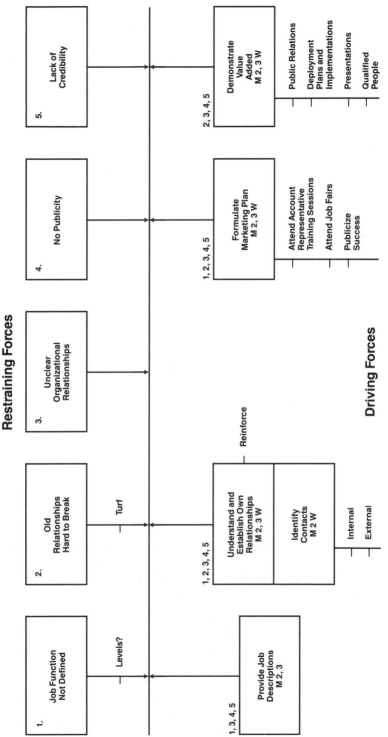

2 — Level of Acceptance and Understanding of Area Planning Is Low

Restraining Forces

Driving Forces

FIGURE 11

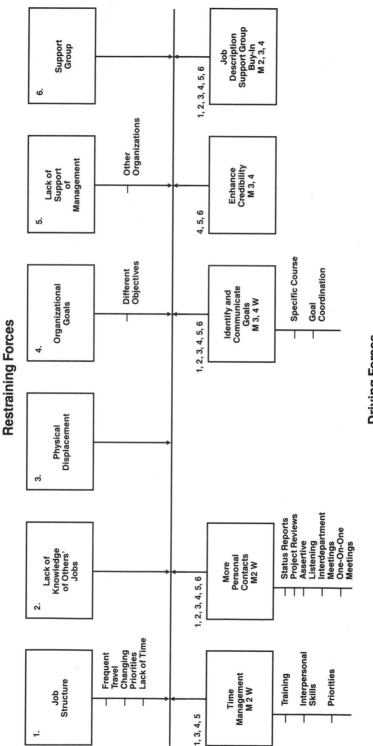

3 — Level of Teamwork Is Insufficient

Restraining Forces

Driving Forces

FIGURE 12

4 — Level of Leverage Over Supporting Organizations Is Insufficient

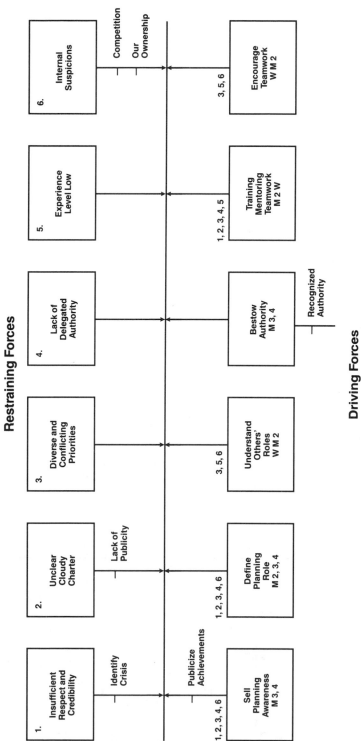

Restraining Forces

Driving Forces

FIGURE 13

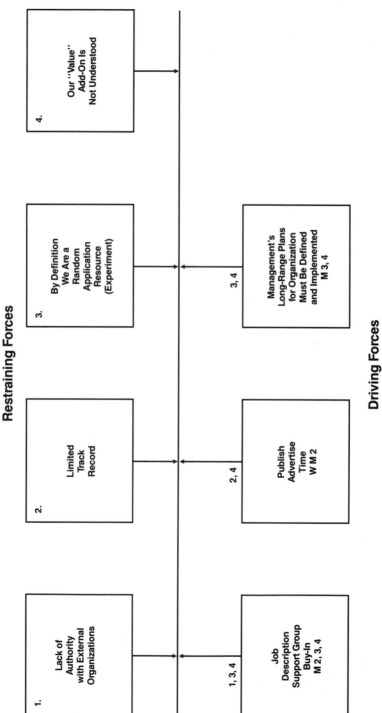

5 — Level of Involvement In Commitment Process Is Low

Restraining Forces

1. Lack of Authority with External Organizations

2. Limited Track Record

3. By Definition We Are a Random Application Resource (Experiment)

4. Our "Value" Add-On Is Not Understood

Driving Forces

Job Description Support Group Buy-In M 2, 3, 4

1, 3, 4

Publish Advertise Time W M 2

2, 4

Management's Long-Range Plans for Organization Must Be Defined and Implemented M 3, 4

3, 4

FIGURE 14

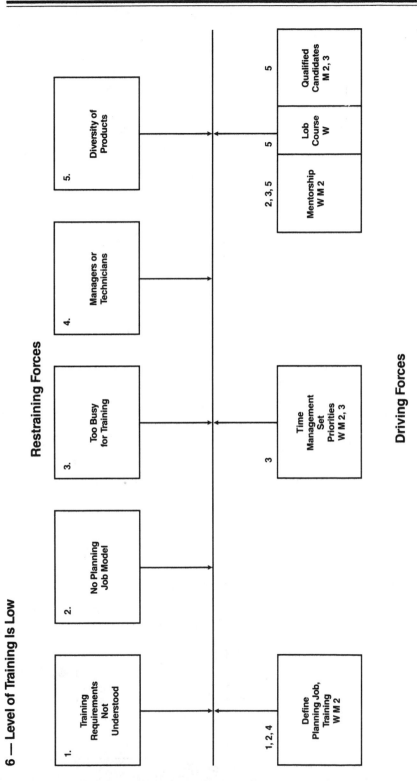

6 — Level of Training Is Low

Restraining Forces

| 1. Training Requirements Not Understood | 2. No Planning Job Model | 3. Too Busy for Training | 4. Managers or Technicians | 5. Diversity of Products |

Driving Forces

| Define Planning Job, Training W M 2 (1, 2, 4) | | Time Management Set Priorities W M 2, 3 (3) | | Mentorship W M 2 (2, 3, 5) | Lob Course W (5) | Qualified Candidates M 2, 3 (5) |

FIGURE 15

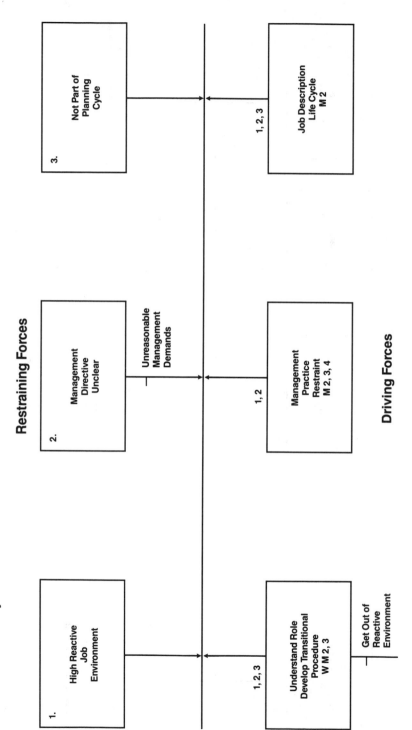

7 — Level of Proactivity Is Low

Restraining Forces

Driving Forces

FIGURE 16

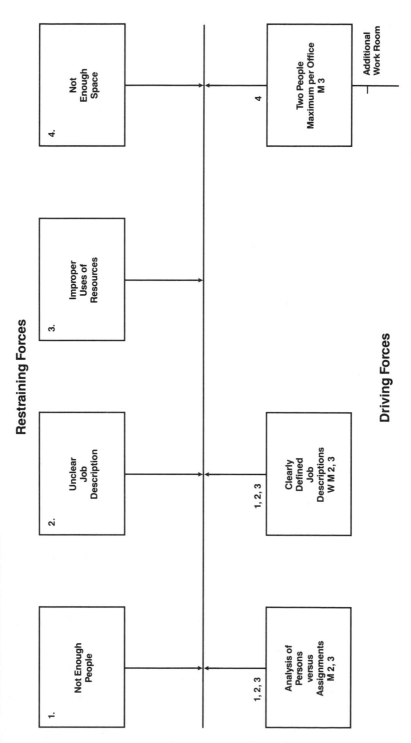

8 — Level of Resources Is Too Low

Restraining Forces

1. Not Enough People

2. Unclear Job Description

3. Improper Uses of Resources

4. Not Enough Space

Driving Forces

Analysis of Persons versus Assignments M 2, 3 — 1, 2, 3

Clearly Defined Job Descriptions W M 2, 3 — 1, 2, 3

Two People Maximum per Office M 3 — 4

Additional Work Room

FIGURE 17

After all the force fields were completed, we summarized the driving forces into management (noted M) or worker (noted W). We asked the group to give its best idea of which management levels could help solve the problems (this is indicated by numbers after the letter M).

The numbers on the top left of each driving force are the restraining forces above that would be affected if the driving force was implemented. We then count the driving forces and find out how many are management, how many are worker, and which levels are involved. In this case, management was listed 37 times and the worker once. Worker was listed jointly with management 21 times. This meant that management, although listed in 99 percent of the cases, had the worker help in 37 percent of the cases. This was not surprising in a group where the workers were high level, highly paid, experienced people working on complex problems. We get much closer to Deming's 85/15 ratio in situations in production-type organizations.

You will recall, the facilitator actually did the cause and effect study and the first force field analysis then "passed the marker" to the first person on the right or left side of the semicircle to do force field analysis number two. In this case, we have presenters for force fields two through eight. We do not have presenters for the cause and effect and first force fields. I always ask for volunteers and always get two. These are usually people who would have liked to participate, thought they were passed by, and then jump at the chance to be a part of the action.

So far, we have added up the management/worker tally and we have assigned a person to discuss the cause and effect and each force field analysis. We are now ready for the presentation to management.

The Visit—Phase III

As mentioned, this is an exciting event. Our group was relieved and ready; their humor was still very evident even though a week had passed since completion of Phase II.

I opened the session with discussions of the management versus worker responsibility summary; management responsibility was 63 percent, worker responsibility was 37 percent. Broken down further, management responsibility was 45 percent lower level, 35 percent middle level, and 20 percent higher level. This did not follow the normal 85/15 rule distribution because this was a relatively small group of technical experts with several years' experience. It's difficult enough to differentiate between worker and management in this highly professional world, so the 63/37 ratio is not surprising.

The next statement I make defines the purpose of this particular session. I told the group that this is an input session from the QAT to management. It's not the time for management to evaluate each statement or commit to specific action. This is the time to make sure management understands the input of the QAT and to clarify any questions.

I reviewed the original brainstorming list of problems and pointed out that all the items listed were causes. The effect of all the group-defined causes was that the organization was not being as effective as possible.

I introduced volunteer number one to walk the group through the cause and effect study, and to define each cause. The remaining force field analyses were covered by each QAT member who acted as facilitator during the QAT session.

After the eighth force field, I went to the easel and wrote the words *WHAT'S NEXT?* as suggested earlier.

I recommended that QRT be established, with a supervisor as chairman. The third-level manager volunteered, named his two immediate subordinates as members, and asked for four volunteers from the QAT and one representative from the staff group.

Eight people became members of the QRT; their first meeting was held immediately after the session. The true test of this entire endeavor will be what the QRT actually does in regard to the driving forces. It is too early to report results of this particular team, but we have shared results throughout this report that show continuous progress in process improvement.

Another Successful Field Trip

An organization in AT&T, known as Quality Management and Engineering Services, sold my service to a division of the Florida Motor Vehicle Agency. The remainder of this chapter will discuss the three phase approach that was implemented in the license division of that organization.

Phase I

The Phase I session was attended by about 80 managers and specialists from within the division. The session went pretty much as usual with one exception. When I discussed the need for a new kind of leadership and quoted John Naisbitt as saying the leader of the next decade will be a coach, teacher, nurturer, and facilitator, a young gentleman in the audience became very interested. He approached me during the break time and stated that he was a member of the armed forces reserve and that his particular unit was teaching the same principles of leadership that I had discussed during the lecture. He was very pleased to hear this reinforced from a brand new source and was not reluctant to have me quote him later on in the session. I felt that this was extremely good input and have used the example provided to me by this young gentleman many times since. The reason for this is that if indeed, the armed forces can change its style of leadership to one of this advanced nature, we in the business world should take note.

Phase II

Six Phase II sessions were scheduled very carefully by the AT&T account representative, Joanne Helme, and the Florida Motor Vehicle Division of License. Each session basically consisted of one day allotted for Phase II, and another half day for wrapping up Phase II and making the Phase III presentation. This schedule worked out extremely well although it was difficult in some ways to complete three sessions in one week. This was done, however, and without fanfare.

Each of the six groups developed about 30 specific driving forces that were ready for implementation. This amounted to generation of 180 good ideas in the six sessions. There was, of course, some duplication among the groups, especially in areas of training, morale building and opening up communication flow. The common ground among the six groups was the fact that they were extremely interested and knowledgeable about the subject matter and about the areas that needed improvement. There was consensus on every point; there were intense moments when very serious matters were discussed; and there were other times when a great deal of humor entered the conversation.

One thing that was different about these sessions is the number of observers who were allowed to attend. Each session contained about 10 observers. Initially there was some problem with this, but as we set ground rules for observing only and no participation or discussion by the observers, it began to work more smoothly.

There was an extreme reluctance on the part of many in the Phase II session to participate in the Phase III session with management. Once the sessions got going, however, the reluctance either disappeared or was substantially dissipated. I recall one individual in particular who talked for 23 minutes about the restraining and driving forces that the group had developed. Of course this was done without any prior preparation, without any notes, and this person actually received a round of applause when the presentation was completed.

Phase III

The six Phase III sessions followed the identical format. I was introduced by the top management person who reiterated his support, total support of the project, and his willingness to listen to the ideas of the employees. The audience included all bureau chiefs within the division and other management people. I then kicked off the session by reminding the audience of the Deming formula with major emphasis on attacking waste, restarts, rework, and workaround. I also reminded them of the common cause, special cause elements of variability and then related the actual percent of common causes and special causes for that particular group. I also went over the summary of the various levels of management that needed to take action. In this particular case it is interesting to note that of the six groups, management action or common cause effort equalled 84 percent and special causes equaled 16 percent. The management action tended to skew toward middle and higher levels, at least that was the opinion of the quality action teams that we worked with.

It is significant to report the high level of management involvement in these Phase III sessions. All sessions were attended by the director, assistant director, bureau chiefs, and other management personnel. This was significant and also appreciated by the employee level groups making the presentations. The management team was active in their participation by asking pertinent questions and indicating total support of the quality action team work.

Quality Resolution/Review Teams

The director appointed the assistant director as chairman of each quality resolution team, who is responsible for addressing the problems coming out of each of the six groups. The assistant director appointed the bureau chiefs to be members of that resolution team, as well as two or three members of the original quality action teams. This was a very positive action because it involved the appropriate levels of management required to make the necessary changes, and it also assured continuity by the participation of several members of the quality action team who are very familiar with the work and recommendations of those teams. The director agreed to meet once a month to review progress of the quality resolution teams and address any problems that were getting in the way of progress. In addition, that particular level agreed to work on establishing future quality action teams, deciding who would be on them, as well as deciding who would facilitate those particular sessions. This effort ensured an ongoing nature to the work so that future problems could be tackled in a similar manner. We call this latter group the quality review team.

Examples of Spread Sheet and the Actual Schedule of Implementation of the Three-Phase Process.

Following are examples of the implementation schedule used during the two-week period in implementing the three-phase process, as well as actual spread sheets which were developed subsequently by the quality resolution team.

Implementation Schedule

Week 1:

Monday/PI Meeting	8:00 A.M.– 12:00 P.M. Kick-Off
PII	1:00 A.M.– 4:00 P.M. Group 1
Tuesday/PII	8:00 A.M.– 12:00 P.M. Group 1
PIII	1:00 P.M. – 3:00 P.M. Group 1
Wednesday/PII	8:00 A.M.– 12:00 P.M. Group 2
PII	1:00 P.M. – 4:00 P.M. Group 2
Thursday/PIII	8:30 A.M.–10:00 A.M. Group 2
PII	1:00 P.M. – 4:00 P.M. Group 3
Friday/PII	8:00 A.M.– 12:00 P.M. Group 3
PIII	1:00 P.M. – 3:00 P.M. Group 3

Week 2:

Monday/PII	8:00 A.M.– 12:00 P.M. Group 4
	1:00 P.M. – 4:00 P.M. Group 4
Tuesday/PIII	8:00 A.M.–10:00 A.M. Group 4
Wednesday/PII	8:00 A.M.–12:00 A.M. Group 5
PIII	1:00 P.M. – 3:00 P.M. Group 5
Thursday/PII	8:00 A.M.– 12:00 P.M. Group 6
	1:00 P.M. – 4:00 P.M. Group 6
Friday/PIII	8:00 A.M.–10:00 A.M. Group 6

Group 1 - Driver Improvement and Financial Responsibility Reviewing Officers.
Group 2 - Records.
Group 3 - Uniform Traffic Citations.
Group 4 - Driver Improvement Field Personnel.
Group 5 - Field Operations.
Group 6 - Field Operations.

Television Interview

The public relations arm of the division made arrangements for a television interview on a program called "The Good Morning Show." Following is the content of that interview:

Q. Mr. Stratton, you've been on board two weeks now and what is your assessment of the Florida Department of Highway Safety and Motor Vehicles? What do you see?

A. A company that has its top management extremely interested in doing something to improve productivity of all their employees. Often companies tackle productivity first, but they are tackling it the right way by putting the quality of work first.

Q. What do you think of the quality? Are they putting out a good product?

A. I haven't looked at their end product. I work with the experts that are closest to that work and I find that the people closest to the work have an enormous amount of skill, energy, and knowledge that needs to be tapped. Getting the management team to understand that about 85 percent of the time the kinds of problems that exist are problems with the process. The people don't need to change, the process needs to be changed.

Q. So you defend the employee then as a victim of bureaucracy?

A. Well, I don't like to use the word bureaucracy. I have worked with over five different companies in the last six years and 93 small groups in that time. The gurus say that 85 percent of the time it's the process and 15 percent of the time it's the people, machines, or tools that need to change.

My data shows that in working with the 93 groups, the data is 82 percent and 18 percent. What I've done is taken that concept out of the textbooks and put it into real practice in these businesses. I am an advocate of the employee, in making sure that that employee is working in a process that is right first and then working with the management team to make that happen.

Q. With 1,600 employees and 5.6 million customers, how can you keep someone motivated when they are dealing with that many people?

A. Many employees can be motivated by opening up the lines of communication. It happens time after time. We find that those people and those experts need to be listened to. They need a management team that will take their ideas and run with it and implement them if they can.

I've worked with six groups—10 people in each group—that's 60 people. They have come up with at least 30 ideas in each group with 180 total things to work on now. The management team knows that about 82 percent of those are their babies. The employees know that they are going to do something about them. That is a very positive thing—opening up the line of communications and at the same time improving morale.

Q. You say you don't want to use the word bureaucracy, but use the word process. What are the key elements that you can streamline and make them more efficient?

A. The first key element is communication. That becomes more efficient right off the bat. I have seen people in the last week stand up in front of the management team and really lay it on the line in terms of saying "Here's what we think needs to be done to make things better." This is the key element—open up the lines of communication.

The kind of things that come out of that are improved morale, improved communication, and improved work processes. Changes can be made, some immediately, but most take an enormous amount of dedication, patience and effort on the part of management to make the change.

See Appendix B for a thorough review of the analysis made and actions taken to dramatically improve the processes with the Florida Motor Vehicles Division of License.

PART 6

A CASE STUDY

Introduction

A while back I used force field analysis to manage a complex corporate project. The mission of the project was to develop new ways to price our three major services. This may seem like a rather easy task at first glance. The complexities, however, of a supply contract that had been on the books for over 40 years, a highly authoritarian headquarters staff, and the three services being provided nationwide by thousands of employees tended to make the task quite complex.

The first mission was to select people with expertise in each of the three services disciplines, as well as to obtain help from major corporate groups. A core group of 18 people was assigned. The group was assembled for a one-week orientation and goal setting and then dispersed in four major locations throughout the company. Three groups specializing in each of the primary services became known as *field teams* and the corporate group became known as the *consulting group.* The field teams embarked on a data-gathering phase that meticulously defined each element of the major services, analyzed the data to assure consistency of cost and price treatment, and made recommendations on how to improve consistency and make way for possible new ways of doing business with the ultimate customer.

The total group met periodically during the life of the project to ensure that each team was touching all the bases and that the overall mission was on track and making progress.

Very early in the life of the project, as project manager I felt a desperate need for help in managing the project effectively. Each field team began to take on its own personality, our corporate bosses were trying to unduly influence the outcome, specific team members began to develop weird traits and actions that were negatively affecting the project, and field locations management was beginning to become an obstacle to progress. I called a friend, Darrell Storholt, at our Corporate Education Center in Princeton and asked for help.

After describing all of the problems in more detail, Darrell suggested use of the force field analysis technique to get our hands on all the balls in the air. In about a week I had categorized each of the problem areas then in existence in terms of "level," discussed earlier in the book, and began to define specific restraining forces.

I didn't know about cause and effect at that time. Now I can see that each of the problem areas defined were actually "causes" and the "effect" was that the overall project was in jeopardy. The cause and effect study is shown in Figure 18.

The force field analysis that follows shows the restraining forces, the driving forces, and actual results of the actions taken. There is no question in my mind, or in the minds of those in control at the time, that the use of force field analysis actually saved the project. The recommendations coming from the project were presented to the highest level policy group in the entire company and were accepted. It is most interesting to note that those recommendations were so revolutionary that they form the foundation of ways of doing business today.

The point here is to explain the use of force field analysis, not to give definitions of the actual recommendations. Over time the recommendations may be augmented or changed completely; the use of force field analysis is the important thing for the reader to understand.

With this in mind, let's now examine each "cause" and its force field analysis.

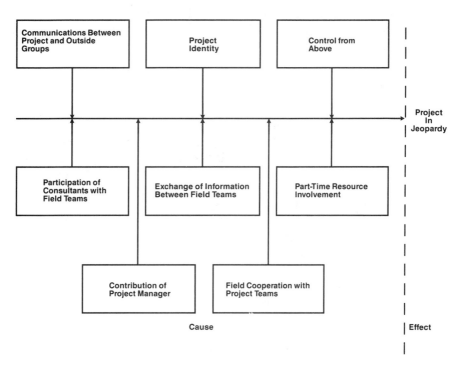

FIGURE 18

Examples of Force Field Analysis

Cause 1

Level of Control from Above

During the initial and early stages of the project there was continuous interaction between the project manager and those directing the project. Although the project got off to a good start after its members were told that control from upper management would be minimal, and that the project members could determine for themselves appropriate action to be taken, various actions led to deterioration of this position. Its overall effect on the project was detrimental and action had to be taken to alleviate the problem of control from above and can best be described in terms of the force field analysis made and the results that occurred.

Restraining Force. Pressure from above for control actually began before the initial start of the project in determining to whom the project manager should report. The approach was to open up the chain of command, make maximum use of whatever level would be necessary in solving the problem, and use the consulting team to solve project-oriented problems. These suggestions were accepted and used throughout the project. In essence, the general manager became the unofficial boss and provided guidance concerning administration of the project.

Other evidence of pressure for control from above can be summarized as follows:

- Pressure on individuals in the sponsoring organization to find out what was going on in the field.
- General concern about keeping closely informed on progress.
- Sponsoring organization attendance at the first project meeting.
- Insistence that the sponsoring organization be represented at the second project meeting in spite of strong feedback that attendance would be detrimental.
- During the project manager's absence early in the project the sponsoring organization enhanced the role of the consultants in terms of administration and control rather than technical content.

The above can be summarized as one restraining force indicated as pressure from above for precise control of the project from an administrative as well as content standpoint.

Driving Force. As mentioned previously, the driving force is a force applied to lessen the pressure and, therefore, aid in decreasing the level of control to a more acceptable level.

- A confrontation between the project manager and the sponsoring organization concerning the sponsoring organization's attendance at project meetings occurred over a period of approximately three weeks.
- A confrontation between the project manager and the general manager occurred; it was indicated that if the need for control from above continued to increase it would be necessary to replace people involved with the project. The general manager advised that this was not an appropriate solution, and that we should make the best of those presently involved with the project rather than expect to get top-notch replacements. The general manager indicated that there was no pressure on him to control or direct the project in any way.
- In line with the above clarification, another driving force was an announcement to the project manager that the need for a common control vehicle, common operation by all teams, and project identity at that stage had been lifted in favor of each team determining its own course of action in line with the objectives set at the initial training session. This announcement had a lasting and favorable impact on the total project in that it was a clear signal that the ball had been given back to the project to determine its own course. There was some apprehen-

sion about this. The group was given responsibility to decide the nature of future project meetings. Regular weekly progress reports were eliminated.

- A confrontation between the project manager and the general manager occurred concerning the role of consultants. It was agreed that the relationship of consultants to the chain of command should be "cooled off."

Results.

- The sponsoring organization agreed not to attend project meetings unless invited.
- Lifting the need for common control, common operation, and project identity had a positive effect on the operation of each team.
- Representatives from the three field teams met and decided on an outline for the final project report, assigned responsibility to individuals involved with the project for common sections of the report, and agreed on the makeup of these sections.
- Project identity evolved naturally among the three field teams. Agreement was reached on a common approach to identity functions in each of the three major areas being examined. Agreement was also reached concerning a tool to be used in defining the concepts, procedures, and implementation arrangements on practices and procedures.
- The general manager had a session with the consultants that helped bring the consultants' roles into perspective; i.e., representing their own discipline and helping and assisting the field teams at the field team's discretion. This was done in line with the project manager's recommendation noted above. In subsequent sessions between the project manager and the consultants, their role was further defined and clarified, and this was communicated to the three field teams. This resulted in a more positive contribution by the consultants to the project.

Restraining Force. The sponsoring organization attempted to organize its three representatives on each field team to meet periodically and discuss all aspects of the project and what was being accomplished by each team. This was also considered a restraining force keeping the level of control from above at a higher level than was acceptable.

Driving Force. The driving force to alleviate this was a confrontation between the project manager and the sponsoring organization that stressed the need for direct contact with each team concerning specific problems related to that team at the initiative of the sponsoring organization. It was indicated that the teams would take initiative when they considered it appropriate, but that it would also be appropriate for the sponsoring organization to make a contribution when, in fact, the sponsoring organization deemed it necessary. This approach was stressed both verbally and in writing to the sponsoring organization.

In addition, the project manager learned how the teams wished to interface with the sponsoring organization.

Results.

- The sponsoring organization agreed not to deal with its three team representatives as a group.
- It also agreed to deal with the individual teams on specific areas concerning contribution to content as a resource rather than on general philosophy or status.

Restraining Force. Another "group" within the sponsoring organization also expressed the desire to organize the same three team representatives to report to them occasionally on status and recommendations.

This was again leveled by a confrontation between the project manager and the group in which the suggestion was not supported, and another suggestion was made to cover this verbally with each individual team.

Results.

- The group agreed not to deal with the three team representatives as a group.
- Contribution by visits to teams as well as periodic discussions on a continuing basis were made by the group.

Restraining Force. The sponsoring organization's attendance at monthly meetings was discussed earlier under pressure from above for control.

Driving Force. The driving force was a confrontation between the project manager and the sponsoring organization.

Results. The sponsoring organization did not attend meetings.

Restraining Force. There was direct interaction with project members by upper management.

Driving Force. The project manager monitored assignments, supported assignments when they were appropriate, and changed them when they were not.

Results. The project remained on target throughout.

Restraining Force. Less guidance by the general manager contributed to the increase in need for control from other levels.

Driving Force. The project manager took the initiative to keep the general manager informed and sought advice where appropriate concerning project administration. Several key factors are significant.

The first was a suggestion to the general manager to meet with the training consultant and get an objective opinion concerning the progress and problems of the project. This meeting clarified the project manager's role in relation to the sponsoring organization. Another suggestion was given to the general manager concerning timing of his field visits and what he should look for in those visits. It was also suggested that feedback be given to the general manager concerning the disruptive influence of the consultants.

Results.

- Prior to the start of the project, concern expressed by the project manager led to securing more appropriate candidates to represent the sponsoring organization in the project. This set the pace for other organizations to follow and had a significant impact on the caliber of people selected to represent other disciplines as well.
- Clarification was provided concerning the suggestion to replace people. This course of action was not taken in favor of improving the individuals and letting them do the job themselves.
- The session with the training consultant clarified the role of the sponsoring organization to be resource-oriented and the role of the project manager to be administration-oriented. The general manager evolved here as the administrative as well as the functional head of the project and the project manager's boss.
- The general manager agreed to replace one team member.
- The general manager made sure the project manager was well informed concerning his field visits both before and after the visit. The project manager initiated contact in *all* instances.
- The general manager took appropriate and timely action concerning definition of the consultant's role.

Cause 2

Level of Project Identity

Restraining Force. In the early stages of the project, the field teams were mainly concerned with geographic moves: getting situated at the new location both at home and at work, determining a plan of action for their individual team in the data gathering phase, and then actually going out in the field to interview key people and organizations in accomplishing the data-gathering operation. These kinds of activities naturally required close coordination among the four people on each field team and did not, in fact, require any major degree of coordination or cooperation between teams. Although a natural condition, this fact was thought of as a restraining force that tended to decrease the level of project identity to a point below that which would be necessary in the development and analysis of actual alternatives that would occur later in the project.

Evidence of high team identity includes the following:

- No meaningful communication between teams in the early months of the project.
- Concern of some teams about what the other teams were actually doing.
- No meaningful use of consultants by the field teams until later in the project.
- A complete takeover by one team in an early project meeting with little or no evidence of discussion regarding participation of all teams before the meeting.
- A tendency of one team to ignore the planning done during the training week concerning schedules and target dates.

Driving Force. An initial reaction was that strong team identity would be detrimental to the project in its early stages as well as in later stages. This was emphasized at the first project meeting. After lengthy consideration and discussion with various management levels as well as the management training organization, it was concluded that high team identity was a natural process in the early stages due to the kinds of activities indicated above and that any force applied by the project manager to unify actions of the teams and make them compatible would be inappropriate. This posture was announced at a project meeting where the need for common identity and control vehicles was lifted. This recognition can be considered a driving force. It was considered that the pressure of time in development of the final package would require total cooperation and the melding of the teams at a later stage in the project.

Results. The project manager and training consultant visited two field teams and discussed communication problems between teams at the initiative of both teams. As a result, five members of each field team initiated and attended a special meeting representing the three field teams and agreed on the final presentation format. They also assigned specific individuals to be responsible for the common areas of the report, and assigned teams the responsibility for sections of the report involving individual team recommendations, implementation arrangement, and a summary section. The group agreed to specific due dates for the outline, first draft, final draft, and final document dates.

Although the meeting only concentrated on common areas and did not delve into the specifics of actual recommendations, it was the first meaningful attempt by participants across the project to get together on their own and work toward a compatible end result.

The second major result that led to an increase in the level of project identity was the evidence of sincere sharing that took place midway into the project. Particular emphasis was devoted to each team's approach in arriving at alternatives and conclusions. Part of this discussion was the development of a matrix including consideration of all elements as well as implementation and project evaluation of alternatives. It was indicated by the group that maximum communication would be vital throughout the remainder of the project, and that all teams should continue to strive for compatibility and a continued common approach. The field teams also gave indication that they were dependent on the consulting team for help in various key areas.

A major concern of the project manager at this point in the project was the possible tentativeness of the outward support for maximum communication between teams, and a desire toward development of a compatible approach.

Restraining Force. It is a main concern of the project manager to influence the teams to get together. See the discussion starting on page 96 for a complete description of the driving forces and results.

Restraining Force. Activity of teams in the early stages of the project requires and enhances team identity. The restraining forces mentioned are appropriate.

Driving Force. The driving force was to respect this as vital in the first half of the project. It was decided that project identity would be more important in the later stages.

Results. Project identity grew steadily throughout the project.

Restraining Force. The teams were reluctant to adopt similar methods of attack due to the individuality of team experiences in the data-gathering stage of the project and, therefore, the lack of real need for communication between teams. Different methods of attack were established to do the actual data gathering.

Field Team A began almost immediately after a brief period of determining what kinds of questions would be asked, the purpose of the meeting with field representatives, and who should make visits and who should be interviewed. As a result Team A placed major emphasis on revising its questions and approach to field visits after initial field visits. It remained on target concerning schedules of visits in line with their original planning. However, in retrospect, Team A concluded that fewer visits would have been sufficient to do the job and so advised Field Team B concerning its planned visits to the field.

Field Team C spent more time developing an extensive questionnaire that it, in turn, sent to key people. This questionnaire received abundant attention and criticisms from many different sources. Because of this, the questionnaire was withdrawn and Field Team C interviewed key people in an effort to answer pertinent questions and concerns. This attempt was not totally satisfactory because of the approach used by Field Team C in obtaining information from those interviewed. Negative feedback was provided to

Team C by the project manager concerning this development as it occurred and as the team was interviewing in the field.

During the first four months, Field Team B decided to place maximum emphasis on developing a firm base of understanding concerning detailed practices and procedures, and its effect on all related organizations. This also included determining the impact of a group studying and developing national guidelines and also a group working on the same endeavor from a divisional standpoint. They tested their ideas on several selected locations before actually developing a comprehensive questionnaire.

Field Team B decided to visit all field locations (45 visits). Much pressure was brought to bear on Team B by the project manager to decrease the visits based on Team A's advice and experience. Subsequently, Team B decided to decrease visits to 25 rather than 45 locations.

Feedback from several key field locations, including an on-site visit, during one interview indicated that the planning time spent by Field Team B was valuable in terms of quantity and quality of information received.

Driving Force. The fact that the teams went in different directions during the data gathering stage and were reluctant to adopt similar approaches was not thought of as a major deterrent to getting the data-gathering job done. This, of course, would change as the effort of each team changed in the actual analysis and development of alternative stages. This was suggested informally to each team at various times and was also mentioned in terms of the kind of meeting that would be held at midpoint. In spite of strong feeling on the part of some project members that results could only be achieved at a project meeting by breaking the group into smaller groups, the project manager believed that the major results would have to occur with the 18 project members working together to arrive at conclusions as to the approach that would be adopted by the project as a whole in the development of actual alternatives. This feeling was supported by a few key project members and actually did occur.

Results. All teams adopted similar methods of attack. Field Teams A and C met two weeks before the project meeting and were well along the way to adopting similar approaches and assuring compatibility.

Field Team B came to the project meeting looking for help as a result of devastating feedback to the team from the project manager regarding the general manager's visit. They received help by way of constructive criticism from each field team.

Restraining Force. There was a feeling of competition between teams. From the start of the project there was an inherent feeling among all three field teams that the end result of the project would be measured in terms of what each team provided rather than what the total project provided as an end product. This led to the lack of communication between teams in the beginning of the project and the desire to come up with the best plan to get the job done first.

Driving Force. This was first brought up early in the project but clear action was not taken by the teams at that point. Agreements were reached to exchange all written material, use conference calls more frequently between teams, and communicate more in setting up meetings. It was also recognized that working closer together would be important to achieve meaningful end results.

The project manager began to identify common problems that required communication between teams as they developed. The key item here was the need to develop a common outline.

Results. Teams interchanged written material and started to discuss common problems more frequently. They achieved agreement on the common outline and the framework for the approach to development of actual alternatives. This was tested from a technical standpoint by a visit made to each field team by the sponsoring organization management. Strong suggestions were made for closer collaboration between teams concerning actual alternatives. This actually occurred and continued throughout the life of the project on a very healthy level.

Cause 3

Level of Communication Between the Project and Outside Groups Such As Consultants and Professors

At the outset of the project it was indicated that it would be feasible and, in fact, compulsory to get advice and consultation from organizations and people outside of the company. This would include consultants from both the legal and academic fields. In addition, it was suggested that the project could benefit from finding out how the job is handled in other industries and this could be determined through actual interviews with these companies. The project members believed this to be a good idea and placed much weight on it in the determination of final alternatives. This was evident in the planning done during training week where much discussion ensued concerning whether this was a field team responsibility, a consulting team responsibility, or a joint responsibility. The level of communication between the project members and people outside the group was restricted in the first month of the project as follows:

- No interview of outside companies.
- No outside consultants.
- No public relations.

The following will describe the restraining forces and driving forces that have eliminated any communication between barriers between the project and outside sources.

Restraining Force. Legal restrictions.

Driving Force. Confrontation with the director to obtain modification of restrictions.

Results. The director modified all restrictions previously. The modifications, however, did not produce any actual communication between the project and outside groups.

Restraining Force. Teams disbelieved the modifications. Although each category was modified to some degree, project members did not pursue any actual knowledge from outside sources at the onset.

Driving Force. Teams gave specific definitions of their needs. On several occasions the project manager tried to get the teams to take advantage of the modifications and make specific recommendations concerning their needs. This was done in the early stage of the project by each team concerning subjects to be discussed with an outside expert. Field teams requested that a consultant team member seek information through the company about the procedures of other organizations.

Results. As indicated, a consultant team member was assigned to obtain information concerning other organizations. This was pursued and results were available to each team.

Restraining Force. There was a high level of control by the sponsoring organization. Due to the sensitive nature of the information being sought, it was decided that the director would be a control point concerning such interchange and data. This is thought of as a restraining force, although a necessary action.

Driving Force. The control at this level was respected as vital and teams were encouraged to report requirements specifically and directly to that level through the consultants. A serious attempt was made here to make sure that this interface dealt with the subject of communication to outside organizations and did not get involved with administration of the work of the project per se.

Results.

- The consultants dealt with the director regarding the use of outside consultants.
- The teams worked through the consultants.
- The team members gained an appropriate level of understanding concerning the need for this control.

Cause 4

Level of Participation of Consultants with Field Teams

This subject received much discussion during training week. At that time, there was a strong feeling among the three field teams that the consultants were trying to put themselves in a supervisory or controlling position concerning review and evaluation of the field teams' work. This was not completely reviewed during training week and remained a consideration to be dealt with throughout the life of the project. It is important at this stage to appreciate the role that was defined by the consulting team during training week and agreed on by the entire group.

Restraining Force. The team believed that the consultants must review and pass judgment on team activities. As indicated above, this began during training week and was prevalent in some degree throughout the remainder of the project. However, the consultants continuously felt that they had a responsibility to oversee the overall project activity to make sure that end results would be practical. This is a delicate task; actions and words could lead field teams to believe the consulting team's role was more controlling in nature than it actually was. As indicated previously, the consultants went overboard at one point which supported the feeling of the three field teams. This feeling and the inappropriate action of consultants was considered a restraining force on the actual contribution of the consulting team.

Driving Force. Teams should be convinced of the real role of the consulting team through major contact with field teams during the development of alternatives stage. This contact essentially came from two major sources: strong pressure from the project manager on field teams to make maximum use of the consultants during the development of alternatives stage, and maximum penetration by the consultants with each of the field teams during the same stage.

Results. Throughout this section field teams have been referred to as all having the same problems. In actuality, there were great differences in attitude among field teams in that some used consultants to maximum advantage sooner than others. Because of the teams' early suspicions that the consultants were trying to take over and the fact that these suspicions were confirmed, the consulting team's effectiveness was seriously hampered. One team, for instance, virtually ignored the potential contribution of two consultants. In the earlier stages of the project, the field teams provided the consultants with specific tasks. This helped to define the role of the consultant specifically.

Restraining Force. There was a lack of specific tasks from field teams to consultants. This was a problem in the earlier stages in the project.

Driving Force. More input from field teams to consultants defined specific tasks.

Results. This input was provided and appropriate action was taken by the consultants.

Restraining Force. There was less direct contact by consultants with field teams during various stages of the project. This was more apparent in the earlier stages of the project when the field teams were interviewing and collecting data, than it was in the latter stages of the project when the actual development of alternatives took place and major activity was started to test for practicality and implementation capability by the consultants themselves.

Driving Force. More field visits by consultants were encouraged, and field teams were encouraged to work with consultants when appropriate. Consultants were assigned specific responsibility for preparation of the general manager's speech. Three consultants were assigned to individual teams.

Results. This was more of a problem with Field Team A than with Teams B or C. This was primarily caused by the fact that Team A prescribed a task to be done by the consultants from early in the project that was not deemed a necessary task by the consultants.

They accepted responsibility to do the job, negotiated for technical assistance from the Corporate Statistical Analysis Organization, and provided Field Team A with substantial data that were used as a base by Team A in answering the original question. This conflict began to subside when Team A realized it would need support, help, and advice from the consulting team.

Restraining Force. The earlier stages of the project were exclusively involved with gathering data. The consultants' main contribution to field teams in the earlier stages was to help them gather data in areas that the field teams believed could be done more appropriately by the consultants.

Driving Force. The project manager decided to wait until the development of alternatives stage of the project before suggesting action on the part of the consultants that would contribute toward successful completion of the project. It was thought here that the field teams would come to realize that the contribution of the consulting team was important to their individual progress. The driving force was allowing the pressure of time to take its course rather than forcing a false and, therefore, insignificant interface between the field teams and the consulting team.

Results. A great change in attitude among the three field teams started midway during the project and continued.

The consultants contributed significantly in the development of alternatives and their crystallization in the final proposal.

The consultants' activity increased significantly through the life of the project in the area of testing for practicality and actual implementation of final alternatives.

Restraining Force. Field team identity was strong in the early stages of the project, and, therefore, the need to identify with the consultants was weak.

Driving Force and Results. See previous comments on this.

Cause 5

Level of Exchange of Information Between Field Teams

Because the individual field teams thought they had enough autonomy to come up with a final product without interface with other teams and without interface with the consulting team, there was less communication than was actually required during the earlier phases of the project between all teams. As indicated previously, this was natural during the data-gathering stage in that various approaches could, in fact, be used to accomplish this particular phase.

Very early in the development of alternatives phase, the lack of adequate communication was recognized by teams as being a serious detriment to the accomplishment of final objectives. The following forces describe attitudes and resulting actions that, in fact, contributed to increase effective communication between all teams.

Restraining Force. There was a feeling of competition between teams. This has been described adequately in previous sections.

Driving Force. The field teams must realize that the feeling of competition exists and that all negative aspects should be eliminated by the teams themselves. This posture began to take place when the problem of competition between teams came up in discussion. At that time, it was agreed that more information should be exchanged, both verbally and in writing.

As the alternatives for Field Teams A and C began to take shape, the project manager stressed compatibility of approaches in his discussion with each team.

Results.

- The competitive attitude lessened to a considerable degree and was most noticeable at key points during the life of the project.
- In addition, the field teams started to visit each other to work toward a more compatible approach.

Restraining Force. Teams were too busy solving their own individual problems in the early stages of the project.

Driving Force. It was thought that the team would recognize the need for a joint thrust on specific areas later in the project.

Results. The elementization and partitioning Field Team C originated, the manner of illustrating alternatives in matrix form as developed by Field Team C, and Field Team B's approach of determining advantages and disadvantages for establishing their alternatives are best examples of this.

Restraining Force. There was a basic feeling of difference in competence among teams. In the early visits, the project manager got the impression from various individuals that a feeling existed concerning the difference in level of competence of individuals on other teams. Specifically the degree of education was mentioned. One team had four members, one of whom had a bachelor's degree, one a master's degree, and two high school degrees as compared to another team whose four members each had master's degrees, including one who had a law degree. Other concerns included the success or failure of teams in their interviewing of field locations.

Driving Force. In each case, the project manager found that one team's evaluation of another in any of the areas mentioned was usually overplayed for reasons that were not quite clear. These reasons could have been the restraining force of unhealthy aspects of competition between teams. The concern about the difference in education, for instance, was definitely the case of pitting one team against another instead of figuring out a way to make maximum use of the educational level on other teams to the benefit of those that, in fact, required it. The project manager's approach was to indicate to each individual that had this concern that the gap between teams, whatever it may be, was not as severe as it may have seemed. He encouraged maximum contact both informally on a one-to-one or team-to-team basis, and also formally at project meetings. The teams were also encouraged to participate more fully in the preparation of agenda items for each meeting.

Results. All talents across the project were used to maximum efficiency in coming up with the end report. This affected the field representatives on each team as well as those representing common disciplines. In the last five months of the project, the consultants were effective in having positive impact on the teams, the general manager's speeches, the final report, and their own home organizations concerning implementation effort.

A healthy type of confrontation also developed between teams concerning problems.

Restraining Force. Teams did not share basic data and ideas in early stages of the project. This was covered in previous comments.

Driving Force. Teams need to recognize this and take action to solve it themselves. An example can be set by sharing information both verbally and in writing.

Results. See previous comments.

Cause 6

Level of Part-Time Resource Involvement

The part-time resource people consisted of representatives from eight major organizations in the company. The training consultant was involved more fully than any other part-time consultant throughout the life of the project. The other part-time resource people were active in varying degrees throughout the project. The level of involvement, however, was a concern in the early stages for reasons that will be evident in the discussion that follows.

Restraining Force. The field team wanted to be autonomous in the early stages of the project. An initial observation of field teams was that they could pretty much handle the task without too much help from either full-time or part-time resources. There was a strong desire to do the job themselves instead of relying on help from other organizations.

Driving Force. The field teams needed to be told that the part-time consultants could do more to support their efforts. The consultants would be a good source for ideas and also would help prepare the way for possible implementation. It was also indicated to the teams that the consultants were really not contributing as much as they could.

Results. All part-time resource organizations became actively involved throughout the life of the project.

Restraining Force. The part-time consultants were somewhat reluctant to initiate help.

Driving Force. A meeting was held with all consultants. Two-way communication was stressed at this time. The general manager participated by encouraging the consultants to initiate help on their own.

Results. There were no apparent problems of lack of support or communication between the part-time resource people and the project. All communication that had been made was positive and help had been obtained wherever required.

Restraining Force. The training consultant was a major participant in the December Training Session held at the Corporate Education Center. However, his efforts in coordinating with the project were minimal early in the project. This changed considerably when pressures were recognized by the project manager.

Driving Force. The project manager had a session with the training consultant indicating need for more contact with the teams.

The project manager kept the training consultant informed with all written material concerning the project and by phone conversations seeking advice or advising on key points throughout the project.

Results. The training consultant attended a key project meeting and was a help in advising key action concerning performance of specific individuals, including the newest member of the project. He advised the project, at that time, that he would be available for consultation on an individual or team basis if desired. He visited the three field teams and offered to discuss problems or concerns about communication between individuals on each team, communication between teams, and consideration of individual growth. This led to a conclusion by both Field Teams B and C that a special project meeting would be appropriate to iron out problems concerning the final project report, what it would include, and who would be assigned responsibility for specific sections.

The training consultant had an extensive private session with the general manager that developed into a discussion participated in by the four levels of management in the sponsoring organization. The result of these combined sessions was that all levels gained a clear understanding of the role of each person and the contribution to be made to the project. Essentially, it was agreed that the project manager would have full administrative responsibility for the project including schedules, objectives, personnel, approach, training, selection, and control of the project, and that the sponsoring organization would have responsibility concerning contribution to and evaluation of the specific content that would be developed by each field team. The fact that the development of content was not scheduled to start until the latter part of the project was stressed, and also that contact with the sponsoring organization during the data-gathering stage would be minimal except for acquiring data within that organization, which had already been accomplished.

The training consultant advised individuals and teams at various points in the project. This tended, in some cases, to improve individual performance, and in other cases, team performance.

As mentioned earlier, the training consultant suggested the force field analysis technique in analyzing various project manager concerns, which helped determine the cause of certain problems and actions that could be taken to alleviate them. This contribution was considered vital to the overall success of the project.

Cause 7

Level of Contribution of Project Manager to Teams

The matrix management combined with a synergistic approach required the project manager to develop a more liberal management style. The Theory Y approach was also appropriate due to the nature of the task. A word about each of these management techniques is appropriate.

Matrix management required that a chain-of-command approach not be used within the project itself. In other words, there was not one individual on each team who reported directly to the project manager concerning results of that particular team. The aspect we are discussing here is the fact that the project members worked in an atmosphere where rank or structure of any kind was not recognized. It was, therefore, important that the impact of the project manager on the various teams be concentrated more toward the developmental mode of operation than either strict control or the opposite which would be relinquishing responsibility for reaching objectives. The developmental mode placed major emphasis on informing, persuading, exploring, coordinating, stimulating, and sharing problems and solutions. Little emphasis was placed on enforcing, dominating, selling, or fighting to maintain maximum control.

The *synergistic approach* mentioned previously makes achieving results through group effort the maximum goal. The definition of a synergistic approach is "the cooperative effort in which the effects are greater than the sum of each part (individual working alone)." This, in effect, is the major reason for lack of structure within the project itself, and securing people with the best talents to represent specific disciplines that could, in fact, meld together as a team as well as a total group of 18 in adjusting themselves to the problem at hand and, in fact, solving it.

The Theory Y approach mentioned earlier refers, of course, to McGregor's more enlightened view of the employee by management. This theory assumes that people generally seek responsibility; that they have a positive capacity for exercising imagination, ingenuity, and creativity; and that they can exercise self-control. Although McGregor's theories address themselves specifically to the average person, the people selected for the project had high credentials in education and/or experience as well as, for the most part, a strong desire to participate in the project.

The following will describe forces that developed that restricted the project manager's role in regard to the above areas, and those forces that were applied to counterbalance them and allow a more adequate contribution.

Restraining Force. Direction from above equates to more control by the project manager in terms of enforcing and dominating. Cause 1 covered most areas where this was predominant; namely, the pressure for actual control of activity within the project from above, the desire of two separate organizations to organize the three people representing the sponsoring organization on the project, attendance of sponsoring organization at meetings, direct interaction with project members, etc. These actions tended to increase the control aspects and, therefore, decrease the developmental mode of operation that was thought to be more in line with the matrix concept, a synergistic approach, and the Theory Y concept.

Driving Force. It was necessary to separate the functions of direction from participation in the content concerning activity from above. As indicated in Causes 1 through 4, attempts were made to involve teams with participation concerning content and any help that the chain of command could give in this area. Confrontation was the course of action taken when any kind of control or action was considered inappropriate.

As indicated above, the sponsoring organization's involvement was limited in the earlier stages when not appropriate, and sought in the later stages when it was appropriate.

Results. Causes 1 through 4 indicated results that were achieved as a result of the preceding driving force. In addition, the project as a whole was totally responsible for establishing a plan of attack including objectives for the entire project and gathering data from various field locations. The sponsoring organization did get involved in the development of alternatives stage and continued throughout the life of the project.

Restraining Force. More overt action by the project manager to control specific activities of teams led to less contribution and support of field teams in the early stages of the project.

Driving Force. A decision was made by the project manager to give maximum freedom to the field teams early in the life of the project. It was decided that the quest for a project identity, a common control vehicle, and adoption of similar approaches would be dropped—this resulted in the field teams developing their own system for controlling these activities. In addition, the need for a weekly progress report was lifted based on field team requests.

The project manager provided direction to individuals and teams as well as the chain of command when appropriate.

Results. As indicated, lifting the need for the items mentioned previously resulted in solid response by the field teams.

The following results highlight some major areas where direction by the project manager was effective:

- Field Team B reduced the number of its visits from 45 to 25; this facilitated meeting project schedules.
- One team member was replaced due to health. The replacement selection facilitated meeting project schedules and also aided the approach, content, and ultimate testing of alternatives for both Field Teams A and C.
- The decision not to replace others facilitated the end product and also helped the involved individuals.
- The need for compatibility was stressed to both Field Teams A and C. This resulted in a strong cohesive plan of attack by both teams.
- Team B was advised concerning the appropriate approach to solve the problem of developing only one alternative. This resulted in the development of several approaches.

- Consultants were advised concerning their role in the development of the interim status report. This resulted in a favorable reaction by field teams and an end product that was highly acceptable.
- Information was provided to the sponsoring organization, resulting in the following action:
  - The need for compatibility between Field Teams A and C was stressed. This was indicated in visits by the general manager and had a significant impact which also resulted in compatibility being established as noted previously.
  - It was indicated that Field Team B was recommending one approach and that decisions should be made concerning this approach. This also resulted in the several approaches being developed by Team B as noted previously.
  - General manager and director visits were recommended and arranged during the early stages of the project through the development of alternative stages. These visits had a significant impact on the quality of work and the content of alternatives. At a later stage it was recommended that the director be more specific concerning the appropriateness of actual alternatives.
  - A system of rewards was developed stressing informal involvement of the general manager in regard to the short-term goals of each individual. This was met with good feelings on the part of project members in that they realized someone on a significant level was concerned about their individual career goals and was willing to be a "willing negotiator" if this could, in fact, help them along the way.
  - As a result of a request for more meaningful involvement of the sponsoring organization concerning content, the director visited each field team and had two of his organizations explore the appropriateness of alternatives from their own organization's viewpoint.
  - All the results indicated previously evolved from the direct or indirect action attempted throughout the life of the project by the project manager.

Restraining Force. A strict chain-of-command approach lessens exposure of the teams to needed input. The best example of this is access to higher levels of management for required input regarding past agreements, current activity, and interpretations of policy and procedures.

There seemed to be a reluctance of individuals and organizations to initiate contributions of the aforementioned nature to the teams. As mentioned previously, the main problems here seemed to be the continuous confusion between direction of what the teams should do and input in the form of suggestions, advice, and criticism concerning content only. The project position from the beginning was to de-emphasize the former in favor of a strictly project-oriented direction for the project and to favor maximum interface with all organizations involving content.

Driving Force. It was necessary to cut through the traditional chain-of-command approach and go directly to the person or persons necessary to get the job done. This related to all organizations indicated previously as part-time resources, as well as those considered full-time resources.

Conversations were used, for the most part, to initiate the above kinds of action although correspondence was initiated at times to serve the same purpose. Both were effective and produced the necessary results.

Results.

- Visit to Field Team A shifted emphasis from detailed problems and concerns to overall problems and concerns.
- Visit to two other organizations stressed need for compatibility between both teams concerning approach.
- Visit to Field Team B indicated the inadequacy of a one-alternative approach in favor of a multiple-alternative approach.
- Visit to each team cleared up the problem of understanding the actual alternatives suggested concerning reliability and practicality from a sponsoring organization standpoint.
- Progressive interface between teams and all the full-time and part-time organizations resulted in better communication and understanding of the alternatives.
- There was a savings in time and money on the part of the project by making maximum use of even intuitive direction received as a result of all visits by higher management. The project manager in these cases utilized the technique of maximum communication between those who visited and those who were visited. This involved clarifying interpretations from both sides as to what was discussed, why, and what action should be taken.

Restraining Force. Pressure was exerted on teams and individuals at times to act in specific areas that may or may not have been appropriate. Examples of this include:

- The consultants were requested to visit Field Team B and determine the appropriateness of interchange of data and further interface between another organization that was allegedly studying the project problem and Field Team B.
- A consultant was asked to perform a task that the project manager was given but had not completed.

- Organizations endeavored to organize the three project members from the sponsoring organization on each team for purposes of reporting to them concerning progress and results.
- The consultants expanded their role to administrative actions.
- The introduction of a new manager led to some confusion regarding the role of the management team. This was temporary in nature and lasted only two weeks.

Driving Force. In all situations, there were attempts to accomplish results and relieve pressure on the teams at the same time. In many cases this clarified what was actually required and specific action or needs were communicated.

Results. The consultants decided that Field Team B had secured necessary input to be knowledgeable about the other organization's activity and also found that the team had elected to maintain an arm's length relationship in that this group had committed itself to a specific approach which in the end could only be considered among many approaches and evaluated at a later date in that framework. The consultants usually discussed jobs that were given to them and made sure that two persons were, in fact, not doing the same thing. Interface with the sponsoring organization was accomplished through other means than organizing the three project members on each team to periodically report in. The consulting role that was heavily leaning toward administration was clarified and changed. To firm this up, discussions were held with the consultants and also assignments were suggested concerning specific interface with each team on the special preparation work.

The role of the new manager was clarified and remained consistent with the role established previously.

Restraining Force. Playing a directive role at meetings was considered less than appropriate in achieving meaningful results. It is a natural tendency for the chairperson of a meeting to enforce or dominate when the going gets rough.

Driving Force. Problem sharing and stimulating maximum discussion was stressed whenever possible.

Results. Some meetings were more productive than others, but the overall trends seemed to be the ability to identify, share, and solve problems in a more efficient manner as time went on. *There was no dramatic difference, however, between the kinds of problems and confrontations that were experienced in reaching solutions during the first week of training and those encountered during the life of the project.*

The individuality of each person remained a very strong force opposing complete unanimity on any given subject. This did not deter the group as a whole in defining problems, arriving at solutions, defining objectives, planning detailed work to accomplish objectives, and producing a significant end result.

Restraining Force. There was continued misunderstanding of the consultants' role by the field teams as well as the consultants themselves. This problem continued throughout the entire project. The main problem here was the inherent fact that the consultants not only represented their own specialty, but necessarily got involved with overall problems from time to time that were of global nature to the project. This was necessary because there was either no one in the project to represent a particular discipline that may have been required, or the problem was general in scope and required a technical type response and/or solution that the consultants could offer in a natural way.

Some of the problem related to misunderstanding is mentioned above, but there was also the problem of competition and strong team identity that also tended to lessen the role of the consultants rather than enhance it. This was mentioned in detail in Cause 4.

The consultants, either through misunderstanding of their role or other pressures, sometimes made premature plans to leave the project or became involved as indicated earlier in an administrative capacity.

Driving Force. The major driving forces to counteract the above restraining type forces were to clarify the consultants' role continuously with the individual field teams when necessary, suggest action to the consultants individually or as a team when appropriate, support appropriate actions by either the field teams or the consultants concerning this specific problem, or attempt to provide constructive criticism when necessary.

Results. Consultants were persuaded by field teams that their presence and action was vital to the project in the training week and later during the project. During the training week, two consultants believed that their efforts were not required and volunteered to abort the project. This never did happen as a result of the interaction between the field teams and the consultants noted previously. An identical feeling occurred later from the same two consultants. Action was taken to clarify the role again including conversations with the project members, the general manager, and the home organizations of the consultants involved. This resulted in holding the consulting team together for the remainder of the project and benefiting from the contribution of the individuals involved.

As mentioned previously, the consulting role had to be defined and clarified. This was accomplished and communicated to each field team, and resulted in a more meaningful stance and contribution by the consultants.

See Cause 4 for more detail concerning the role of the consultants in the project.

Restraining Force. Another restraining force was the inability of a minority of members to direct themselves or handle the inherent conflicts of matrix management. This had a tendency to impede team progress at times when major attention was placed on individuals' problems and maximum attention to these problems rather than project objectives. Included in this was some confusion when team members did not have a technical boss to go to to solve a specific technical problem. Team members seemed to be reluctant in the early stages to get the technical-type problem solved in their home organization. This resulted in some procrastination and loss of time, but was not critical to achieving end results.

The fact that each group was placed together at one time produced conflict in the early stages in just plain getting along with one another. The group had to develop its own norms and rules and informal structure.

The uncertainties of the task itself tended to create some tension among team members. Although all experienced the same kind of tension, a greater number exhibited an ability to handle this than did not.

Some were concerned about rewards and accommodations in the earlier stages of the project. This again was a minority of members, but nevertheless the subject received abundant attention.

In addition to these, there was misunderstanding of matrix management, a concentration on the negative rather than positive aspects, belittling of the project manager, attempts to leave the project prematurely as noted earlier, concern about splitting the group in four separate geographic areas rather than one, and an attempt to meld the 18 members or a portion of them in one geographic location at a premature stage.

Driving Force. A specific log was not maintained concerning the frequent contact with individuals and teams that tended to either solve the above type problems or keep them at least neutral. All the action, however, can be classified as either confrontation with individuals when appropriate, working through key individual team members to solve team type problems, or confrontation with an entire team. The training consultant was utilized most effectively in all the areas noted above. He participated with the project manager in discussions with teams and had individual sessions with some team members that tended to keep the overall project objectives in accurate perspective.

Results. The four teams remained intact geographically throughout the entire year and accomplished all objectives. The specific results caused by the above action are too numerous and personal to mention. Most of the areas discussed, however, in each of the eight concerns had a bearing on the driving forces mentioned here.

Restraining Force. Low level of communication between teams was a serious problem from time to time throughout the project. This related to some of the restraining forces noted earlier, especially in Causes 4 and 5. This came about in the stages when plans were being made to gather data in the field, prepare the agenda for project meetings, exchange meaningful information concerning alternatives, make decisions concerning the level of testing required to meet project goals, and select a digest committee to prepare a summary report of project recommendations. All of these resulted in varying degrees of communication, but only reached maximum efficiency under pressure of one kind or another.

Another problem related to low level communication was the tentativeness of agreement between teams even when it was reached. Compatibility seemed to be lost at one stage and had to be bolstered through suggestions from the project manager for Field Teams A and C to become better coordinated.

Driving Force. The approach here was twofold. First, the communication problem had to be attacked by having the training consultants visit all field teams. The purpose of this kind of visit was to open up the problem of communication to determine why it existed and what could be done about it in general rather than any specific terms. The second manner of addressing the communication problem was to solve specific problems as they occurred.

Results.

- All project meetings with the exception of two were based on maximum communication between field teams, what subject should be discussed, the level of time involved, and whether the total group should be involved or subgroups with definition of specific subjects for both.
- As noted earlier, Field Teams A and C became compatible after they were asked to do so. This actually did occur in an efficient way. Another example is the communication to Field Team B by each of the other teams concerning their plan of attack on expanding final alternatives to more than one specific conclusion. This occurred.
- Each team tackled the testing problem in different ways using various approaches. A definition of the testing to be completed was confirmed with the sponsoring organization and communicated to each team. This aided the accomplishment of testing objectives both during the project and after.
- Based on some specific suggestions, each team changed its representative on the digest committee to a more appropriate person.

Restraining Force. The total group had an overall tendency to have meetings, make agreements, and then not follow through or take appropriate action in regard to those agreements. This relates to the last item discussed, namely, lack of or a low level of communication, but differs to the extent that this item relates to agreements being made at meetings and then not followed. This, in some cases, relates to poor communication, but cannot be considered as the chief primary reason.

Driving Force. Continuous follow-up was made to assure appropriate action at appropriate times concerning many subjects. The highlights of these are covered below under *Results.*

Results.

- The initial planning done during the training week to accomplish project objectives remained firm throughout the project. Detailed plans to arrive at this that were made by each team varied from following the general plan to ignoring it with varying degrees in between. The detailed plans, however, were originated, revised, and monitored so that overall project dates and objectives were, in fact, accomplished.
- The subject of what level of information was required at various stages got much attention and was agreed to at various times. In spite of much discussion and many changes, the desired level was reached and a highly satisfactory report was given.
- As indicated earlier, the subject of testing got much attention and several attempts to define it failed. This required continuous effort and work with each team and the chain of command to arrive at a satisfactory and accepted definition.
- The final report format received much attention in the early stages of the project and was resolved for the most part when members from each field team met to define the actual format. This remained the same until the latter stages of the project when format only became important concerning the final digest report.
- Evidence of agreeing on a subject and not following through on the agreement was the consultants' role. This was explored in Cause 4 which indicated in detail the steps that were taken to alleviate the continued misunderstanding of the consultants' role. The overall result was effectuated in specific cases only, but remained a general problem throughout the life of the project.
- Another example of this phenomenon was the establishment of a digest group to work on recommendations of what a summary report should include. This went from an eight-person committee to a four-person committee; from a one-month project to a one-day project; from a relocation of people and families to no relocation. The basic agreement which was sound when originated and adhered to in spite of the above shifts was to come up with a summary report for the project including a description of alternatives and recommendations by the three teams. This was accomplished.

Restraining Force. Heavy travel, especially in the first part of the project, caused people to be away from home for extended periods on a repetitive basis. In some respects, this caused problems on the home front, the details of which are unknown.

Driving Force. A letter was originated from the general manager to the spouses of those involved in the project. This letter recognized the spouse's role as being an important one to the success of the project, and recognized the need for extensive travel on the part of every project member. This letter was well received.

Results. As indicated previously, the letters were well received and tended to ease frustration and aid in understanding the position of those involved in the project.

Restraining Force. There was a general feeling that "home" organizations were not considering performance ratings and promotional opportunities as they should. The distance from the "home boss" caused a feeling of being forgotten and tended to cause a gap concerning personal development discussions. This became known as the "out-of-sight out-of-mind syndrome."

Driving Force. The project manager had discussions with each functional boss prior to rating time and was assured that ratings either remained the same or were actually increased for all those involved in the project. This was communicated to individuals that seemed to have a high concern about rating treatment.

In addition, the project manager interviewed each individual concerning short-term goals, and, where appropriate, shared problems concerning growth with these individuals. Maximum use was made of the training consultant in this area, and interviews were set up with at least three of the project members. Where appropriate, discussions centered on submitting specific people for promotion. These cases involved persons of long service whose chances for promotion were slight even though they may have deserved it fully.

Results.

- All persons were treated fairly by "home" organizations regarding appraisal. No appraisal was changed downward. Some were changed upward.
- Communication of this to those individuals who were concerned seemed to help. The personal development discussions with the project manager and also the training consultant was a very positive action that led to better contributions by these individuals.

Cause 8

Level of Field Cooperation with Project Teams

This involves all organizations related to the project either directly or indirectly. This includes the full-time and part-time organizations.

All organizations more or less responded to direct questions mainly through necessity of answering in a formal way, but two organizations very often initiated action on their own to involve themselves in a productive and positive way with the project.

In addition, the management training consultant involved himself in the project in the same manner as noted above, namely, responding when asked for advice and help, but also initiated positive action. The best example of this is the time spent with individuals in the project in helping them understand their current situation which helped them to contribute in a more positive way to the project. These sessions also helped individuals as far as short-term and long-term growth.

Restraining Force. The position of related organizations was, in most cases, to wait for the teams to contact them before responding. This was noted previously, and in summary relates to the problem of waiting rather than initiating action to help project teams when necessary.

Driving Force. Two-way communication was encouraged as being appropriate. This subject was stressed by the project manager and general manager to all part-time resource organizations. This aided in some ways, but for the most part it remained a project responsibility to get action from these organizations in one way or another.

When a particular organization reacted favorably, was a special help, or initiated action in one way or another, recognition was usually made by either the field team or the project manager, or even the general manager where appropriate. This tended to maintain that level of cooperation throughout the life of the project.

Results.

- Most field and headquarters organizations cooperated fully with the project teams in the many interviews that took place in the data-gathering stages of the project.
- The management Training Organization as noted was a consistent help to the project, to field teams, and to individuals — both in responding and initiating.

Restraining Force. Field Team B was the last of the project teams to get out in the field in the data-gathering stage. This was considered restraining for two reasons. One, the level of cooperation Team B would get from the field was unknown; and, two, their timing appeared to be off as far as initiating this kind of contact.

Driving Force. The project manager decided to hold off before applying pressure to Field Team B to make the field visits. The reasoning was that the team was spending a lot of time determining the correct approach and coming up with a questionnaire that would be all-inclusive and would prevent the need for future follow-up visits.

In other words, the team attempted to do a quality job in-house before making actual field visits.
Results.

- Field Team B completed plans for visitations and actually finished all visits in good time. These visits were well within project target dates, although it did put pressure on Team B in the development of the alternatives stage.
- Based on actual on-site visitations to field locations by the project manager with Field Team B and the favorable feedback to the general manager from key managers in the field, Team B exhibited maximum preparedness and, therefore, accomplished a great deal in each of its field visits. They enhanced the project image and accomplished the data-gathering phase in a most satisfactory manner.

Restraining Force. There was some field dissatisfaction with Field Team C's approach in the early stages of the data-gathering phase. The project manager received bad feedback from several sources that pointed out this dissatisfaction specifically.

Driving Force. This negative feedback was passed on to Team C by the project manager during a field visit. The project manager got the team's viewpoint on this and also checked, based on the team's suggestion, with an organization that had recently been interviewed.

Results. The overall feeling was that the Field Team C approach really contributed to the problem, and they revamped their plan of attack to eliminate any negative aspects in future visits.

Restraining Force. There was some need on the part of other organizations for more information concerning the project. This was mainly apparent in the early stages of the project.

Driving Force. It was decided that maximum saturation by verbal communication with all field organizations would be necessary. This was accomplished by the project teams, the project manager, and the general manager in conferences and also informal contacts, and also with the part-time resource organizations.

Results. Most organizations were cordial and cooperative in a meaningful way with the project teams.

Summary

Ninety-four results have been shared in this chapter. The idea that results can only be reported by use of numbers is a highly mistaken notion. John Naisbitt said the manager's new role is to coach, to teach, to nurture[9]. I would add "to facilitate." The results spelled out in this chapter are examples of what can happen when these traits are put to use.

Dr. Deming has said that the unknown and unknowable numbers are the ones that are most devastating. In this case it is not known what would have happened if action was not taken as illustrated in each driving force. It is highly probable that the project would have failed and the wealth of information, data, and recommendations would have been lost.

In this new economic age it has now become vital for managers to step back, take a hard look at what they are doing, and make rapid changes to ensure that pride returns to all places of work.

The recommendations of this project were accepted by the highest policymaking body over 15 years ago. The management process described was and still is avant-garde. We are now hearing phrases like partnershipping, servant leadership, and finding "moments of truth." These all refer to the kind of process we have been referring to throughout this book. Some will never understand or accept this process—others will. I hope the latter prevail over time.

PART 7

ON LEWIN

Most quality practitioners are finally recognizing that force field analysis has a place in quality improvement. The problem is they have placed it among the list of tools in the wrong place. This technique when placed together with cause and effect provides an extremely powerful tool to improve quality not only in production but in the white-collar area that has virtually been ignored over the past 30 years.

Learning about force field analysis is not an easy task. It was discovered by behavioral scientist Dr. Kurt Lewin in the thirties. His work is documented in a book entitled *Field Theory and Social Science*[4] compiled by his friend Dorwin Cartwright in the fifties.

To date I have utilized cause and effect/force field analysis (CE/FFA) very successfully in five different companies in such diverse groups as sales, marketing, engineering, installation, market planning, public relations, customer service, legal, human resources, accounting, billing, and manufacturing.

Most have worked with cause and effect given to us by Dr. Ishikawa.[3] I would like to share with you in this chapter my understanding of Dr. Lewin's work. I have taken key quotes from the book *Field Theory and Social Sciences,* that I will comment on with the objective of reaching a better understanding of its application in today's environment.

Page viii

> He discusses many basic problems of scientific method which all social scientists face and he *proposes solutions* not so much on the basis of absolute "right or wrong" as in terms of what will make the scientist most productive.

Comment: I italicized "proposes solutions." This is exactly what we do in the CE/FFA process—*propose solutions.* One facilitator, when making her presentation to the management team by explaining all restraining and driving forces, said, "It is refreshing to concentrate on solutions rather than just talk about the problems as we usually do."

Page ix

> By never ending series of small excursions into the unknown.

Comment: When using the CE/FFA process, it is not necessary for the facilitator to be an expert in the area being examined. I recall working with a company in the personnel department. Two weeks after the session I received a letter asking permission to use CE/FFA in a real estate firm owned by the employee's mother. A month later I received a call expressing great appreciation. CE/FFA worked in a real estate situation. These "excursions into the unknown" are not only challenging and rewarding but *fun.* It's great to be with experts who really do know what needs to be done to make things better—it's great to expose them to a process that is dynamic and one that helps each group zero in on areas of improvement.

Page ix

> The life space of a group, therefore, consists of the group and its environment as it exists for the group.
>
> The life space is defined so that at any given time it includes all facts that have existence and excludes those that do not have existence for the individual or group under study.

Comment: I like to work with homogeneous groups. This can be defined as a group that works in the same process. Examples include accounting, billing, production (specific product), legal, customer service (same customer), or market planning. It is a much more difficult task, but when processes can be defined and employees can be selected from different disciplines that interact on that process, then by all means tackle the process improvement task using CE/FFA. Save this until you have a few successful homogeneous groups under your belt.

The "life space" that Lewin discusses is important to consider when putting a group together in the first place. Including all facts that have existence for a particular group, *at a particular time*, is most important. The facts that exist at a particular time must be dealt with.

Excluding facts that do not have existence in my experience means clearly separating those areas that appear to be problems that are not actual causes of the effect being explored. Very often these kind of phenomenon can be readily exposed by a group in the CE/FFA setting.

Page 45

> Field theory is probably best characterized as a method: namely, a method of analyzing casual relations. It is this discovery that is important to understand—among others. What may appear to be a relatively insignificant factor, when combined with the forces and factors surrounding the entire situation, the original observation may be anything but casual.

Comment: As mentioned, in my work with over 100 small groups, I have found that even the smallest point or fact when placed in proper perspective of the entire situation becomes easier to understand and therefore solve or learn to cope with.

Building scientific constructs, I believe, relates to the definition of restraining forces and then identifying the driving forces that can counteract the restraining forces and result in change.

Page 60

> An analysis which starts with the situation as a whole.

Page 63

> Instead of picking out one or another isolated element within a situation, the importance of which cannot be judged without consideration of situation as a whole, field theory finds it advantageous, as a rule, to start with a characterization of the situations as a whole.

Comment: Through our experience and education we often omit looking at the situation as a whole and "zero in" on the supposed solution. Even people in the highest positions fall into this trap. *Zeroing in* when done by the wrong person for the wrong reasons can have devastating effects on the final outcome, as did the example cited. This type of management has recently been referred to as *micro-management mentality.* (Scherkenbach—General Motors) and *laser beam management* (Muscari—ALCOA). I would suggest this kind of management is prevalent in American business.

Failure to step back and look at the situation as a whole is one of the most serious mistakes made today. Lewin's approach demands looking at the entire situation; considering all the variables in existence at a particular time. How many times have you been sidetracked by the expert who "zeroed in" on only one aspect of a problem and totally ignored many other contributing factors. Force field analysis just doesn't allow myopic thinking. It is most surprising to find very few that understand this important principle.

As a practical example on how I use this vital concept, consider the following. When I first meet with a small group of experts from a given area of expertise I ask them, "What kind of problems are you encountering in getting your job done?" The group is asked to brainstorm this so all ideas are allowed. What usually happens is the group lists *causes* as in a classic cause and effect study. The effect ends up being the end result of all of this. We then refine the causes by combining like causes, eliminating some, redefining others, and then even rank ordering the causes. I have been justifiably cautioned (by Bill Scherkenbach) about this rank ordering. One must not place undue emphasis on the rank ordering result. We do it primarily to give the group the chance to refine the causes during the rank ordering. I find this almost always happens and therefore makes rank ordering a useful exercise.

The major point here is that the resulting cause and effect study truly does look at the total situation or as Dr. Lewin puts it, "the situation as a whole."

This definitely helps avoid the pitfall of considering only a portion of the problem. The portion, by the way, that may be most apparent, or in other cases a particular person's favorite chestnut.

My feeling is that cause and effect, better than any known technique, helps the user characterize situations "as a whole." This situation can then be attacked vigorously using Lewin's force field technique. As I have said many times the combination of these two separate and distinct disciplines is indeed powerful and useful in many different environments. I cannot think of a place where it would not be effective.

Page 256

> Whenever a resultant force exists, there is either locomotion in the direction of that force or a change in cognitive structure equivalent to this locomotion. The reverse also holds: whenever a locomotion or change of structure exists, resultant forces exist in that direction.

Comment: The key here is that a structure can only change as a result of the forces (positive-driving) acting upon it. Locomotion equals change. The structure changes when driving forces act upon the structure. Structure can also be thought of as the situation being examined at the time.

When a group uses CE/FFA to examine their structure or situation they first determine causes, then the effect. The next step is to do a force field analysis on each cause. This requires a determination of why the structure or situation exists as it does at this time. Something Lewin calls restraining forces holds the structure in a static state—which has no movement.

The next step is to determine what *driving* forces can be applied against any or all of the restraining forces to affect locomotion or change.

Page 259

> Driving and Restraining Forces. The forces toward a positive, or away from a negative, valence can be called *driving forces.* They lead to locomotion. The locomotions might be hindered by physical or social obstacles. Such barriers correspond to *restraining forces.* Restraining forces, as such, do not lead to locomotion, but they do influence the effect of driving forces.

Comment: See previous comment.

Dr. W. Edwards Deming states that for continuous improvement to occur one must start with a theory. My theory is that Ishikawa's and Lewin's methods, when combined, provide a disciplined approach that helps capture the enormous skill and knowledge of those closest to the work. We need to learn how to tap this skill and knowledge instead of suppressing it as we may have done in the past.

In no way do I wish to represent myself as a thorough expert on Dr. Lewin's teaching. His writing is most difficult. What I hope we have done is utilize his thoughts in a modern constructive way to help people and organizations "see" the big picture and be able to concentrate on continuously improving situations, processes, and relations.

Review

Introduction

- Production, cost cutting, meeting schedules, and managing defects comes first—not quality. This must change dramatically in the nineties.
- Two things drive me in this regard. One is the notion that those closest to the work really have an enormous amount of skill, energy, and knowledge that needs to be tapped.
- The second is the theory of variability. Dr. W. Edwards Deming first taught me this in his four-day lecture and the concept was later reinforced by reading his work *Out of the Crisis*.[2]
- Here is a way, here is a method, here is a procedure that will launch you into meaningful quality improvement. It has had a seven-year successful track record in more than one industry. It is ready to be implemented in *many* others including the government, the military, hospitals, and schools at all levels.

Part One – The Steps

- In a talk to about 300 people at Oklahoma State University I asked, "How many of you have a degree in quality improvement?" To no one's surprise no one raised their hand.
- It will take a lot more than the alphabet soup approach to get through quality improvement. We have SPC, QC, QA, JIT, MBO, GD, DOE, OA, TEI, CTR, BM, STC, SQC, PMP, SQA, SQE, EDI, STSM, and still little meaningful progress.
- Management thinks the programs will do it and most are extremely reluctant to become actively involved.
- Dr. Deming is preaching for the transformation of the American style of management. This goes far beyond the aforementioned alphabet soup method.
- As John Naisbitt said, "The job of the manager of the nineties is to coach, teach, and nurture." Later on Naisbitt added the attribute "to facilitate." As mentioned Tom Peters said, "We have failed to tap our work forces' potential."
- I strongly feel that a combination of the 10 previous ideas makes for a direction in the nineties that is powerful, meaningful, and focused; a direction that will ensure American industry regains the number one position.

The Deming Formula

- If you improve your quality you improve your productivity automatically—it's a chain reaction. You do this by lowering waste, lowering restarts, lowering rework. When this finally happens you then can capture markets with higher quality, lower cost of goods and services. This will allow you to stay in business and provide more jobs.

The 85/15 Rule

- At one time Dr. Deming attributed 85 percent of the reason for variability to the process and 15 percent of the reason to people, machines, and tools.
- Bill Scherkenbach who wrote *The Deming Route to Quality and Productivity*[10] reminds us that management is responsible for the entire pie—not just the 85 percent aimed at improving the process.
- It is far best to be invited in to implement quality improvement than to force your way in.
- I did several things to help the "invitation" come sooner.
- This has mushroomed into a massive effort involving every major organization in the company.
- What does matter is that the implementor believes in the method and that it works.
- This is dangerous because it allows the rest of the management team to say, "Let the champion worry about quality."
- Far too many managers are still delegating quality to the quality control department or to the quality professional, or even worse to the consultant.
- My method has worked in five different companies that I know of and possibly more by use of the written material I have provided since 1986.

Record and Tell About Successes

- My best success story involves an organization that literally survived being eliminated because of the work they did over a three-year period in improving the quality of their operation.
- In all of the work the most important improvements cannot be measured.
- *Kaizen* means improvement. Imai tells us that this improvement occurs in the East every day.
- Again the top is not the CEO but the middle manager in charge of a large responsibility. If that person is just BSing, his team knows it and nothing will happen—absolutely nothing. I have seen this happen time after time.
- My advice is don't give up.

Wait for the Phone to Ring

- I guarantee that as you record and tell about successes the phone will literally ring off the hook.

Part Two – The Process

- The CE/FFA (cause and effect/force field analysis) technique allows those closest to the issues to identify problems, their causes, and the forces affecting improvement.

Phase I

- The purpose of this session is to help the management team understand its role in implementing and supporting quality improvement.
- We don't lose sight of the fact that higher management should get involved in 10 percent of the cases; employees can help in 15 percent of the cases; and middle and lower management levels can act on the remaining 75 percent.
- One thing that will not happen unless you have the CEO's full understanding, support, and active involvement is you will not turn the company around.

Phase II

- In a recent lecture Deming stated that the common cause/special cause idea originally came from Walter A. Shewhart of the former Bell Telephone Laboratories.
- The numbers are not important. Deming says it is 85/15; Juran says it is 80/20; in my work with over 100 small groups it comes out to be 82/18. Remarkably close numbers!
- In my 30 years of business experience, when a defect occurred we usually looked for "who" did it.
- I didn't comprehend the experiment until months after I saw it, but the bead experience inferred that management must remove the red beads from the system—blaming the employee doesn't accomplish anything.
- It is very important to go to management with suggested solutions—not just problems. This is not something new.
- Employees closest to the work often have very good ideas about what these solutions are and can make solid recommendations. If we stop at the problem definition as presented in the classic cause and effect, we miss the opportunity for needed input.
- It is recommended that the senior-level manager open this session and set the tone.
- The best way facilitators learn is by doing it. This is why we give as many people as possible the opportunity to actually lead the force field analysis session.

Phase III

- "It took me six months at 'charm school' to learn how to talk with such authority. How did you do this in 10 hours?"

Phase IV

- The purpose of this examination is to pinpoint measurable areas of the process, build a data base in these measurements, identify potential or real problem areas, and take action to correct and prevent future problems.

Part Three – The Facilitator

Facilitator Responsibilities

- The facilitator must create an atmosphere that allows free and open group discussions.
- All discussions should be free of any type of facilitator censorship.
- As facilitator, your opinions are not appropriate; you are seeking the group's ideas.
- Another bit of advice is that it's really best if you, as facilitator, are not an expert on the problem being explored.

Drawing the Cause and Effect Diagram

- I have never, in over 100 sessions, seen less than five or more than 12 causes developed.
- The reason for this is what looks like something different on a brainstorm list can sometimes fit into a major cause either as part of it or other times as an example of how the major cause manifests itself.

Drawing the Force Field Analysis

- Then tell the group to think of this line as "the level of" line.
- At this point the facilitator hands the marker to the QAT member sitting on the right or left side of the arc. This usually comes as a great surprise to everyone.
- Let's talk for a moment about the QAT participation in the Phase III management presentation.
- It is important to understand why we go to such extremes to have everyone participate.

- The group unanimously requested and agreed that we meet on Sunday to finish up. This is an example of the real discipline that occurs during these sessions.
- Usually we come pretty close to Deming's original 85/15 management/worker ratio. My data of over 100 groups says it's 82/18, remarkably close.
- Now let's discuss the management data from the facilitator's standpoint.
- The overriding thing to carry with you is the notion that those closest to the work do have great ideas that need to be tapped.
- At the time of this writing she is singlehandedly implementing this process in a 10,000-person division of AT&T.

Part Four – Use of Cause and Effect with Force Field Analysis

- Effects are those quality problems or defects that occur on the specific job to which each group is assigned (page 45).
- The key is to put the right group of people together to examine that problem (page 47).
- After the group has determined the number one quality problem, the facilitator draws a cause and effect diagram on the pad and asks the group to suggest major causes of the problem to be studied (page 47).

Part Five – Anatomy of a Successful Field Trip

- The talk went well. No talk is ever exactly the same. Many times I find myself reacting to a positive or negative gesture and inserting a comment that wasn't thought of previously. In this particular talk it appeared the group was seeking more definitions of Deming's "drive out fear" point (page 58).
- The other Deming point that many people challenge is the elimination of numerical goals and work standards. This group was no exception. Some say, "You only get what you measure." I would say, "And that's all you get!" Time and time again in my 30 years of experience I have seen people who could do more than they were asked to do (page 59).
- We had a situation where someone had the idea of motivating engineers to do a better job by drawing cartoons of engineers making mistakes. When management began to understand that the process the engineers were working on was the problem, not the engineers, the cartoons disappeared almost overnight. The

important thing to understand from this experience is how to use the data when involving employees (page 59).

- Presentation to Management. I told the group that the presentation to management is an input session from the QAT to management. It's not the time for management to evaluate each statement or commit to specific action. This is the time to make sure management understands the input of the QAT and to clarify questions (page 73).
- I recommended that QRT be established with a supervisor as chairman. The third level manager volunteered, named his two immediate subordinates as members and asked for four volunteers from the QAT and one representative from the staff group (page 73).

Part Six – A Case Study

- I didn't know about cause and effect at that time. Now I can see that each of the problem areas defined were actually "causes" and the "effect" was that the overall project was in jeopardy. The cause and effect study is shown in Figure 18 (ms. p. 93).
- The point here is to explain the use of force field analysis, not to give definitions of the actual recommendations. Over time the recommendations may be augmented or changed completely; the use of force field analysis is the important thing for the reader to understand (page 93).
- The point here is to explain the use of force field analysis, not to give definitions of the actual recommendations. Over time the recommendations may be augmented or changed completely; the use of force field analysis is the important thing for the reader to understand (page 93).
- As mentioned earlier, the training consultant suggested the force field analysis technique in analyzing various project manager concerns which helped determine the cause of certain problems and actions that could be taken to alleviate them. This contribution was considered vital to the overall success of the project (page 96).
- The aspect we are discussing here is the fact that the project members worked in an atmosphere where rank or structure of any kind was not recognized. It was, therefore, important that the impact of the project manager on the various teams be concentrated more toward the developmental mode of operation than either strict control or the opposite which would be relinquishing responsibility for reaching objectives (page 97).
- The definition of a synergistic approach is "the cooperative effort in which the effects are greater than the sum of each part (individual working alone)." This, in effect, is the major reason

for lack of structure within the project itself, and securing people with the best talents to represent specific disciplines that could, in fact, meld together as a team as well as a total group of 18 in adjusting themselves to the problem at hand and, in fact, solving it (page 97).

- The Theory Y approach mentioned earlier refers, of course, to McGregor's more enlightened view of the employee by management. This theory assumes that people generally seek responsibility; that they have a positive capacity for exercising imagination, ingenuity, and creativity; and that they can exercise self-control (page 97).
- A strict chain-of-command approach lessens exposure of the teams to needed input. The best example of this is access to higher levels of management for required input regarding past agreements, current activity, and interpretations of policy and procedures (page 99).
- There was a savings in time and money on the part of the project by making maximum use of even intuitive direction received as a result of all visits by higher management. The project manager in these cases utilized the technique of maximum communication between those who visited and those who were visited. This involved clarifying interpretations from both sides as to what was discussed, why, and what action should be taken (page 100).
- In all situations, there were attempts to accomplish results and relieve pressure on the teams at the same time. In many cases this clarified what was actually required and specific action or needs were communicated (page 101).
- There was no dramatic difference, however, between the kinds of problems and confrontations that were experienced in reaching solutions during the first week of training and those encountered during the life of the project (page 101).
- The major driving forces to counteract the above restraining type forces were to clarify the consultants' role continuously with the individual field teams when necessary, suggest action to the consultants individually or as a team when appropriate, support appropriate actions by either the field teams or the consultants concerning this specific problem, or attempt to provide constructive criticism when necessary (page 102).
- In addition to these, there was misunderstanding of matrix management, a concentration on the negative rather than positive aspects, belittling of the project manager, attempts to leave the project prematurely as noted earlier, concern about splitting the group in four separate geographic areas rather than one, and an attempt to meld the 18 members or a portion of them in one geographic location at a premature stage (page 103).

Another Successful Field Trip

- This chapter will discuss the three-phase approach that was implemented in the license division of that organization.
- The reason for this is that if, indeed, the armed forces can change its style of leadership to one of this advanced nature, we in the business world should take note.
- There was consensus on every point; there were intense moments when very serious matters were discussed; and there were other times when a great deal of humor did enter the conversation.
- There was an extreme reluctance on the part of many in the Phase II session to not want to participate in the Phase III session with management.
- It is significant to report the high level of management involvement in these Phase III sessions.
- The management team was active in their participation by asking very pertinent questions and indicating total support of the quality action team work.
- Often companies tackle productivity first, but they are tackling it the right way by putting the quality of work first.
- Getting the management team to understand that about 85 percent of the time the kinds of problems that exist are problems with the process. The people don't need to change, the process needs to be changed.
- I am an advocate of the employee, in making sure that that employee is working in a process that is right first, and then working with the management team to make that happen.
- The management team knows that about 82 percent of those are their babies. The employees know that they are going to do something about them.
- The kind of things that come out of that are improved morale, improved communication, and improved processes.
- This is exactly what we do in the CE/FFA process—propose solutions.
- It's great to be with experts who really do know what needs to be done to make things better—it's great to expose them to a process that is dynamic, and one that helps each group zero in on areas of improvement.
- As mentioned, in my work with over 100 small groups, I have found that even the smallest point or fact when placed in proper perspective of the entire situation becomes easier to understand and therefore solve or learn to cope with.
- Through our experience and education we often omit looking at the situation as a whole and "zero in" on the supposed solution.
- This type of management has recently been referred to as *micro-management mentality* (Scherkenbach—General Motors) and *laser*

beam management (Muscari—ALCOA).
- The major point here is that the resulting cause and effect study truly does look at the total situation or as Dr. Lewin puts it, "the situation as a whole."
- Locomotion equals change. The structure changes when driving forces act upon the structure.
- Dr. W. Edwards Deming states[2] that for continuous improvement to occur one must start with a theory.

Closing Comments

To date I have worked with over 100 small groups and used the CE/FFA process successfully. I have used force field analysis to manage extremely complex projects as illustrated in Part Six. Although the process is useful in production-oriented situations I have found it to be extremely useful in the white-collar area. Accounting, billing, market planning, customer service, sales, legal, and public relations are examples.

Some questions were asked in the Introduction that I would like to address specifically in these closing comments:

- *How do you get management's attention to act decisively in helping workers do a better job to break down barriers that prevent quality excellence?*

This is not a one-shot situation. It is good to gain common ground through use of the same language. This can be attained by attending the many courses that are available and by reading the books referred to in this book. It is everyday practice of the principles learned that is of utmost importance. Some have asked, "Why does a company have to have its back against the wall before it gets into meaningful quality improvements?" Unfortunately, this is the case at times. But as Dr. Juran suggests, it is easier to achieve actual improvement when your process is in control rather than trying to figure out what to do when the process is in chaos.

So how do you, as quality practitioner, get management's attention? James Houghton, president of Corning Glass Works, suggests that you "discuss your cause, not your tools." He also advised, "Take the quality message to the top person in your organization as a *solution* to some of the organization's quality problems—take a position and point out the consequences of inaction."[15]

As cited earlier in this book, the top person need not be the CEO. Seek out what I call the location head—the person in charge of a specific function. You must have this person on your side. When I first started I called a friend who was location head. He cooperated fully and progress was attained. Then word began to spread to other organizations; people who I have never met call me. The conversation, however, is the same: "Please help me improve the quality of my operation." Then we go into the phases discussed in this book.

The use of employees and first-line supervisors on quality action teams followed by the use of quality resolution and review teams involving management definitely helps break down the barriers that prevent quality excellence. Workers end up doing a better job because the weaknesses in the process are identified and management does something to fix the process.

- *How do you get workers to participate in managerial decisions?*

As mentioned previously, John Naisbitt, Michael MacCoby, and Douglas McGregor all discuss the importance of participative management for now and the future.

Use of the CE/FFA process described in this book gets worker participation in a disciplined way. It is better than MBWA, brainstorming, the Gordon technique, or cause and effect and force field analysis used separately. The combination is what gives the power to this process. Seventy-five groups have used this tool without failure. It has given workers and lower levels of supervision the great opportunity to have a say in what needs to be done to fix the process—and this is participation at its best. We merge these workers with management in our Phase III session where good participation usually takes place on the management side.

- *How do you get out there and ask the questions to get the workers' ideas crystallized?*

You use a trained facilitator in the CE/FFA technique. This is better than the casual conversation the boss gets involved in in walking around. Please don't misunderstand. Walking around may be fine, but there must be more to get solid input. In the 100+ sessions of six to 10 hours each, I have seen anywhere from 25 to 94 ideas created in each session. On the average this equates to over 5,000 recommendations—all aimed at fixing the process, not the air conditioning, or cleaning windows, or providing privileged parking, or Sunday afternoon picnics, or the texture of toilet paper! Some ask if I did a Pareto analysis on the 5,000 recommendations. The answer is no! These 100+ groups all came from different organizations. The management of those organizations analyzed the recommendations to discover what they could do. I advise the management team that nothing in business can be considered *trivial.* If Ray Kroc believed this, McDonald's would have gone bankrupt 20 years ago. Clean trays, cooks wearing hats, and clean rest rooms are not trivial in the customer's eyes. Cleanliness and consistency of service and taste are the hallmarks of McDonald's worldwide success.

So, if we end up with a list of 30 recommendations, I recommend going after the easiest first. Why let something wait that can be fixed in 24 hours! Tackle the harder items later with a planned approach that will get the job done over a period of time. Assign someone responsible, agree on a target date, track that date, and record any possible cost savings.

- *How do you, as manager, unleash the worker's creative ideas to solve problems?*

First, give them time and opportunity to use the CE/FFA process with the help of a trained facilitator. Second, *listen* to the ideas, and third, take action. Unless this cycle is completed you will have done more harm than good. Dr. Deming has stated that American management doesn't want to step out and take a chance to help improve things. "It's easier to do nothing," he said.[16] We can no longer take this route. Management at all levels must now take ownership of the process and in one small step at a time act to improve it. I think we are closer to a now or never situation than ever before. Time is running out!

- *How does management set in motion a way to implement these ideas so that the work can be done better?*

This entire book is about showing "a way" to improve quality that works. If you have started your reading here, as I do occasionally, go back to page one and start at the beginning. You will discover "a way" that dramatically gets workers/supervisors and higher management together on preventing defects and controlling variability. The end result can be higher productivity, lower cost, and higher quality goods and services. This can result further in companies staying in business and providing more jobs. The latter, of course, is Dr. Deming's formula. Dr. Deming made this statement in one of his lectures:

> You are living in the most underdeveloped country in the world—just think what the United States could do if every employee was allowed to make a maximum contribution and management managed the way they should.[17]

If this book just helps nudge us in the direction Dr. Deming has been pointing, it will have been worth the effort.

__PREFACE__
TO APPENDICES

The following are examples of using the discipline of cause and effect/force field analysis (CE/FFA) in administration areas such as information systems that address the problems of application outages and training; systems engineering that addresses the problem of the organization not being as efficient as it should be; systems testing that addresses the problem of lower than wanted product quality; systems development that also addresses the problem of the organization being less effective. The next six CE/FFAs are done by one company, Florida Motor Vehicle Division of License. All six involve different departments' views of how to improve the service of issuing licenses to the public. Specific actions follow each CE/FFA that were taken by bureau chiefs and then staffs to help solve the problems defined.

The examples are all presented as developed by each group. There are differences in format and technique. All follow the CE/FFA pattern close enough to reach overall understanding of the problem.

APPENDIX A

SECTION ONE

MIS APPLICATION OUTAGES

QUALITY ACTION TEAM PRESENTATION

**MIS QUALITY IMPROVEMENT PROCESS
APPLICATION OUTAGES**

Scope: Application outages are the focus of this QAT since it more precisely identifies an impact to our customer base. Application outages are composed of several elements of which two main categories compose the majority of the underlying issues. The first category is application maintenance which is the global term defined by business systems related to activities usually performed by programmer analysts in order to keep production systems running correctly and on schedule. Problem process identification is performed by the data center by opening an on-line incident via the problem tracking facility. The second category is post-implementation and correction which typically follows immediately after production implementation and allows for a stabilization period. Problem process identification is performed by the customer based upon a discrepancy in the design or programming stage.

The task of the Application Outages QAT will be to identify and eliminate the internal failure costs of quality within the application development life-cycle.

Quality Action Team Members from:

QAT facilitator
Business systems
Data management
Data center
Operations support
Technical support
Customer community

Source: TEST. UT. LIB. APPLQAT (APPLQAT)

CAUSE AND EFFECT

Effect: Application systems fail to meet customer needs, causing high cost and low customer satisfaction

Top categories

PROJECT PLANNING AND CONTROL
- Estimating Is Incorrect
- Managing Customer Expectations Is Poor
- Excessive Re-planning
- Deadlines Can Take Precedence Over Quality
- Poor Monitoring and Control

CUSTOMER REQUIREMENTS
- All Affected Customers Not Involved
- Customers Can't Define Needs
- Changing Business Requirements
- Poor Communication

ANALYSIS
- Incomplete Analysis
- Incomprehensible
- Lack of Business Knowledge
- Poor Integration of Applications
- Poor Make/Buy Decisions

DESIGN
- Poorly Integrated Applications
- Inflexible Designs
- Poor Design Skills
- Lack of Overall Business Knowledge
- Lack of Feedback/Review on Design

IMPLEMENTATION (CODE & TEST)
- Lack of Customer Commitment & Involvement
- Lack of Training
- Time to Market Too Long
- Inadequate Testing
- Complex Environment
- Poor Coding

Bottom categories

CHANGE CONTROL
- Poor Change Control Process
- Inadequate Standards
- Lack of Test Procedures
- Lack of Tools
- Slow Turnaround
- Execution Errors
- Scheduling Errors

ONGOING OPERATIONAL PROBLEMS
- Too Many Scheduling Errors
- Execution Errors
- Poor Monitoring of Errors
- Printing and Distribution Problems
- Inefficient Jobs and Programs
- Operator Errors

METHODOLOGY AND STANDARDS
- Inadequate StorageTek Documentation
- Lack of Training on Methodology and Standards
- Lack of Common Environments
- Multiple Methodologies
- Lack of Conformance

TOOLS AND TRAINING
- Lack of Common Reusable Modules
- Not Enough Useful MIS Tools
- Lack of MIS Staff Training
- Inadequate Training on StorageTek Applications

END USER APPLICATIONS
- Inadequate Ad Hoc Reporting Tools
- Lack of Support
- Lack of Visibility
- Lack of Control

1.1 LACK OF SYSTEMATIC PROJECT PLANNING & CONTROL RESULT IN EXCESSIVE TIME TO MARKET

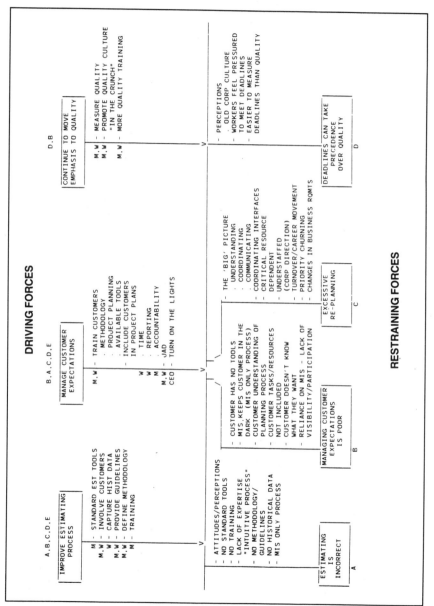

1.2 LACK OF SYSTEMATIC PROJECT PLANNING & CONTROL RESULT IN EXCESSIVE TIME TO MARKET

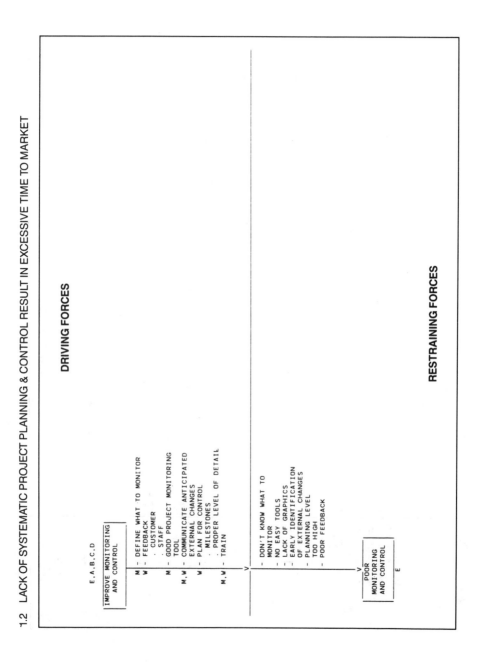

DRIVING FORCES

E.A.,B.C.D

IMPROVE MONITORING
AND CONTROL

M - DEFINE WHAT TO MONITOR
W - FEEDBACK
    . CUSTOMER
    . STAFF
M - GOOD PROJECT MONITORING
    TOOL
M,W - COMMUNICATE ANTICIPATED
    EXTERNAL CHANGES
W - PLAN FOR CONTROL
    . MILESTONES
    . PROPER LEVEL OF DETAIL
M,W - TRAIN

V

- DON'T KNOW WHAT TO
  MONITOR
- NO EASY TOOLS
- LACK OF GRAPHICS
- EARLY IDENTIFICATION
  OF EXTERNAL CHANGES
- PLANNING LEVEL
  TOO HIGH
- POOR FEEDBACK

V
POOR
MONITORING
AND CONTROL

E

RESTRAINING FORCES

2. IDENTIFICATION OF CORRECT CUSTOMER REQUIREMENTS IS TOO LOW.

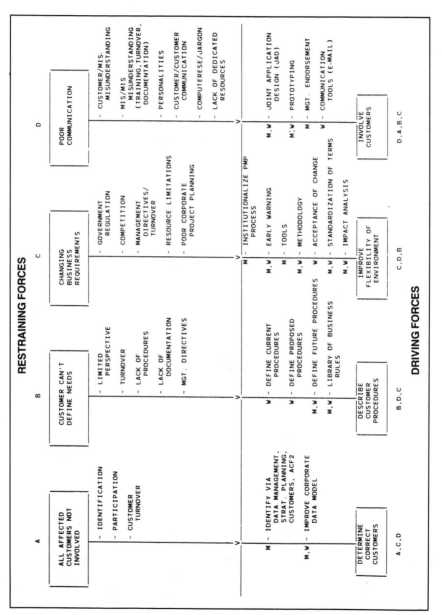

3. DUE TO POOR ANALYSIS, THE LEVEL OF SUBSEQUENT CHANGES IS TOO HIGH.

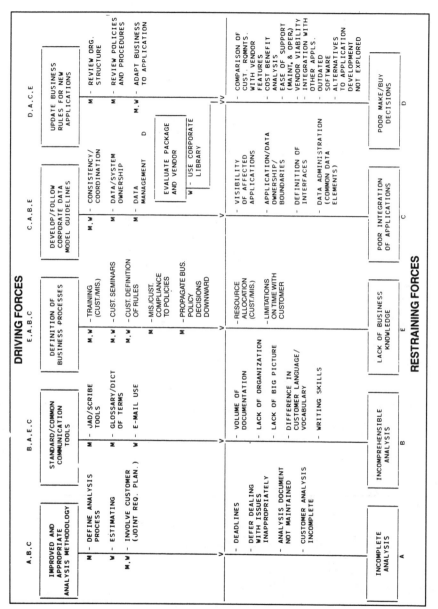

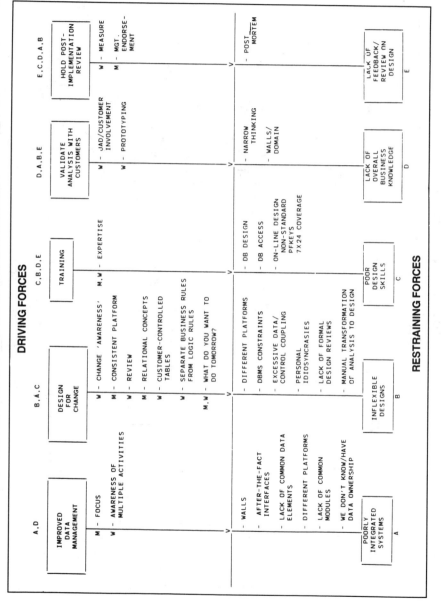

4. DUE TO POOR DESIGN, THE LEVEL OF SUBSEQUENT CHANGES IS TOO HIGH.

5.1 CUSTOMER SATISFACTION WITH THE CODING AND TESTING PROCESS IS TOO LOW.

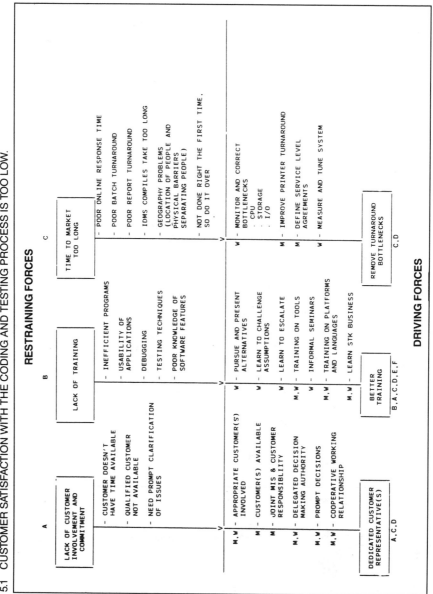

5.2 CUSTOMER SATISFACTION WITH THE CODING AND TESTING PROCESS IS TOO LOW.

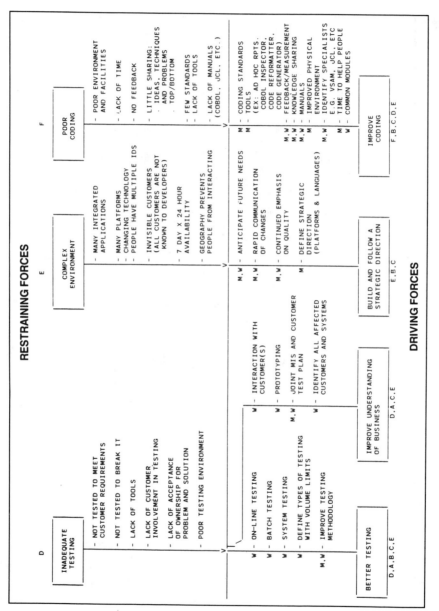

RESTRAINING FORCES

D — INADEQUATE TESTING
- NOT TESTED TO MEET CUSTOMER REQUIREMENTS
- NOT TESTED TO BREAK IT
- LACK OF TOOLS
- LACK OF CUSTOMER INVOLVEMENT IN TESTING
- LACK OF ACCEPTANCE OF OWNERSHIP FOR PROBLEM AND SOLUTION
- POOR TESTING ENVIRONMENT

E — COMPLEX ENVIRONMENT
- MANY INTEGRATED APPLICATIONS
- MANY PLATFORMS
- CHANGING TECHNOLOGY
- PEOPLE HAVE MULTIPLE IDS
- INVISIBLE CUSTOMERS (ALL CUSTOMERS ARE NOT KNOWN TO DEVELOPERS)
- 7 DAY X 24 HOUR AVAILABILITY
- GEOGRAPHY PREVENTS PEOPLE FROM INTERACTING

F — POOR CODING
- POOR ENVIRONMENT AND FACILITIES
- LACK OF TIME
- NO FEEDBACK
- LITTLE SHARING:
  · IDEAS, TECHNIQUES AND PROBLEMS TOP/BOTTOM
- FEW STANDARDS
- LACK OF TOOLS
- LACK OF MANUALS (COBOL, JCL. ETC.)

DRIVING FORCES

BETTER TESTING — D.A.B.C.E
- W — ON-LINE TESTING
- W — BATCH TESTING
- W — SYSTEM TESTING
- W — DEFINE TYPES OF TESTING WITH VOLUME LIMITS
- M.W — IMPROVE TESTING METHODOLOGY

IMPROVE UNDERSTANDING OF BUSINESS — D.A.C.E
- W — INTERACTION WITH CUSTOMER(S)
- W — PROTOTYPING
- M.W — JOINT MIS AND CUSTOMER TEST PLAN
- W — IDENTIFY ALL AFFECTED CUSTOMERS AND SYSTEMS

BUILD AND FOLLOW A STRATEGIC DIRECTION — E.B.C
- M.W — ANTICIPATE FUTURE NEEDS
- M.W — RAPID COMMUNICATION OF CHANGES
- M.W — CONTINUED EMPHASIS ON QUALITY
- M — DEFINE STRATEGIC DIRECTION (PLATFORMS & LANGUAGES)

IMPROVE CODING — F.B.C.D.E
- M — CODING STANDARDS
- M — TOOLS (EX: AD HOC RPTS. COBOL INSPECTOR. CODE REFORMATTER. CODE GENERATOR)
- M.W — FEEDBACK/MEASUREMENT
- M.W — KNOWLEDGE SHARING
- M.W — MANUALS
- M — IMPROVED PHYSICAL ENVIRONMENT
- M.W — IDENTIFY SPECIALISTS E.G. VSAM, JCL, ETC
- M — TIME TO HELP PEOPLE
- W — COMMON MODULES

6. BENEFITS OF THE CHANGE CONTROL PROCESS ARE TOO LOW.

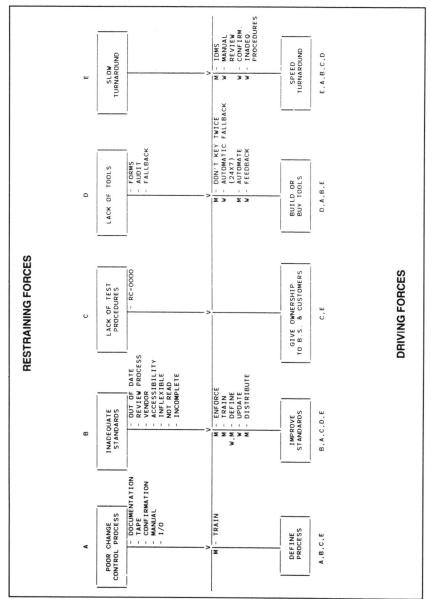

7.1 THE LEVEL OF ONGOING OPERATIONAL PROBLEMS IS TOO HIGH.

DRIVING FORCES

A, B, D, G — IMPROVE THE SCHEDULING PROCESS

- M,W – IMPROVE STDS. / GUIDELINES
- M,W – ANALYZE NEW SCHED. PKG. (HOLIDAY SCHED.)
- W – REVIEW & IMPROVE SCHED. PROCESS
- W – AUTOMATE MORE APPLICATIONS
- W – PROVIDE TRAINING (OPERATIONS & PROGRAMMERS)

B, A, D, G — REDUCE EXECUTION ERRORS

- M – RETHINK BETA TEST ENVIRONMENT (BETTER TEST PLANS)
- M – MANAGE OUR SUPPLIERS
- M – INSTALL RELIABLE HARDWARE
- M,W – IMPROVE PROBLEM TRACKING SYSTEM
- M – BETTER JOBSCAN TOOL (CHECK ACF2)
- M,W – IMPROVE DISCIPLINE OF HOT IDS
- M – PROVIDE 24X7 CHANGE CONTROL
- W – TEST "ALL" PGMS. & JCL FOR PROD.
- M – PURCHASE HIGHER GRADE MEDIA & MEDIA EVALUATION MACHINE.

C, A, B, D, E, G — ACCURATELY MONITOR OPERATIONAL ERRORS

- W – REDEFINE PROBLEM TRACKING SYSTEM
- M,W – MONITOR ONLINE SYSTEMS (NO RESOURCES)
- M,W – DEFINE/ANALYZE STATISTICAL REPORTING
- M – SELECT TOOLS

D, A, B, G — IMPROVE RECOVERY PROCESS

- W – IMPROVE RECOVERY PROCESS
- M,W – REFINE RECOVERY PROCESS
  - TRAIN
  - AUTOMATE
  - ENFORCE
- W – DOCUMENT SYSTEM INTERFACES (FLOWS)
- M,W – PROVIDE "HELP" FACILITY (PF1)
- W – DESIGN FOR FAILURE PREVENTION
- M – AUTOMATE RECOVERY
- M – PROVIDE FOR REPORT REPRINT
- W – PRACTICE RECOVERY
- M,W – BREAK DOWN WALLS (COMMUNICATION)

RESTRAINING FORCES

A — TOO MANY SCHEDULING ERRORS

- POOR STANDARDS
- UNTESTABLE SCHEDULES
- CUSTOMER/PGMR DOCUMENTATION
- MANUAL CHG. CONTROL PROCESS CUMBERSOME
- SPECIAL REQUESTS
- SCHEDULING CONSISTENCY
- INFLEXIBLE SCHEDULING PACKAGE
- NO TRAINING/ORIENTATION

B — TOO MANY EXECUTION ERRORS

- LACK OF PROBLEM REPORTING GUIDELINES
- UNTESTABLE ACF2
- LACK OF CONTROL ON HOT IDS (NOT USING CHANGE CONTROL PROC.)
- NO 24X7 CHANGE CONTROL
- UNTESTED PGMS./JCL
- TOO MANY HARDWARE/ MEDIA/MICROCODE PROBLEMS

C — POOR MONITORING OF ERRORS

- PROBLEM TRACKING CUMBERSOME
- DATA CENTER ONLY DESIGN
- NO CURRENT CAPABILITY TO MONITOR ONLINE SYS.
- NO PERSONNEL ASSIGNED TO MONITOR ONLINE ERRS.
- LACK OF PROBLEM TRACKING STATISTICAL ANALYSIS
- MANY AREAS NOT BEING EFFECTIVELY MONITORED
  - CHANGE CONTROL
  - DBA
  - BUSINESS SYSTEMS
- LACK OF TOOLS
- PROBLEM TRACKING ELEMENTS INCOMPLETE (NO FYI)

D — PROBLEMS WITH RECOVERY

- INCORRECT DOCUMENTATION
- PROC. NOT FOLLOWED PERSONNEL IN D.C. NOT TRAINED
- LACK OF PERSONNEL
- COMPLEX INTERFACES
- LACK OF CHK. & CONTROL POINTS BETWEEN SYSTEMS
- AFFECTED CUSTOMER NOT NOTIFIED
- CAN'T CREATE RPT. WITHOUT RERUN
- MANUAL FILE RECOV.
- UNTESTED RECOVERY PROCEDURES
- POOR INTERDEPART-MENT COMMUNICATION

7.2 THE LEVEL OF ONGOING OPERATIONAL PROBLEMS IS TOO HIGH.

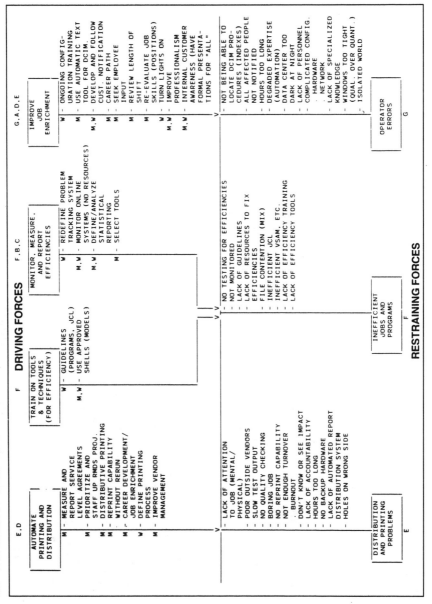

8.1   INADEQUATE AND UNENFORCED STANDARDS, & THE LACK OF A COMMON METHODOLOGY
RESULT IN LOW CUSTOMER SATISFACTION

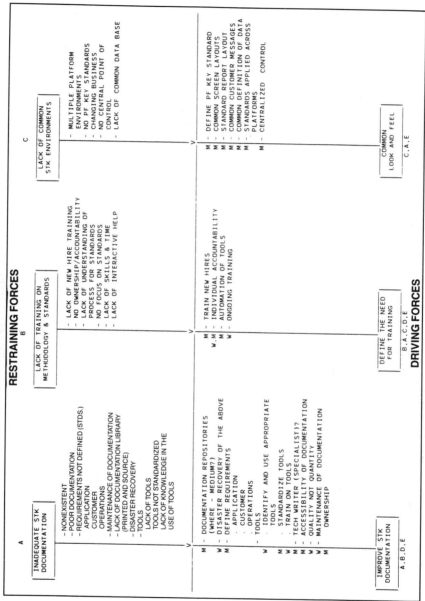

RESTRAINING FORCES

A

INADEQUATE STK
DOCUMENTATION

- NONEXISTENT
- POOR DOCUMENTATION
- REQUIREMENTS NOT DEFINED (STDS.)
  APPLICATION
  CUSTOMER
  OPERATIONS
- MAINTENANCE OF DOCUMENTATION
- LACK OF DOCUMENTATION LIBRARY
  (PRINTED AND SOURCE)
- DISASTER RECOVERY
- TOOLS
  LACK OF TOOLS
  TOOLS NOT STANDARDIZED
  LACK OF KNOWLEDGE IN THE
  USE OF TOOLS

M – DOCUMENTATION REPOSITORIES
    (WHERE – MEDIUM?)
W – DISASTER RECOVERY OF THE ABOVE
M – DEFINE REQUIREMENTS
    . APPLICATION
    . CUSTOMER
    . OPERATIONS
W – TOOLS
    . IDENTIFY AND USE APPROPRIATE
      TOOLS
M – . STANDARDIZE TOOLS
W – . TRAIN ON TOOLS
M – TECH WRITER (SPECIALIST)?
M – ACCESSIBILITY OF DOCUMENTATION
W – QUALITY NOT QUANTITY
W – MAINTENANCE OF DOCUMENTATION
M – OWNERSHIP

B

LACK OF TRAINING ON
METHODOLOGY & STANDARDS

- LACK OF NEW HIRE TRAINING
- NO OWNERSHIP/ACCOUNTABILITY
- LACK OF UNDERSTANDING OF
  PROCESS FOR STANDARDS
- NO FOCUS ON STANDARDS
- LACK OF SKILLS & TIME
- LACK OF INTERACTIVE HELP

M – TRAIN NEW HIRES
W,M – INDIVIDUAL ACCOUNTABILITY
M – AUTOMATION OF TOOLS
W – ONGOING TRAINING

C

LACK OF COMMON
STK ENVIRONMENTS

- MULTIPLE PLATFORM
  ENVIRONMENTS
- NO PF KEY STANDARDS
- CHANGING BUSINESS
- NO CENTRAL POINT OF
  CONTROL
- LACK OF COMMON DATA BASE

M – DEFINE PF KEY STANDARD
M – COMMON SCREEN LAYOUTS
M – STANDARD REPORT LAYOUT
M – COMMON CUSTOMER MESSAGES
M – COMMON DEFINITION OF DATA
M – STANDARDS APPLIED ACROSS
    PLATFORMS
M – CENTRALIZED CONTROL

IMPROVE STK
DOCUMENTATION

A.B.D.E

DEFINE THE NEED
FOR TRAINING

B.A.C.D.E

COMMON
LOOK AND FEEL

C.A.E

DRIVING FORCES

8.2   INADEQUATE AND UNENFORCED STANDARDS, & THE LACK OF A COMMON METHODOLOGY
      RESULT IN LOW CUSTOMER SATISFACTION

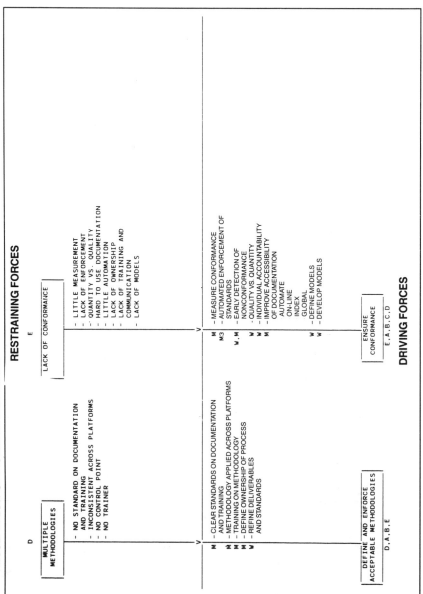

RESTRAINING FORCES

E

LACK OF CONFORMANCE

- LITTLE MEASUREMENT
- LACK OF ENFORCEMENT
- QUANTITY VS. QUALITY
- HARD TO USE DOCUMENTATION
- LITTLE AUTOMATION
- LACK OF OWNERSHIP
- LACK OF TRAINING AND
  COMMUNICATION
- LACK OF MODELS

D

MULTIPLE METHODOLOGIES

- NO STANDARD ON DOCUMENTATION
  AND TRAINING
- INCONSISTENT ACROSS PLATFORMS
- NO CONTROL POINT
- NO TRAINER

M - MEASURE CONFORMANCE
M3 - AUTOMATED ENFORCEMENT OF
     STANDARDS
W, M - EARLY DETECTION OF
       NONCONFORMANCE
W - QUALITY VS. QUANTITY
M - INDIVIDUAL ACCOUNTABILITY
M - IMPROVE ACCESSIBILITY
     OF DOCUMENTATION
       AUTOMATE
       ON-LINE
       INDEX
       GLOBAL
W - DEFINE MODELS
W - DEVELOP MODELS

M - CLEAR STANDARDS ON DOCUMENTATION
     AND TRAINING
M - METHODOLOGY APPLIED ACROSS PLATFORMS
M - TRAINING ON METHODOLOGY
W - DEFINE OWNERSHIP OF PROCESS
W - REFINE DELIVERABLES
     AND STANDARDS

ENSURE
CONFORMANCE

E, A, B, C, D

DEFINE AND ENFORCE
ACCEPTABLE METHODOLOGIES

D, A, B, E

DRIVING FORCES

9.1   INADEQUATE TOOLS AND TRAINING RESULT IN LOW CUSTOMER SATISFACTION.

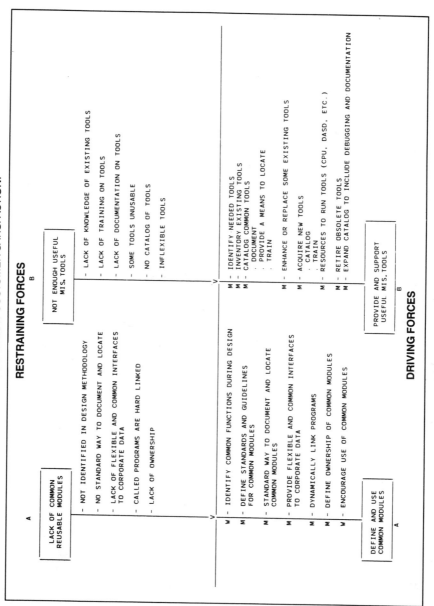

RESTRAINING FORCES

A   B

LACK OF COMMON
REUSABLE MODULES

- NOT IDENTIFIED IN DESIGN METHODOLOGY
- NO STANDARD WAY TO DOCUMENT AND LOCATE
- LACK OF FLEXIBLE AND COMMON INTERFACES TO CORPORATE DATA
- CALLED PROGRAMS ARE HARD LINKED
- LACK OF OWNERSHIP

NOT ENOUGH USEFUL MIS. TOOLS

- LACK OF KNOWLEDGE OF EXISTING TOOLS
- LACK OF TRAINING ON TOOLS
- LACK OF DOCUMENTATION ON TOOLS
- SOME TOOLS UNUSABLE
- NO CATALOG OF TOOLS
- INFLEXIBLE TOOLS

DRIVING FORCES

W - IDENTIFY COMMON FUNCTIONS DURING DESIGN
M - DEFINE STANDARDS AND GUIDELINES FOR COMMON MODULES
M - STANDARD WAY TO DOCUMENT AND LOCATE COMMON MODULES
M - PROVIDE FLEXIBLE AND COMMON INTERFACES TO CORPORATE DATA
M - DYNAMICALLY LINK PROGRAMS
M - DEFINE OWNERSHIP OF COMMON MODULES
W - ENCOURAGE USE OF COMMON MODULES

DEFINE AND USE COMMON MODULES

A

M - IDENTIFY NEEDED TOOLS
M - INVENTORY EXISTING TOOLS
M - CATALOG COMMON TOOLS
  . DOCUMENT
  . PROVIDE A MEANS TO LOCATE
  . TRAIN
M - ENHANCE OR REPLACE SOME EXISTING TOOLS
M - ACQUIRE NEW TOOLS
  . CATALOG
  . TRAIN
M - RESOURCES TO RUN TOOLS (CPU, DASD, ETC.)
M - RETIRE OBSOLETE TOOLS
M - EXPAND CATALOG TO INCLUDE DEBUGGING AND DOCUMENTATION

PROVIDE AND SUPPORT USEFUL MIS. TOOLS

B

9.2 INADEQUATE TOOLS AND TRAINING RESULT IN LOW CUSTOMER SATISFACTION.

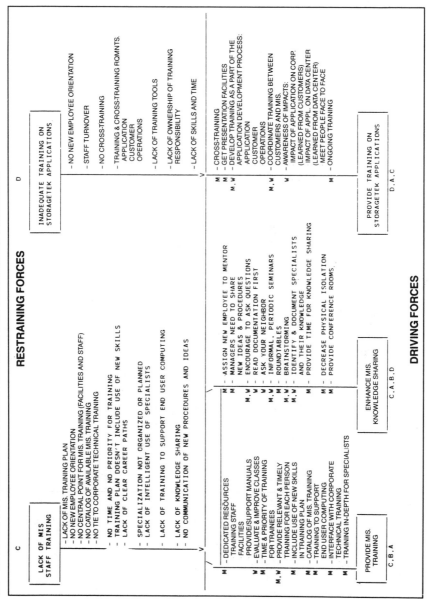

10. THE LEVEL OF SATISFACTION WITH END USER APPLICATIONS IS TOO LOW.

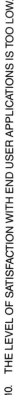
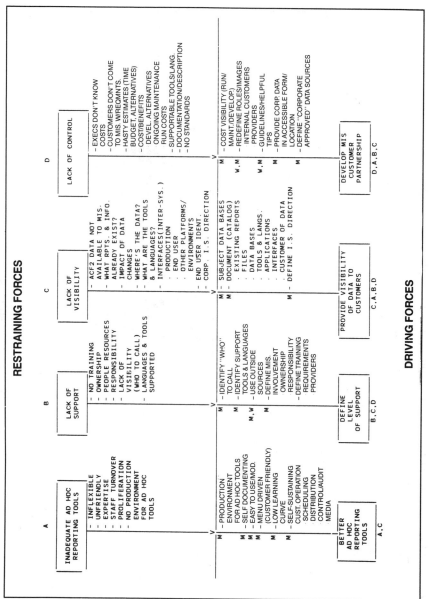

Major Opportunities for Improvement

- Training.

- Tools.
  –Problem management and change management

- Resources.
  –People
  –Time
  –Machines

- Get close to customer.
  –Identify
  –Communicate
  –Commitment
  –Learn STK business (face-to-face customer contact)

- Culture.
  –Recognition
  –Accountability/ownership
  –Information about STK (future direction)
  –Knowledge sharing
  –Respect for each other
  –Tear down walls (physical locking is detrimental to this goal)
  –Job enrichment
  –Common shared goals corporate-wide

- Methodology and guidelines.
  –Estimating
  –Planning
  –Measurement/monitoring
  –Documentation
  –Testing

Application Outages QAT
Quality Action Team Data

Typical results:
  Management = 85%
  Workers = 15%

Our action team results:
  Major driving forces = 53
  Detail driving forces = 257

Management actions	= 270 items	= 79%
Worker actions	= 70 items	= 21%
Total	= 340 items	

SECTION TWO

MIS TRAINING

QUALITY ACTION TEAM PRESENTATION

Training Quality Action Team

Team members:
Since the need for training touches all of MIS, it was felt that a broad representation would best suit this QAT. The following organizations participated:

> Data center
> Business systems
> Hardware services
> DPIC
> Software support
> Data management
> Data center

Scope:
The scope of this QAT is the need for training in MIS. At the same time, it is hoped that this QAT will serve as a model for other organizations within StorageTek to address training.

Justification:
Training is fundamental to avoiding failures (i.e., Quality).
The MIS Training Survey.

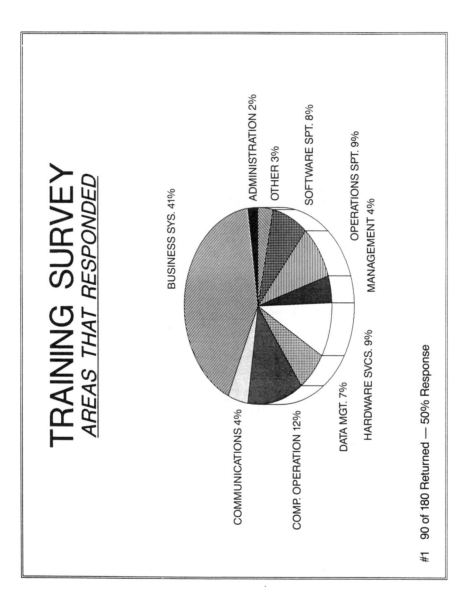

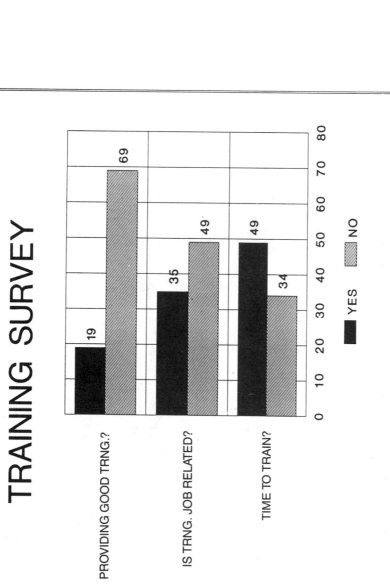

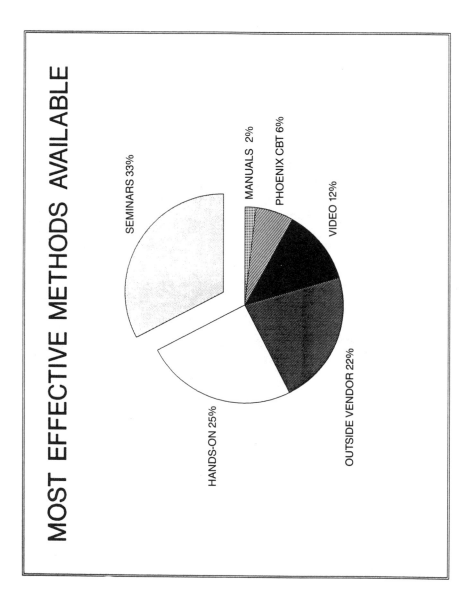

MOST EFFECTIVE METHODS AVAILABLE

SEMINARS 33%

MANUALS 2%

PHOENIX CBT 6%

VIDEO 12%

OUTSIDE VENDOR 22%

HANDS-ON 25%

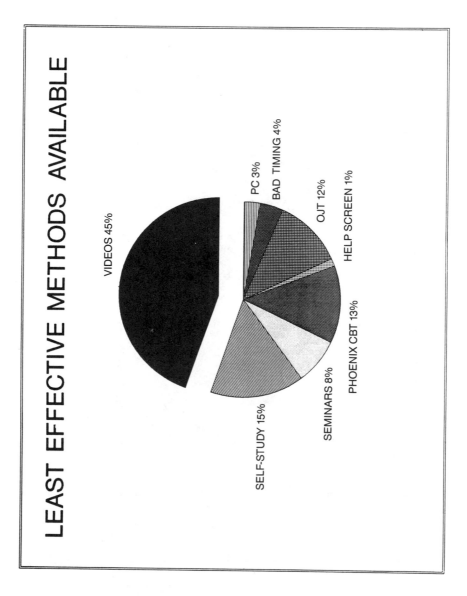

LEAST EFFECTIVE METHODS AVAILABLE

VIDEOS 45%

PC 3%

BAD TIMING 4%

OJT 12%

HELP SCREEN 1%

PHOENIX CBT 13%

SEMINARS 8%

SELF-STUDY 15%

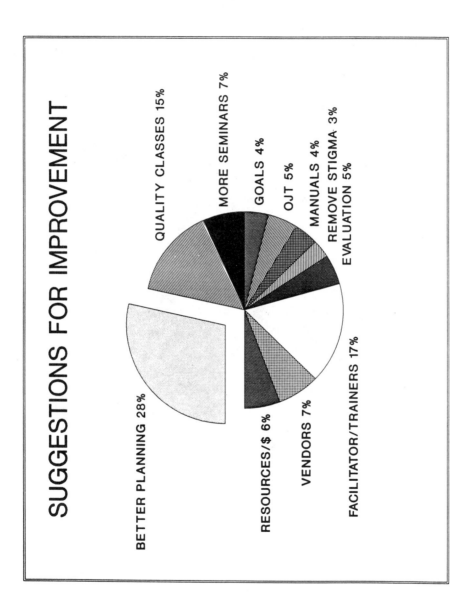

SUGGESTIONS FOR IMPROVEMENT

BETTER PLANNING 28%

QUALITY CLASSES 15%

MORE SEMINARS 7%

GOALS 4%

OJT 5%

MANUALS 4%

REMOVE STIGMA 3%

EVALUATION 5%

FACILITATOR/TRAINERS 17%

VENDORS 7%

RESOURCES/$ 6%

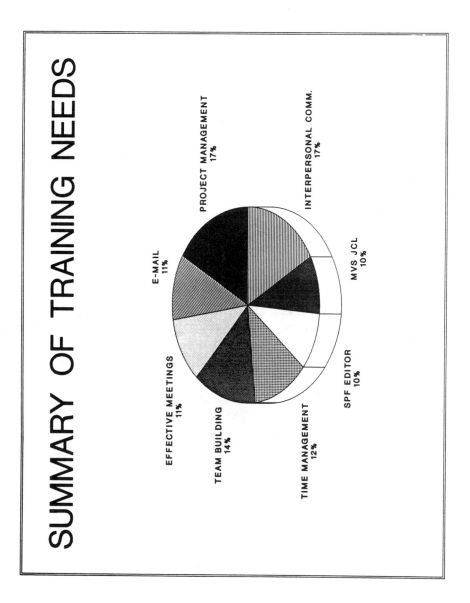

SUMMARY OF TRAINING NEEDS

PROJECT MANAGEMENT
17%

INTERPERSONAL COMM.
17%

E-MAIL
11%

MVS JCL
10%

EFFECTIVE MEETINGS
11%

TEAM BUILDING
14%

TIME MANAGEMENT
12%

SPF EDITOR
10%

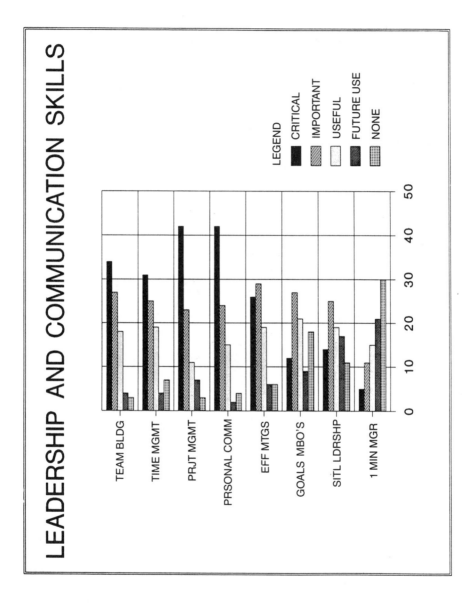

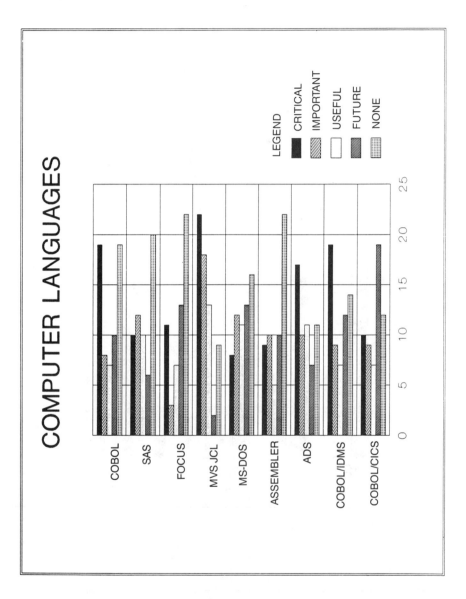

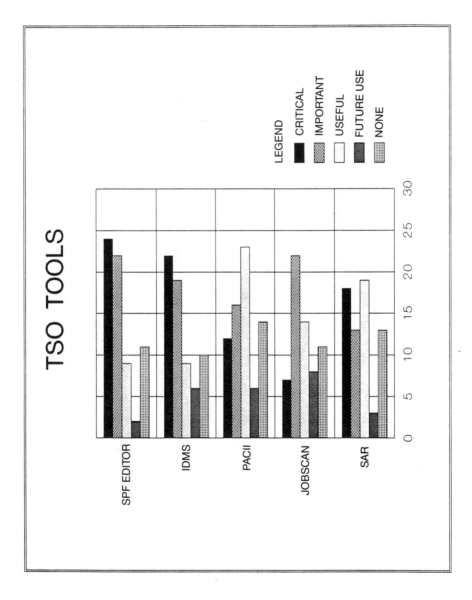

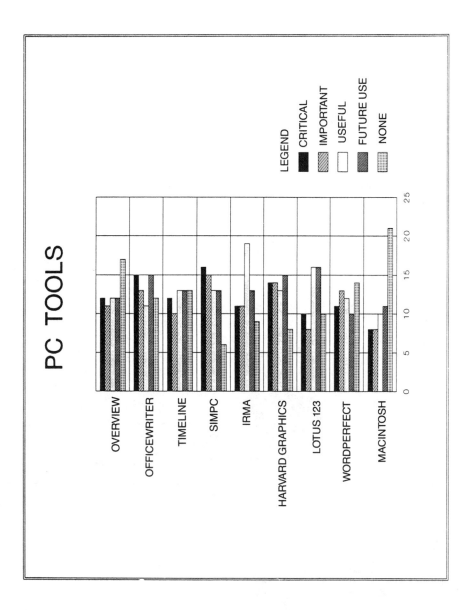

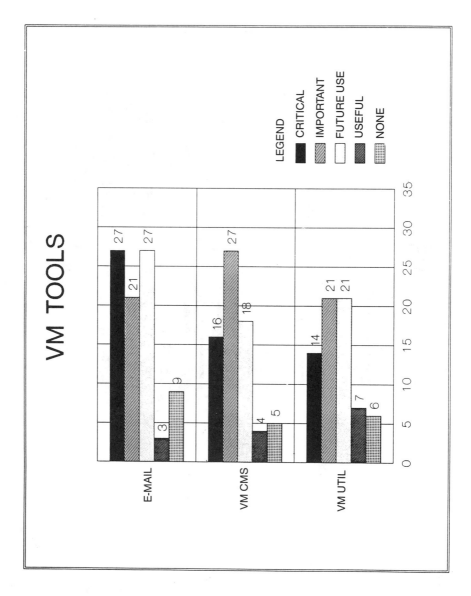

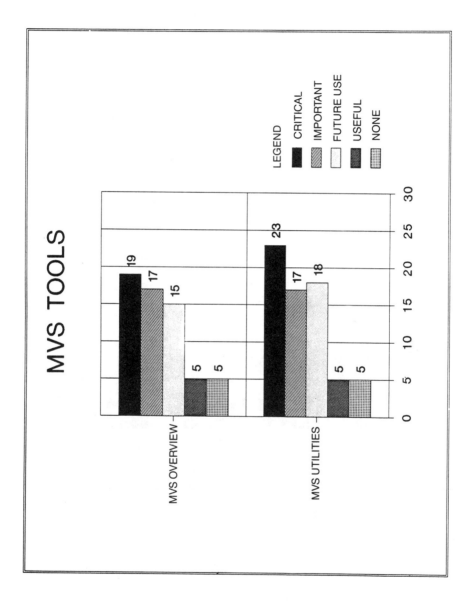

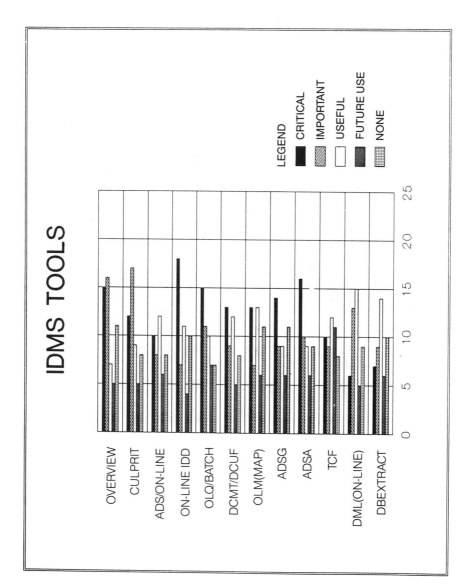

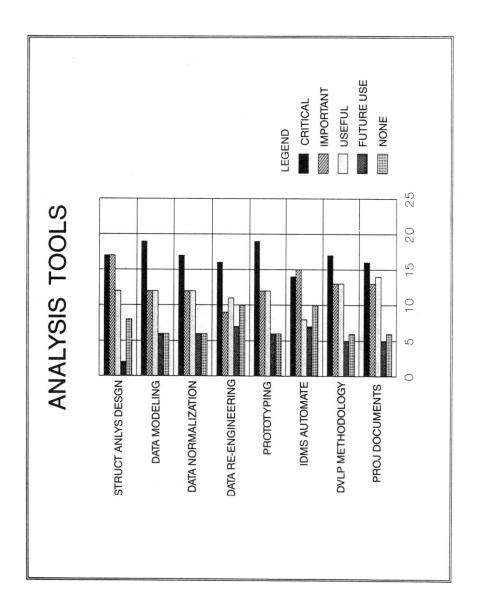

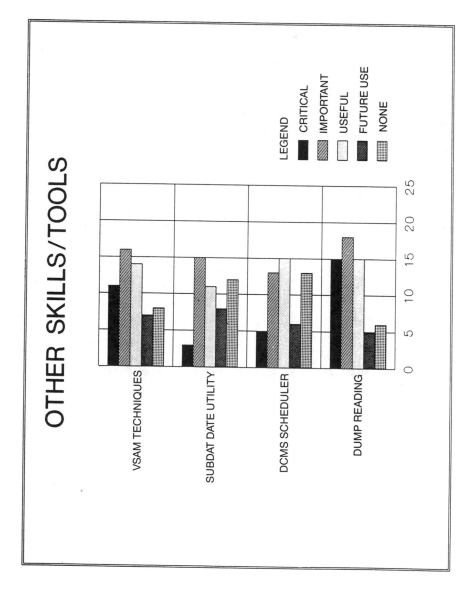

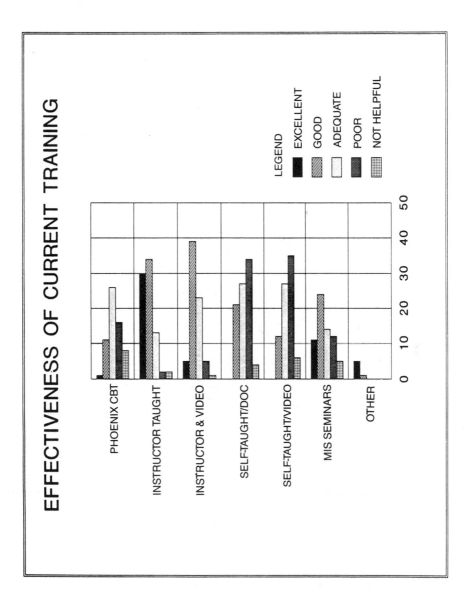

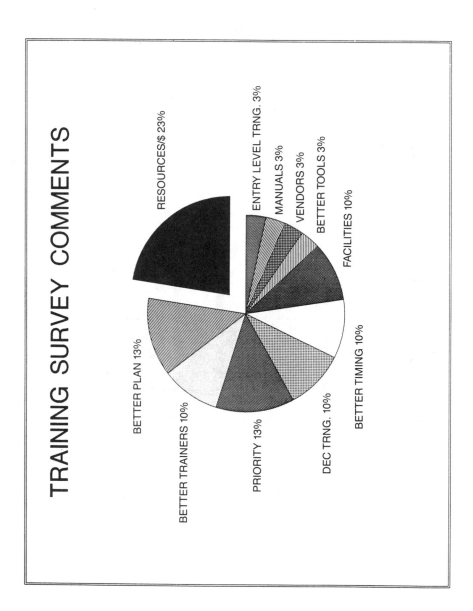

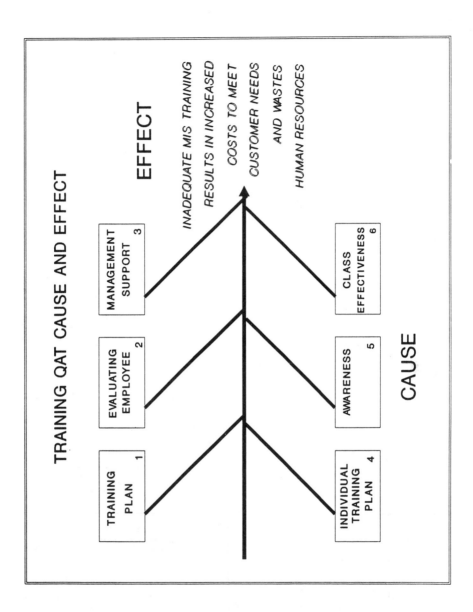

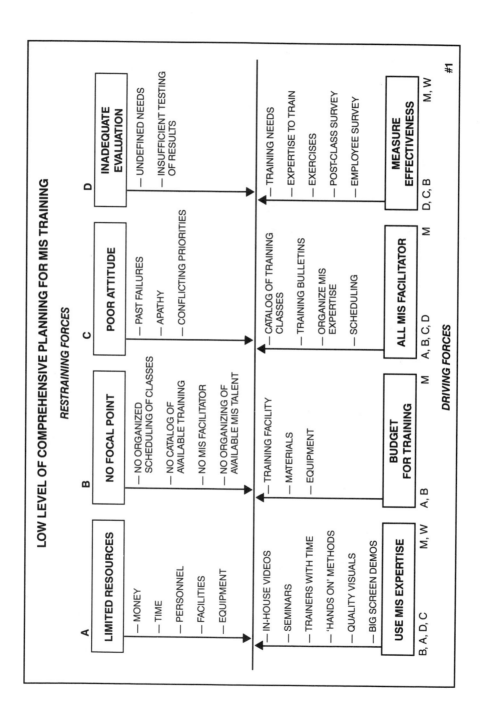

LOW LEVEL OF COMPREHENSIVE PLANNING FOR MIS TRAINING

RESTRAINING FORCES

A
LIMITED RESOURCES   B, A, D, C   M, W
— MONEY
— TIME
— PERSONNEL
— FACILITIES
— EQUIPMENT

B
NO FOCAL POINT
— NO ORGANIZED SCHEDULING OF CLASSES
— NO CATALOG OF AVAILABLE TRAINING
— NO MIS FACILITATOR
— NO ORGANIZING OF AVAILABLE MIS TALENT

C
POOR ATTITUDE
— PAST FAILURES
— APATHY
— CONFLICTING PRIORITIES

D
INADEQUATE EVALUATION
— UNDEFINED NEEDS
— INSUFFICIENT TESTING OF RESULTS

USE MIS EXPERTISE   B, A, D, C   M, W
— IN-HOUSE VIDEOS
— SEMINARS
— TRAINERS WITH TIME
— 'HANDS ON' METHODS
— QUALITY VISUALS
— BIG SCREEN DEMOS

BUDGET FOR TRAINING   A, B   M
— TRAINING FACILITY
— MATERIALS
— EQUIPMENT

ALL MIS FACILITATOR   A, B, C, D   M
— CATALOG OF TRAINING CLASSES
— TRAINING BULLETINS
— ORGANIZE MIS EXPERTISE
— SCHEDULING

MEASURE EFFECTIVENESS   D, C, B   M, W
— TRAINING NEEDS
— EXPERTISE TO TRAIN
— EXERCISES
— POST-CLASS SURVEY
— EMPLOYEE SURVEY

DRIVING FORCES

#1

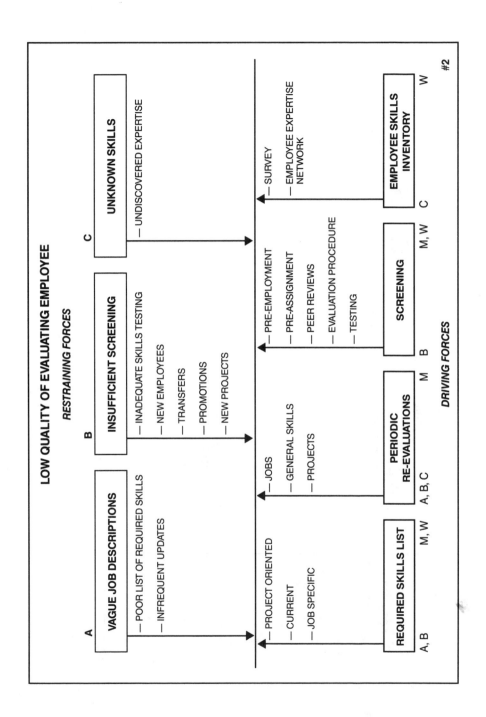

LOW QUALITY OF EVALUATING EMPLOYEE

RESTRAINING FORCES

A VAGUE JOB DESCRIPTIONS
— POOR LIST OF REQUIRED SKILLS
— INFREQUENT UPDATES

B INSUFFICIENT SCREENING
— INADEQUATE SKILLS TESTING
— NEW EMPLOYEES
— TRANSFERS
— PROMOTIONS
— NEW PROJECTS

C UNKNOWN SKILLS
— UNDISCOVERED EXPERTISE

DRIVING FORCES

REQUIRED SKILLS LIST — A, B
— PROJECT ORIENTED
— CURRENT
— JOB SPECIFIC
M, W

PERIODIC RE-EVALUATIONS — A, B, C
— JOBS
— GENERAL SKILLS
— PROJECTS
M

SCREENING — B
— PRE-EMPLOYMENT
— PRE-ASSIGNMENT
— PEER REVIEWS
— EVALUATION PROCEDURE
— TESTING
M, W

EMPLOYEE SKILLS INVENTORY — C
— SURVEY
— EMPLOYEE EXPERTISE NETWORK
W

#2

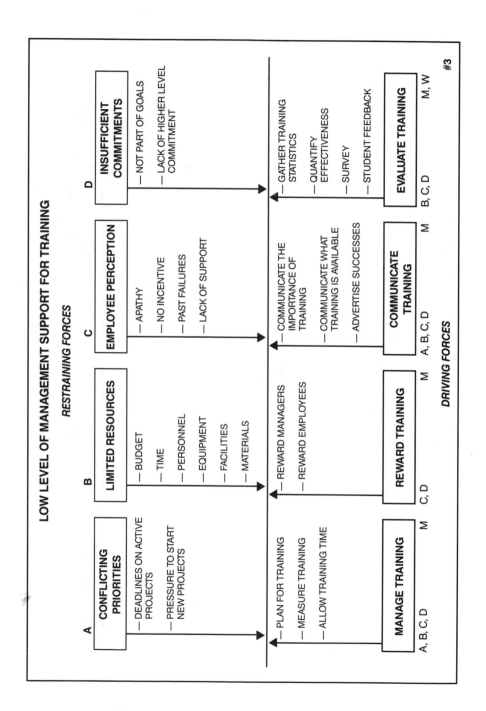

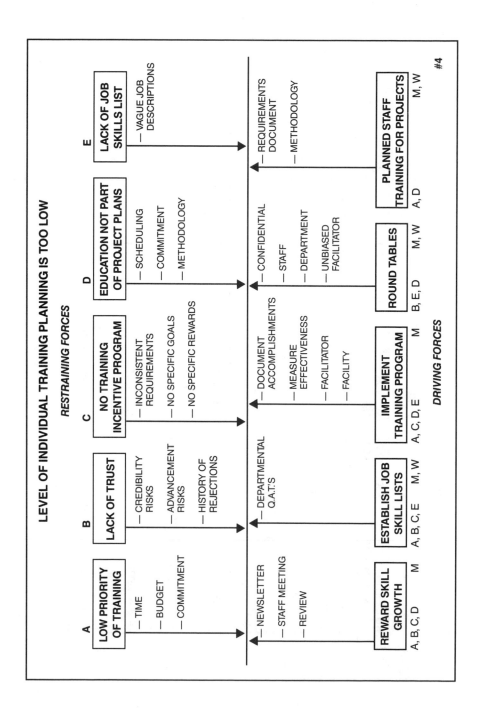

LEVEL OF INDIVIDUAL TRAINING PLANNING IS TOO LOW

RESTRAINING FORCES

A — LOW PRIORITY OF TRAINING
— TIME
— BUDGET
— COMMITMENT

B — LACK OF TRUST
— CREDIBILITY RISKS
— ADVANCEMENT RISKS
— HISTORY OF REJECTIONS

C — NO TRAINING INCENTIVE PROGRAM
— INCONSISTENT REQUIREMENTS
— NO SPECIFIC GOALS
— NO SPECIFIC REWARDS

D — EDUCATION NOT PART OF PROJECT PLANS
— SCHEDULING
— COMMITMENT
— METHODOLOGY

E — LACK OF JOB SKILLS LIST
— VAGUE JOB DESCRIPTIONS

DRIVING FORCES

REWARD SKILL GROWTH — A, B, C, D — M
— NEWSLETTER
— STAFF MEETING
— REVIEW

ESTABLISH JOB SKILL LISTS — A, B, C, E — M, W
— DEPARTMENTAL Q.A.T:S

IMPLEMENT TRAINING PROGRAM — A, C, D, E — M
— DOCUMENT ACCOMPLISHMENTS
— MEASURE EFFECTIVENESS
— FACILITATOR
— FACILITY

ROUND TABLES — B, E, D — M, W
— CONFIDENTIAL
— STAFF
— DEPARTMENT
— UNBIASED FACILITATOR

PLANNED STAFF TRAINING FOR PROJECTS — A, D — M, W
— REQUIREMENTS DOCUMENT
— METHODOLOGY

#4

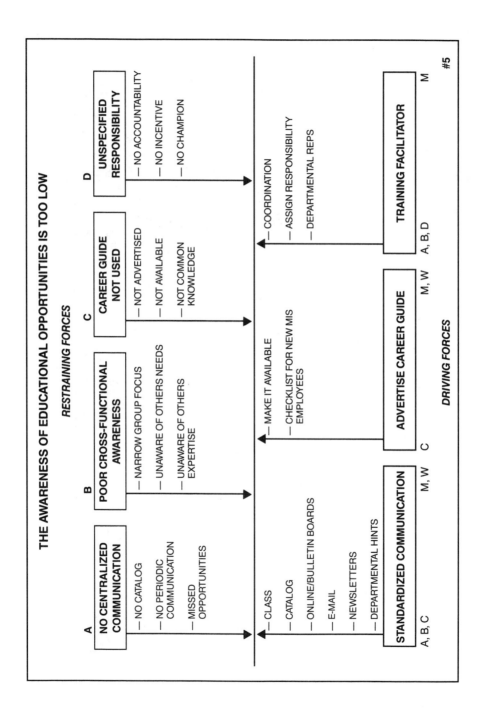

THE AWARENESS OF EDUCATIONAL OPPORTUNITIES IS TOO LOW

RESTRAINING FORCES

A
NO CENTRALIZED COMMUNICATION
— NO CATALOG
— NO PERIODIC COMMUNICATION
— MISSED OPPORTUNITIES

B
POOR CROSS-FUNCTIONAL AWARENESS
— NARROW GROUP FOCUS
— UNAWARE OF OTHERS NEEDS
— UNAWARE OF OTHERS EXPERTISE

C
CAREER GUIDE NOT USED
— NOT ADVERTISED
— NOT AVAILABLE
— NOT COMMON KNOWLEDGE

D
UNSPECIFIED RESPONSIBILITY
— NO ACCOUNTABILITY
— NO INCENTIVE
— NO CHAMPION

STANDARDIZED COMMUNICATION
A, B, C
— CLASS
— CATALOG
— ONLINE/BULLETIN BOARDS
— E-MAIL
— NEWSLETTERS
— DEPARTMENTAL HINTS

ADVERTISE CAREER GUIDE
C
M, W
— MAKE IT AVAILABLE
— CHECKLIST FOR NEW MIS EMPLOYEES

TRAINING FACILITATOR
A, B, D
M
— COORDINATION
— ASSIGN RESPONSIBILITY
— DEPARTMENTAL REPS

DRIVING FORCES

#5

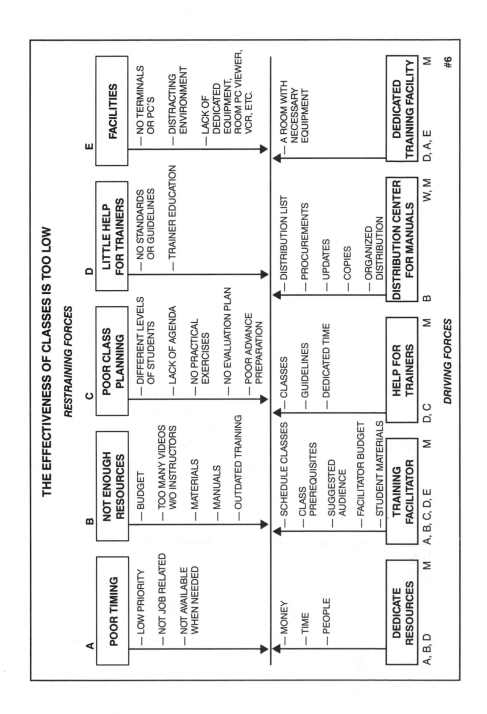

THE EFFECTIVENESS OF CLASSES IS TOO LOW

RESTRAINING FORCES

A	B	C	D	E
POOR TIMING	**NOT ENOUGH RESOURCES**	**POOR CLASS PLANNING**	**LITTLE HELP FOR TRAINERS**	**FACILITIES**
— LOW PRIORITY	— BUDGET	— DIFFERENT LEVELS OF STUDENTS	— NO STANDARDS OR GUIDELINES	— NO TERMINALS OR PC'S
— NOT JOB RELATED	— TOO MANY VIDEOS W/O INSTRUCTORS	— LACK OF AGENDA	— TRAINER EDUCATION	— DISTRACTING ENVIRONMENT
— NOT AVAILABLE WHEN NEEDED	— MATERIALS	— NO PRACTICAL EXERCISES		— LACK OF DEDICATED EQUIPMENT, ROOM PC VIEWER, VCR, ETC.
	— MANUALS	— NO EVALUATION PLAN		
	— OUTDATED TRAINING	— POOR ADVANCE PREPARATION		

DRIVING FORCES

DEDICATE RESOURCES	**TRAINING FACILITATOR**	**HELP FOR TRAINERS**	**DISTRIBUTION CENTER FOR MANUALS**	**DEDICATED TRAINING FACILITY**
— MONEY	— SCHEDULE CLASSES	— CLASSES	— DISTRIBUTION LIST	— A ROOM WITH NECESSARY EQUIPMENT
— TIME	— CLASS PREREQUISITES	— GUIDELINES	— PROCUREMENTS	
— PEOPLE	— SUGGESTED AUDIENCE	— DEDICATED TIME	— UPDATES	
	— FACILITATOR BUDGET		— COPIES	
	— STUDENT MATERIALS		— ORGANIZED DISTRIBUTION	
A, B, D	A, B, C, D, E	D, C	W, M	D, A, E
M	M	M	W, M	M

#6

Training Quality Action Team

Force Field Analysis Summary

Typical Results:
  Management = 85%
  Workers   = 15%

Our QAT results:
  Major driving forces   = 26
  Detail supporting driving forces = 83

  Management actions 81   = 97.5%
  Worker actions 2   = 2.5.%

Training
Quality Action Team Recommendations

(1) Bring in MIS training facilitator(s). Some duties of this position follow:
   (a) Create a catalog of MIS training opportunities.
   (b) Create an inventory list of MIS training expertise.
   (c) Organize and coordinate a schedule for classes and seminars.
   (d) Publicize training program through newsletters, bulletins, E-mail, etc.
   (e) Meet with functional groups to determine needs and tailor training.
   (f) Appoint departmental representatives.
(2) Set up a dedicated MIS training facility with the necessary equipment.
   (a) A room which is conducive to learning.
   (b) PCs with IRMA boards, and coaxial cable to the mainframe (or perhaps just terminals to the mainframe).
   (c) VCR, whiteboard, and overhead projector.
   (d) Big screen capability for demonstrations (e.g., PC viewer).
(3) Set up a focal point for the automatic distribution of technical manuals.
(4) Make use of MIS training expertise (for seminars and classes).
   (a) Ask for volunteers to be trainers within MIS.
   (b) Set up reward/recognition system for trainers and trainees.
(5) When possible, provide training opportunities with the following qualities:
   (a) A facilitator who interacts with students on the subject matter.
   (b) Hands-on exercises.
   (c) Provide current materials (e.g., technical manuals).

(6) Follow-up training with real work-related assignments which use new skills.
(7) Follow up with systematic evaluation to measure training effectiveness.
(8) Enthusiastic management support for the training program. Encouraging employees to get training and to pass on training to others.

SECTION THREE

INFORMATION STORAGE ENGINEERING
QUALITY PRESENTATION
PHASE III

Cause & effect focus

Leadership
Company culture
Planning
Product reliability/quality
Resources
Teamwork
Training

Problems

- Lack of experience.
- Lack of tools for high reliability products.
- High visibility bandwagon.
- Too many bosses/no bosses.
- Micro management.
- Piece of responsibility rather than process.
- Lack of established priorities (sticking by them).
- Doing too many things.
- Too many meetings.
- Lack of accountability.
- Lack of follow-through.
- Too much process (i.e., bureaucracy).
- Lack of consistency in planning (execution).
- Too many customers and suppliers.
- Sharing of resources.
- Not enough training.
- External perception.
- Common goals.
- Perspectives (strategy).
- Lack of technology development.
- Lack of teamwork (including support groups).
- Favoritism (within support groups).
- Fear.
- Product diversity and organizational structure.
- Shortage of critical skills.

Summary

Percent		Tally
83	**Management** (67)	卌 卌 卌 卌 卌 卌 卌 卌 卌 卌 卌 卌 卌 | |
17	**Worker** (14)	卌 卌 | | | |
	Management	
19	Level 1 (35)	卌 卌 卌 卌 卌 卌 卌
51	Level 2 (42)	卌 卌 卌 卌 卌 卌 卌 卌 | |
	Level 3 (53)	卌 卌 卌 卌 卌 卌 卌 卌 卌 卌 | | |
30	Level 4 (55)	卌 卌 卌 卌 卌 卌 卌 卌 卌 卌 卌

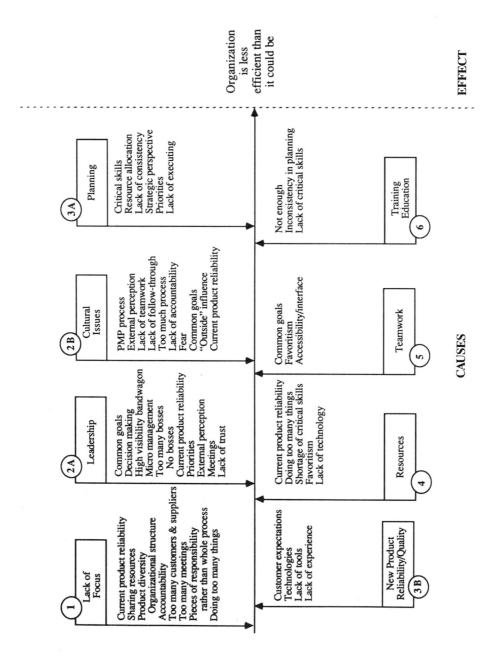

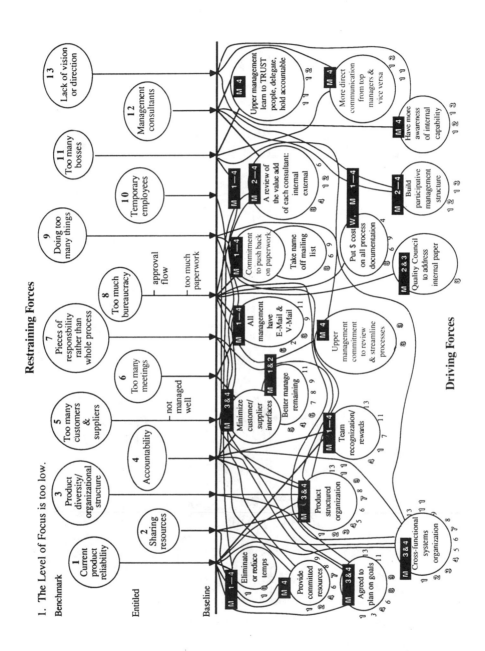

1. The Level of Focus is too low.

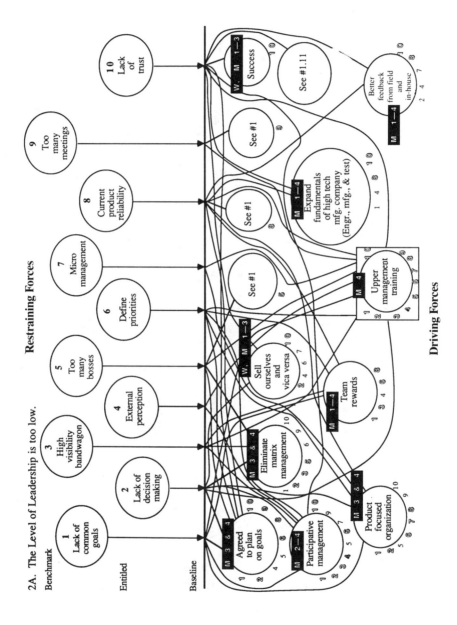

2A. The Level of Leadership is too low.

Restraining Forces

Driving Forces

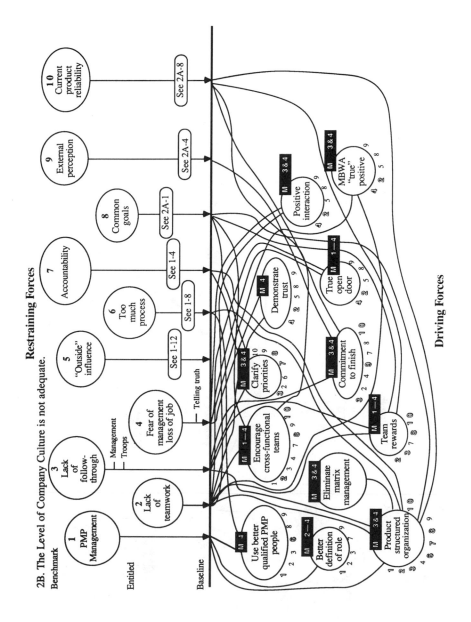

Restraining Forces

2B. The Level of Company Culture is not adequate.

Benchmark

Driving Forces

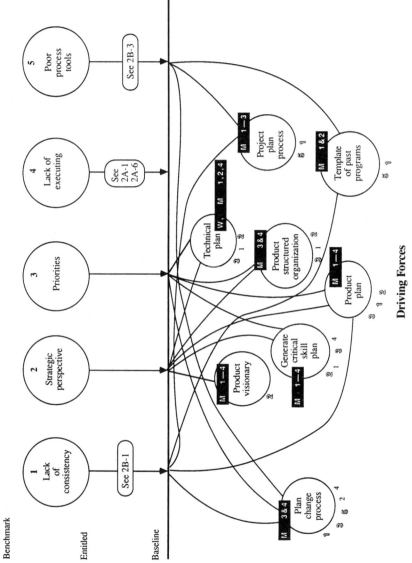

3A. The Level of Planning is too low.

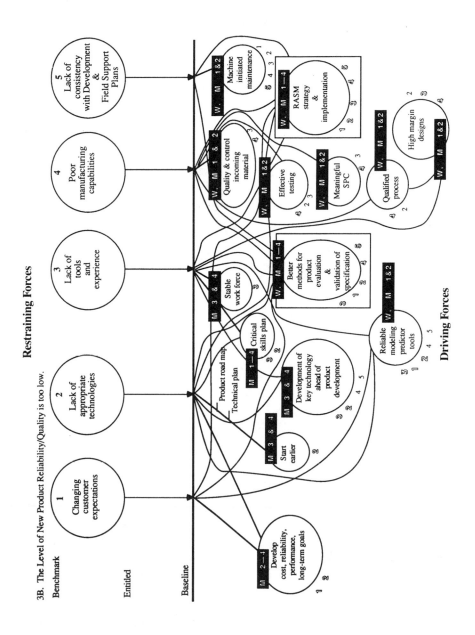

Restraining Forces

3B. The Level of New Product Reliability/Quality is too low.

Benchmark

Entitled

Baseline

Driving Forces

4. The Level of Resources is too low.

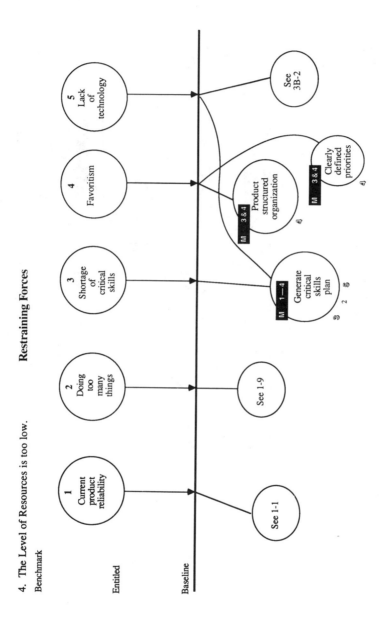

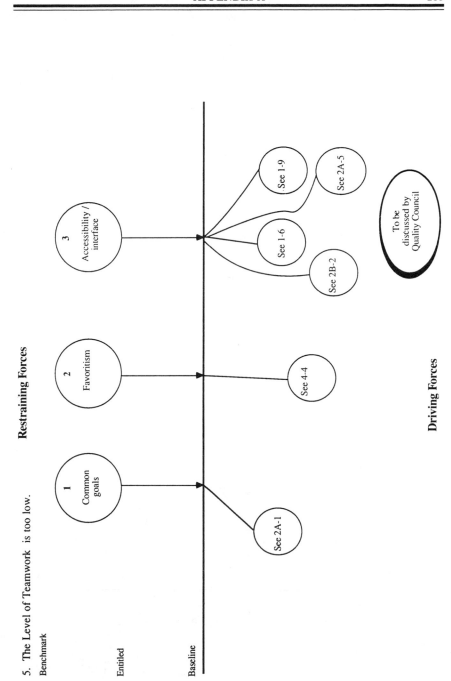

5. The Level of Teamwork is too low.

Benchmark

Entitled

Baseline

Restraining Forces

1 Common goals

2 Favoritism

3 Accessibility / interface

See 2A-1

See 4-4

See 1-9

See 1-6

See 2A-5

See 2B-2

To be discussed by Quality Council

Driving Forces

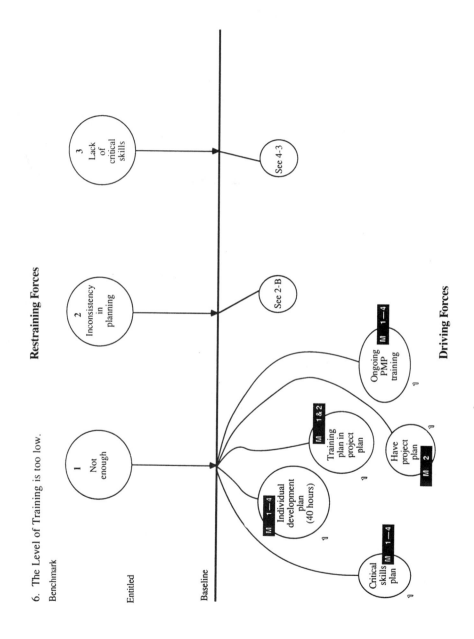

Restraining Forces

6. The Level of Training is too low.

Benchmark

Entitled

Baseline

1 Not enough

2 Inconsistency in planning

3 Lack of critical skills

See 2-B

See 4-3

Driving Forces

Ongoing PMP training   M 1—4

Training plan in project plan   M 1 & 2

Have project plan   M 2

Individual development plan (40 hours)   M 1—4

Critical skills plan   M 1—4

SECTION FOUR

CROSS-FUNCTIONAL TEAM OF
TESTING SPECIALIST ANALYSIS

Problems

- Not a team player.
- Number of design problems too high.
- Development not using results to improve process.
- Premature ship.
- Keep discovering same problems.
- Inadequate tools (resources).
- Not eliminating "bugs."
- "Bugs" found too late to fix.
- Rationalization of problems.
- Not enough time to test.
- Inconsistent process.
- Not enough acceptance by development for validation respon-
  sibility.
- Lack of leadership (no authority).
- Trying to test in quality.
- Entry/exit milestones not enforced.
- Lack of scheduled priorities.
- Funnel effect.
- Keep doing it the same (wrong) way.
- Upper management perception problem.

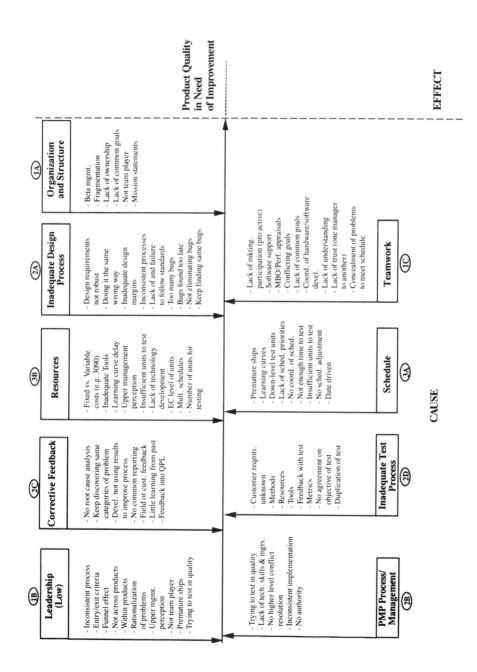

List of Driving Forces
with Greatest Impact

Item

Testing part of team for Dev. Gate Review
test plan of programs.

Definition of test responsibility.

Empowered teams.
MBO/cost accounting.

Common knowledge base.
Data base access.
All failures reported.

Consolidated test plan.

GA transition team.

Test operating plan = program plan + fixed base.
Management of fixed base.

Master schedule of programs.

Program management job description.

Include corrective actions and regression.
Loops in schedules.
Honest assessment.

Test R&D group.

Change management.

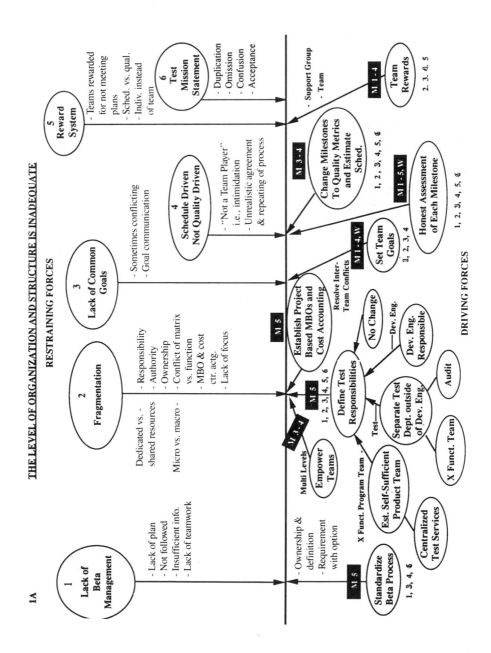

Driving Forces:
• Definition of test responsibility.

Definition:
• Test responsibility within product teams can be defined into two areas needing upper management decisions:
  (1) Given a product team working on a product or task who represents TESTING?:
  (a) Program Management or
  (b) Engineering or
  (c) Test.

  (2) Assuming representation on the team, where do the testing resources (manpower and capital equipment) reside? How are they allocated/assigned to projects?
  (a) Distributed.
  (b) Centralized.
  (c) Hybrid.

Issues:
• There is no assigned responsibility on a cross-functional program team representing and accountable for all of test. There is no *wrong* decision on who should be accountable for test.
• Distributed testing resources are what we have today (see attached chart). The positive aspects of distributed resources are:
  (1) Closeness to engineering.
  (2) No organizational changes are necessary, status quo, no turf issues.
  (3) Career path for testing personnel favors movement into engineering or manufacturing.
  (4) Minimize "police" mentality of testing, in other words testing authority is dispersed.
• Centralized testing resources are combining the test groups, outside of AME, into one department. The positive aspects of centralizing are:
  (1) Common test philosophy.
  (2) Focused test spokesman and leadership.
  (3) Recognized authority level.
  (4) Ease of development of test technology.
  (5) Consolidated knowledge base.
  (6) Favors testing oriented career path.
  (7) Favors test process enhancement/improvements.
  (8) Formalize relationships between test and the rest of the company.
  (9) Centralize budget control and visibility of test.
  (10) Establishes singular interface.

- Investigate compromise/alternative between distributed and centralized.

Driving Forces:
- Empowered team.
- MBO/cost accounting.

Definition of empowered team:
- Product/product line basis.
- Multi-leveled team structure.
- Cradle to grave.
- "Own" the product.
    (1) Quality perspective.
    (2) Business perspective.
        (a) Authority.
        (b) Product plan.
        (c) Business reviews.

    Team rewards

Issues:
- Cultural change.
- Allow failure.
- Compensation issues in doing team rewards.
- Training issues.
- Communication paths.
- Accounting changes.

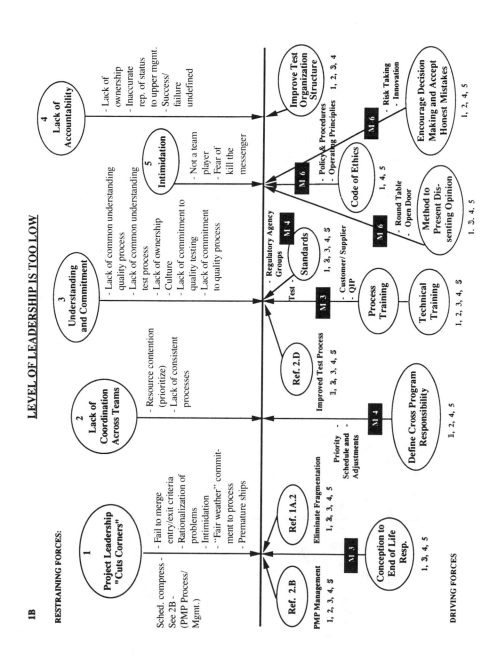

LEVEL OF LEADERSHIP IS TOO LOW

1B

RESTRAINING FORCES:

1 — Project Leadership "Cuts Corners"
- Fail to merge entry/exit criteria
- Rationalization of problems
- Intimidation
- "Fair weather" commitment to process
- Premature ships

Sched. compress - See 2B - (PMP Process/ Mgmt.)

2 — Lack of Coordination Across Teams
- Resource contention (prioritize)
- Lack of consistent processes

3 — Understanding and Commitment
- Lack of common understanding quality process
- Lack of common understanding test process
- Lack of ownership
- Culture
- Lack of commitment to quality testing
- Lack of commitment to quality process

4 — Lack of Accountability
- Lack of ownership
- Inaccurate rep. of status to upper mgmt.
- Success/ failure undefined

5 — Intimidation
- Not a team player
- Fear of kill the messenger

DRIVING FORCES

Ref. 2.B   M 3   Conception to End of Life Resp.
1, 2, 3, 4, 5   1, 3, 4, 5

PMP Management
1, 2, 3, 4, 5

Ref. 1A.2
1, 3, 4, 5

Eliminate Fragmentation
Priority - Schedule and Adjustments -

Define Cross Program Responsibility
1, 2, 4, 5

M 4

Ref. 2.D
1, 2, 3, 4, 5

Improved Test Process
1, 2, 3, 4, 5

M 3   Test -
- Regulatory Agency Groups -
- Customer/ Supplier -
- QIP

Standards
1, 2, 3, 4, 5

Process Training

Technical Training
1, 2, 3, 4, 5

M 4   Improve Test Organization Structure
1, 2, 3, 4

M 6   Policy & Procedures
- Operating Principles   1, 2, 4, 5

Code of Ethics
1, 4, 5

M 6   - Round Table
- Open Door
Method to Present Dissenting Opinion
1, 3, 4, 5

Encourage Decision Making and Accept Honest Mistakes
- Risk Taking
- Innovation
1, 2, 4, 5

M 6

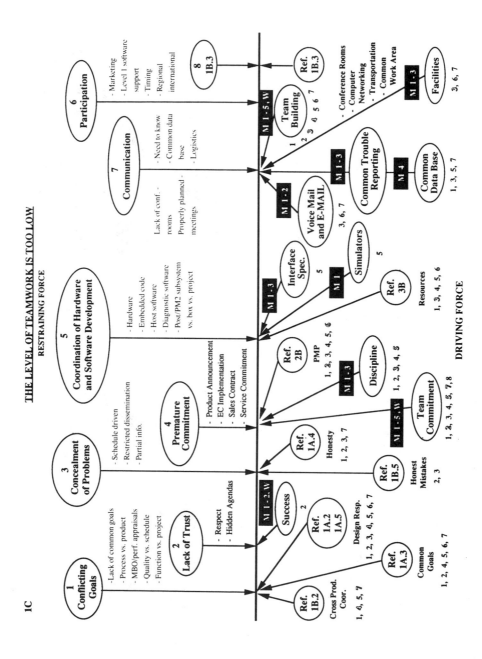

THE LEVEL OF TEAMWORK IS TOO LOW

Driving Forces:
- Common knowledge base.
- Data base access.
- All failures reported.

Definition:
- All problems recorded from conception to end-of-life in a data base that is easily accessible, i.e., Dev. Engr., Mfg., CSE, Test, etc.
- All test reports listed in data base.
- Common corporate severity code definition.
- Common problem definition format.

Issues:
Data
- Who defines?
- Who owns?
- Data collection enforcement.

Analysis/Feedback/Reports
- Who defines?
- Who gets?
- Usage enforcement.
- Data blizzard vs. information.

Who Owns System (Headcount)
- Hardware.
- Application software.
- Data guardian.

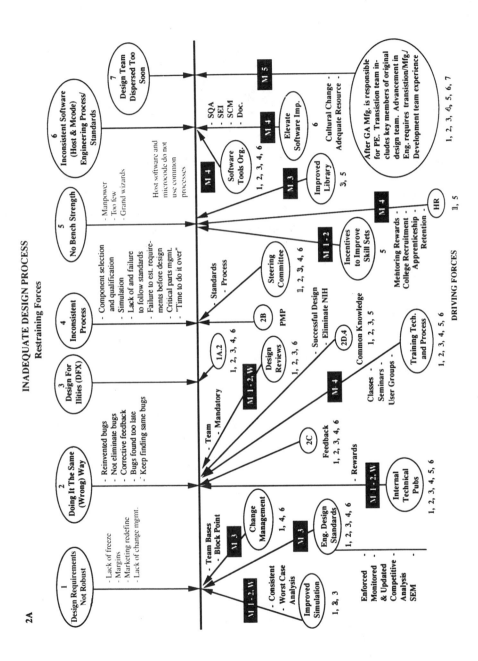

INADEQUATE DESIGN PROCESS
Restraining Forces

Driving Forces:
- GA transition team.

Definition:
- When a product goes GA, manufacturing should assume product engineering responsibility.
- Key development engineers transfer to P.E. for a product transition period.
- Transition team/mfg./development experience is necessary for engineering advancement.

Issues:
- Cultural change?
- Adequate resources?
- Retention of employees?
- Cost accounting?

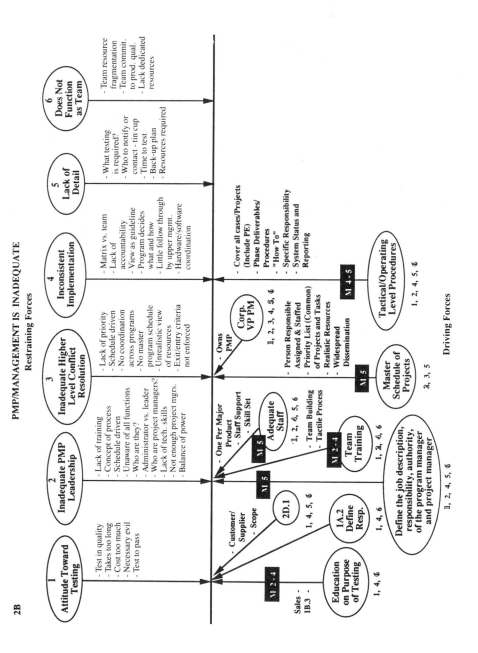

PMP/MANAGEMENT IS INADEQUATE

Driving Forces:
- Program management job description.
- Tactical/operating level PMP procedures.

Definition:
- Program management's job needs to be described including responsibility, authority, interfaces, and relationships to other functions.
- Operating level PMP defined and consistent across programs.

Issues:
- Is the program/project manager the *leader* of the "empowered" product team? If not, who is?
- Who makes the decision to elevate an issue to the next team level?
- Are there multi-level teams?
- What skill set is required for program manager—more technical?

Driving Forces:
- Cross program master schedule management.

Definition:
- A master schedule of programs needs to be established to ensure minimum conflict of resources.
- Process to resolve conflicts between programs needs to be defined.
- Realistic resources reflected in master schedule.

Issues:
- Trade-offs need to be made at program management level to ensure lower priority projects are not "starved" of resources.
- Changing of schedules may result in resource conflict.

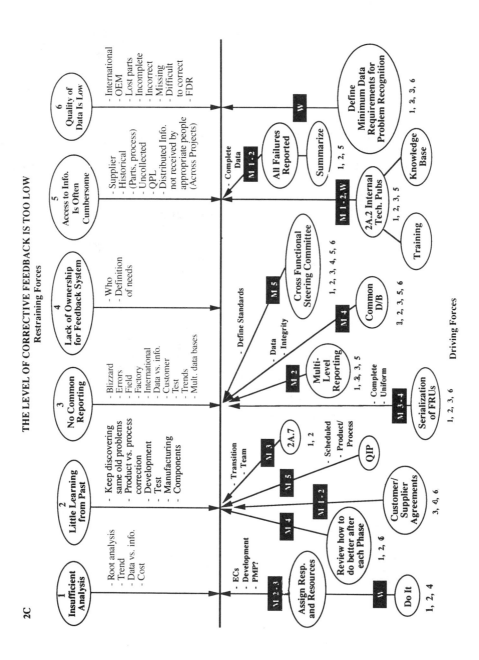

THE LEVEL OF CORRECTIVE FEEDBACK IS TOO LOW

INADEQUATE TEST PROCESS

RESTRAINING FORCES

2D

1 Inadequate Agreement on Objective of Test

Sample size -
- Problem discovery vs. prod. validation
- Test & development do not agree
- Test & manf. do not agree
- Test box not subsystem

2 Duplication of Tests
- Improper scope
- Restart
- Regression

3 Test Omissions
- Missing resources, growth
- Improper scope
- Lacking technology
- Lack of vision
- Schedule compression
- Restart/regression
- Inadequate test skills

4 Inadequate Corrective Feedback
- In test
- In project
- No common reporting format
- No report archive/analysis

5 Inadequate Product Definition
- Too late
- "Better than IBM"
- Customer req. not known

6 Inadequate Test Methods
- Test to pass
- Inadequate Test R & D
- Changes
- Resources
- Tools
- Inadequate test skills

7 Changing Environment
- EC '92
- IBM
- Cust. env.
- Green team
- RASM

DRIVING FORCES

- Environment
- Techniques
- Standards
- Systems
- Tools

Establish Test Technology R & D Group — M 4

- Dissemination of Info.
- Competitive Research
- Market Research
- Resources
- Tools

Plan for Change — M 4

- Func. Spec.
- CAB
- Margins

Define Product — M 1 - 4 W

Include "Post Mortum After GA" — M 1 - 5 W

- Competitive Analysis
- Doc. Control System
- Product Content

- Analysis (Periodic)
- Format
- Archive

Common Knowledge Base

M 2 - 3

M 5

Corp. Std. Severity Codes

Add International "FDR"

Upgrade Test Skills — M 3

Define Failure Loops — W

- Flow Charts
- Restart/Regression

Block Point Changes — M 4

Consolidated Test Plan and Schedule — M 1 - 2 W
- "Boiler Plate"
- Coordinated

Define Scope of Test Groups — M 3 - 4
- Dev./Test
- Test/Mfg.
- Within Test Groups

Statistically Determine Prod. Oper. Margins — W

Capability Ratios

Customer Supplier Agreements — M 1 W

1, 2, 3, 4, 6

Driving Forces:
- Consolidated test plan.

Definition:
- A consolidated test plan outlines in detail what tests are to be performed in order to qualify a new design as validated.
- Tests include: HIT, SIT, SAT, EVT, CPAT, DVT, PVT, HALT, competitive analysis, subassembly life test, BETA, LAP.

Issues:
- Tied closely to "definition of test responsibility." Who does what testing?
- Need outline of typical plan, definition of test, sequence of tests.
- Who enforces and monitors specific plans? (i.e., PVST).
- Life testing?
- Who maintains the "standard" plan?

Driving Forces:
- Test R&D group.

Definition:
- Establish a centralized research and development group to improve testing tools and methods.

Issues:
- Testing technology needs to keep pace with rapid advancement of complex products (e.g., channel emulator, code evaluation tools, error injection methods).
- Design in testability.

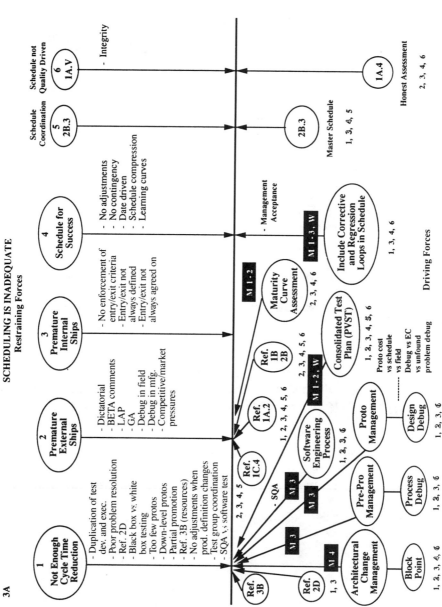

SCHEDULING IS INADEQUATE
Restraining Forces

Driving Forces:
- Change management.

Definition:
- Process and design changes.
- Change management encompasses changes to the product contract, program schedule, program cost, block pointing changes during the test process, and marketing requirement changes.

Issues:
- Testing resources are often overlooked when changes are made.
- Testing is often not involved in the change decision.
- Constant change in machine code levels confuses the integrity of the testing process.
- Block pointing changes will increase effectiveness of test resources.
- Management approval of proposed changes.
- Who tests ECs? Who owns product? Who is responsible to verify value and correctness of change?

Driving Forces:
- Include corrective actions and regression loops in schedules.
- Honest assessment.
- Change milestones to quality metrics and estimate schedule.

Definition:
- When scheduling a project, realistic regression test time for problem resolution needs to be planned.
- Scheduling requires an honest assessment on how much time it will take to design and debug.

Issues:
- Alternatives need to be planned in order to reduce the cycle time it takes to regression test.
- The project team should be quality goal-oriented as well as schedule driven.
- How monitor/define entry/exit of milestones.

3B

THE LEVEL OF RESOURCES IS INADEQUATE
Restraining Forces

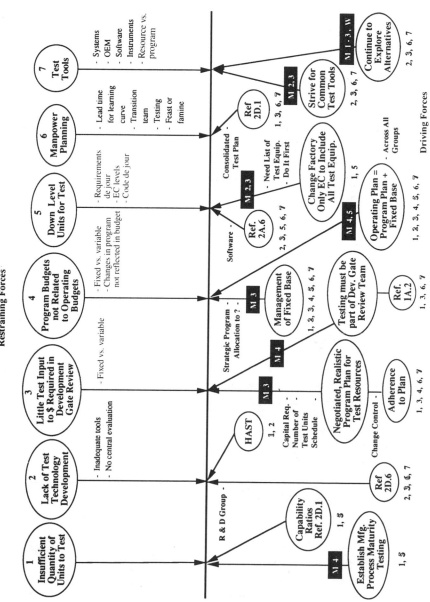

Driving Forces

Driving Forces:
- Testing part of team for dev. gate review.
- Negotiated, realistic program plan for testing resources.

Definition:
- Identification of resources needed to accomplish testing should be part of program budgets and ROI study.
- Realistic assessment of resources vs. testing criteria vs. objectives vs. schedules.
- Early identification and planning of capital resources.

Issues:
- Overlapped testing resources not taken into consideration for GA date (e.g., Program #1 and Program #2 both require same resource at same time in order to meet GA date).
- Allocation and management of testing fixed asset pool with respect to program charges.
  (1) Cancellation of Program #1 may increase cost to other programs.
  (2) Shared resources must be managed between programs.
  (3) Trade-offs of shared vs. dedicated resources.

Driving Forces:
- Operating plan = program plan + fixed base.
- Management of fixed base.

Definition:
- The testing resources defined in the program plan established at the dev. gate review need to be the starting point for the annual testing operating plan.
- Shared testing resources between programs establish the fixed base (i.e., capital equipment, test technology, and specialized man power).

Issues:
- Who manages the fixed base?
  (1) Strategic resource.
  (2) Cost overhead.
  (3) When to resell.
  (4) When to upgrade.
- Testing input at the dev. gate review is a prerequisite.
- Changes in the program plan may modify the needed testing resources.

SECTION FIVE

SYSTEMS DEVELOPMENT

Quality Action Team Data

Typical results:
  Management = 85%
  Workers   = 15%

Systems development team results:
  Management = 90%
  Workers   = 10%*
*Workers were measured as part of "All" category

Actual team results (total of 38 driving forces)
  Executive-level management (1) 24%
  (CEO & Exec. V.P.)

  Middle-level management (2-3-4)43%
  (Corp. Off., V.P., Director)

  Low-level management (5-6)   33%
  (First & Second Level)

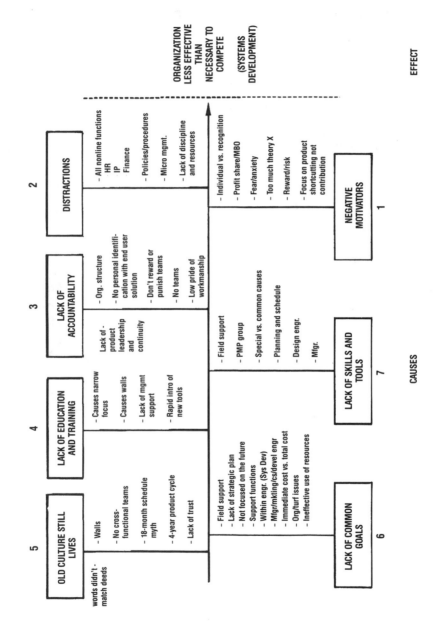

#1 - The Level of Negative Motivators Is Too High

Driving Forces

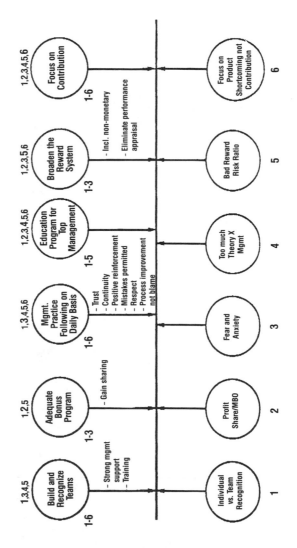

Restraining Forces

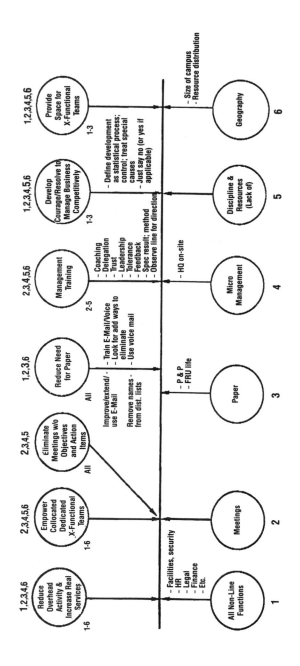

#2 - The Level of Distractions Is Too High

Driving Forces

Restraining Forces

#3 - Lack of Accountability: (Accountability Is Low)

Restraining Forces

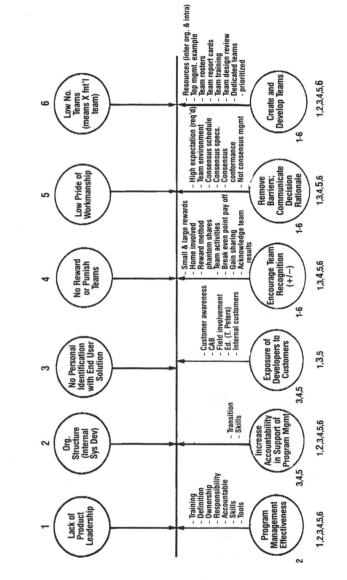

Driving Forces

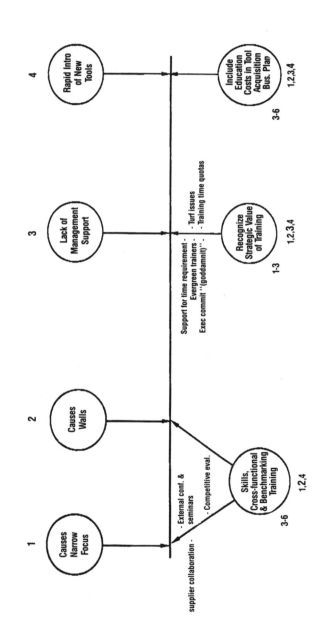

#4 - The Level of Education and Training Is Too Low

Restraining Forces

1   Causes Narrow Focus
2   Causes Walls
3   Lack of Management Support
4   Rapid Intro of New Tools

- External conf. & seminars
- Competitive eval.

supplier collaboration -

Support for time requirement -
Evergreen trainers -
Exec commit "(goddamnit)" -

- Turf issues
- Training time quotas

Skills, Cross-functional & Benchmarking Training
3-6
1,2,4

Recognize Strategic Value of Training
1-3
1,2,3,4

Include Education Costs in Tool Acquisition Bus. Plan
3-6
1,2,3,4

Driving Forces

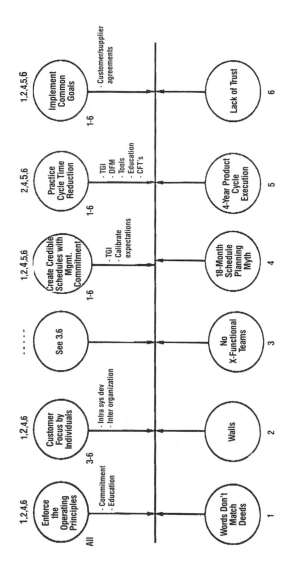

#5 - Old Culture Still Lives

Driving Forces

Restraining Forces

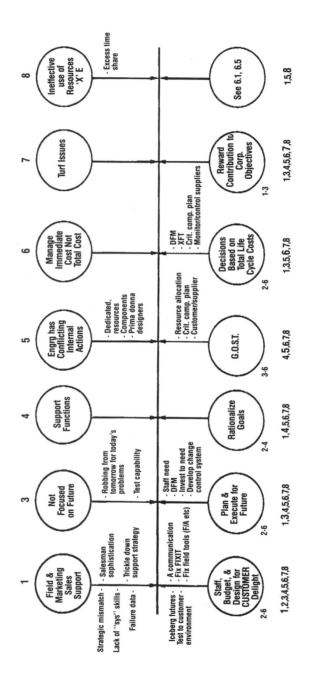

#6 - The Level of Common Goals Is Too Low

Restraining Forces

Driving Forces

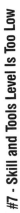

#7 - Skill and Tools Level Is Too Low

Restraining Forces

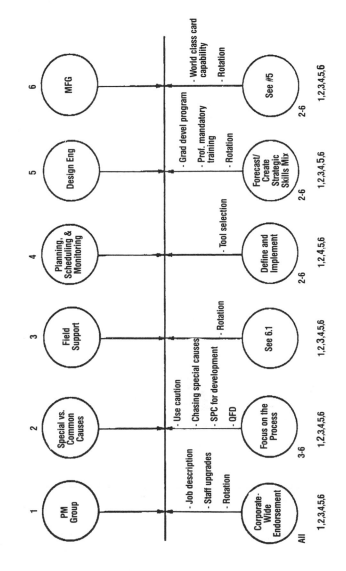

Driving Forces

__APPENDIX B__
SECTION ONE

Quality Service Improvement—Group I

DI & FR Reviewing Officers

Quality Resolution Team

Quality Review Team

Group I—Quality Service Improvement
DI & FR Reviewing Officers

Cause #1—The Level of Records Management Is Too Low

Restraining force

Driving forces

(1) Not posting new items correctly or timely.

(1) Change posting procedures in records.
  - (a) If record not there, don't do anything—give to supervisor.
  - (b) Handle specials first.
  - (c) Measure quality before quantity (records).
  - (d) Emphasize importance of accuracy to management team.

(2) Unable to obtain records and files quickly.

(1) Keep filing up to date.

(2) Sufficient people to pull tickets for review officers.

(3) Unable to locate money ($15 and up).

(1) Have money go to bureaus involved faster.
  - (a) Have money go direct to bureau.
  - (b) Get money lists out faster (DAS).

(4) Volume of records/workload.

(1) Come to work to work (give a full day's work).

(5) Poor training in the courthouse about records.

(1) Traffic ticket coordinators be more involved with problems with tickets/clerks.

(2) Court clerks come to GHQ for training in completion and distribution of UTCs.
  - (a) Higher management arrange this.

(3) More field training with UTC coordinators.

Cause #2—The Level of Training Is Too Low

Restraining force

Driving forces

(1) Lack of communication with DL offices.
   (a) DL supervisor fails to communicate to employees training provided.
   (b) GHQ fails to ensure distribution of written changes to employees.

(1) DL supervisors need to distribute written information to employees.
   (a) Copy updated information to field examiners

(2) Exercise training received in GHQ.
   (a) Distribute written information.
   (b) Employees initial messages sent to field.

(2) Inadequate time to train.
   (a) Lack of funds.

(1) Completion of all basic training.
   (a) Trainer determines when training is completed.

(3) Lack of "focus" training for secretaries and clerks.

(1) Appoint a designated trainer.

Cause #3—The Level of Public Awareness Is Too Low

Restraining force

Driving forces

(1) Public is unaware of law changes.
   (a) Mail is not reaching public due to address changes.

(1) Insert flyers in notices from department.
   (a) Update and revise laws on original FR notices.
   (b) Provide insurance agents with information.
   (c) Give DL offices inserts.
   (d) Give Tag offices inserts.

(2) Public does not understand laws.

(OTHER DRIVING FORCES SHOULD IMPROVE THIS)

(3) Lack of media coverage.

(1) Public information officer should periodically advise the public of law changes.
(a) TV commercials.
(b) Newspapers.
(c) Radio advertisement.

(4) Lack of explanation of laws by dept. personnel.

(1) Personal contact by telephone and other means.
(a) All department personnel need training on dealing effectively with the public.
(b) Personnel need clarification of the laws so they understand them.
(c) More in-service training.
(d) More staff meetings.

Cause #4—The Level of Locating Mail Is Too Low

Restraining force

Driving forces

(1) Poor routing of mail.
(a) Improper routing by mail clerks.
(b) FR reviewing officers are not getting mail addressed to them within the bureau.
(b) Mail clerks are not paying attention to "Personal & Confidential" mail and the attention lines on envelopes and letters.

(1) Better education of mail handlers.

(2) Route mail to reviewing officer to whom it is addressed.

(2) Getting information too late.

(1) Pay closer attention to "Personal and Confidential" mail.

(2) Treat special mail with priority.
  (a) Check envelopes and correspondence for reviewing officer's name for special handling.
  (b) Stress the importance of correct handling of the mail to mail clerk.

(3) Poor distribution of mail in bureau.
  (a) Poor reviewing of mail.

(1) Place office symbols on "reply to:" line.
  (a) Color code envelopes for each bureau.

Cause #5—The Level of Phone System Is Too Low

Restraining force

Driving forces

(1) No direct lines to court (Broward, Dade, Palm Beach).
  (a) State phone book does not provide SUNCOM for Broward.
  (b) Security numbers required to access Broward County clerk's office.

(1) Provide review officers with updated telephone numbers.

(2) No standard system for log out.
  (a) Special assignment, schools, staff meetings.

(1) Set up log-out system.

(3) No corrective action against duty shirkers.

(1) Supervisors to take corrective action.
  (a) Follow-up on activity.

(4) Measuring number of calls is wrong (evaluations).

(1) Measure overall quality of work over quantity in evaluating employee's performance rating.

(5) Monitoring of calls.

(1) Management by walking around (MBWA).

Cause #6—The Level of Use of Funds Is Too Low

Restraining force

1. Improper use of funds.
   (a) Unnecessary office equipment.
   (b) Unnecessary travel expense for short-term training.
   (c) Creating unnecessary positions.
   (d) End-of-year spending.

Driving forces

(1) Use funds for upgrades, raises or bonuses.

Cause #7—The Level of Hard Timing the Public Is Too High

Restraining force

(1) Being rude.

(2) Not listening.

(3) Not providing enough information or wrong information.
   (a) Insufficient information.
   (b) Partial information.

Driving forces

(1) Training and supervision.
   (a) Understand the public's problem.
   (b) Put yourself in the public's shoes.

No recommendation given.

(1) Review record before advising.
   (a) Provide DL number to next office before transferring call.

(2) Provide uniform guidelines for (FR) review officers.
   (a) Accept verification of SR-21 by phone.

(3) Give all review officers the authority to clear suspensions by phone.
   (a) Allow DI review officers to clear suspension after research with clerk's office. FR review officers already clear their suspensions.

(4) Sending public to DL office
    unnecessarily.
    (a) Vice Versa—DL offices tell
        the public to call GHQ
        instead of helping them
        while they are already
        there.

TO: Director
           Division of Driver Licenses

FROM: Assistant Director
           Division of Driver Licenses

SUBJECT: Quality Resolution Team (QRT) Report for Group I

The Quality Resolution Team for Group I has thoroughly discussed all of the suggestions from Quality Action Team #I for the improvement of the quality of service to the public from the Division of Driver Licenses.
Following are the resolutions:

CAUSE #1: LEVEL OF RECORDS MANAGEMENT IS TOO LOW.

Restraining Force #1: Not posting new items correctly or timely.

Resolution: Bureau Chief of Records will retrain the video look-up section to ensure that they are only placing driver license numbers on D-6's and uniform traffic citations when there is 100 percent certainty that the number matches the person named on the ticket or D-6.

A person's full name and date of birth *must match exactly* on both the ticket or D-6 before the number is placed on the look-up document.

This will eliminate placing violations and D-6 suspension on the wrong driving record.

This policy is effective immediately. Quality is much more important than quantity.

Resolution: Bureau Chief of Uniform Traffic Citations will retrain the UTC coders to be more accurate and careful on coding the dispositions. They must write clearly so the keypunch operators can read the code numbers. Quality is much more important than quantity.

Resolution: Bureau Chief of Driver Improvement will reemphasize to section to handle special request cases in a timely manner. Close cooperation between sections is a must, and it will improve the quality of service to the public.

Resolution: All bureau chiefs will initiate training sessions within each of the bureaus to keep employees abreast of current policies and law changes.

Restraining Force #2: Unable to obtain records and files quickly.

Resolution: The review officers in Financial Responsibility will be given top priority when they request a record from their files. The FR Administrator will discuss with the first-line supervisor the importance of records being delivered to the review officer in a timely manner. In all probability the review officers are on the phone with a problem driver or waiting to return a call as soon as possible. Quality service is involved.

Restraining Force #3: Unable to locate money ($15 and up).

Resolution: Bureau Chief of Financial Responsibility will work with Fiscal to establish a money reporting system similar to that now working in the Bureau of Driver Improvement.

Resolution: Financial Responsibility Officer will contact Driver Improvement, and review the money reporting method they have developed to see if it can be tailored to FR's use.

Restraining Force #4: Volume of records/workload.

Resolution: Due to the tremendous workload of the review officers in Financial Responsibility and Driver Improvement, all officers must give a full day's work every day of top-notch quality service.

It is imperative that the first-line supervisors in both bureaus be aware of the attitudes of employees and strive to set examples of quality service.

Dr. Deming emphasizes that management must lead the way. Only management can initiate improvement in quality and productivity. Workers on their own can achieve very little.

Driver Improvement has developed a telephone call back system that may be of assistance to Financial Responsibility.

Restraining Force #5: Poor training in the courthouse about records.

Resolution: The UTC Specialists (4 of them statewide) work full-time with the 67 county Clerk of Courts on disposition of tickets, D-6's, computers, etc. They are aware of the need for constant instruction to clerk employees. We will reinforce this awareness.

Resolution: The Bureau of Uniform Traffic Citations will hold training seminars in GHQ for all bureau employees on the uniform traffic citation issuance, accountability, reporting, and dispositions. This training will begin as soon as possible and not later than April 1.

CAUSE #2: LEVEL OF TRAINING IS TOO LOW.

Restraining Force #1: Lack of communication with driver's license offices.
  a. Driver License supervisors fail to communicate to employees training provided.
  b. GHQ fails to assure distribution of written changes to employees.

Resolution: All bureau chiefs will stress to all levels of supervisors the need to distribute written information (law changes, policy changes, bulletins, etc.) to all employees. This will take effect immediately.

Resolution: The Bureau of Field Operations and the Bureau of Driver Improvement will initiate a policy to have all field employees read and initial messages from headquarters.

Resolution: Both bureaus will begin a numbering system of all teletype communication messages that will establish an orderly communications link from GHQ with the field. This policy will be implemented immediately.

Resolution: To prevent the review officers from being inundated with calls from examiners in the field on DL policy procedure and problem solving questions, the review officers will ask of the examiner making the call, "Have you discussed this with your supervisor?" The intent is not to refuse to help, but to have the examiners in the field seek this information from the immediate supervisor. This process will expedite the handling of telephone calls and also inform the supervisor at the driver license office of the need for special training for the examiners seeking information.

Restraining Force #2: Inadequate time to train.
                              a. Lack of funds.

Resolution: All five bureau chiefs within the Division of Driver
            Licenses will designate an employee to be the trainer
            to train all new employees within the various sections.

            The designated trainer's position description will be
            amended to include training duties. DHSMV Training
            Manager will be contacted to provide "Train the
            Trainer" programs for these people. These trainers will
            be designated by March 15.

Resolution: Lack of funds for training is not a problem this present
            budget year. Money is available now for training
            material, etc.

Restraining Force #3: Lack of "focus" training for secretaries, clerk
                         typists, and clerks.

Resolution: Instructions will be given to review the training mate-
            rial along with the method and need for training the
            clerks and clerk typists in Financial Responsibility to
            ensure adequate training. This will be accomplished by
            April 1.

CAUSE #3: LEVEL OF PUBLIC AWARENESS IS TOO LOW

Restraining Force #1: Public is unaware of law changes.
                         a. Mail is not reaching public due to address
                         changes.

Resolution: Print information flyers on the new laws to mail out
            in Financial Responsibility suspension notices and
            Driver Improvement revocation and suspension notices.

Resolution: Information flyers could also be mailed out in each piece
            of general correspondence from DHSMV to the public.

Resolution: Provide information flyers to all driver license offices
            and Florida Highway Patrol stations statewide for hand-
            out material.
Resolution: DHSMV Publicity Director is coordinating the publicity
            effort in distribution of the new financial responsibility
            law change.

Restraining Forces #2: Public does not understand laws.
            #3: Lack of media coverage.

Resolution: DHSMV Publicity Director will coordinate all of the news releases to the media (paper, radio, and T.V.) on the new financial responsibility law changes and all other law changes.

Restraining Force #4: Lack of explanation of laws by department personnel to the public.

Resolution: Employees of the Division of Driver Licenses will receive extra training in telephone technique. We will combine all bureau training effort for this extra training.

Resolution: All bureaus have training managers established.

Resolution: Bureau chiefs will ensure that their training managers set up and conduct ongoing training sessions for employees on the following: how to deal effectively with the public; clarification of Florida traffic laws and division policies. In addition, various other training sessions can be conducted that will improve the quality of service from the Division of Driver Licenses.

Resolution: The five bureau training managers will meet from time to time as the need arises to combine their efforts, resources, skills, knowledge and abilities in developing in-service training programs for division employees.

Resolution: The Department of Highway Safety & Motor Vehicles has resources available now in the form of training aids, film, tapes, and catalog that should be made available to the training staff for their use.

CAUSE #4: LEVEL OF LOCATING MAIL IS TOO LOW.

Restraining Force #1: Poor routing of mail
            a. Improper routing by mail clerks.
            b. FR review officers are not getting mail addressed to them within the bureau.
            c. Mail clerks are not paying attention to "Personal and Confidential" mail and the attention lines.

Restraining Force #2: Getting the mail too late.

Resolution: Retrain mail handlers. Each mail handler will be retrained and informed of the importance of the mail. Especially the "P & C" mail. Advise the mail route people that review officers are waiting on special documentation contained in the P & C mail that is important to a person's driving record. This type mail should not be treated as routine. It should be expedited. This will be implemented as soon as possible.

Resolution: Financial Responsibility Officer will contact Driver Improvement on their process of mail handling and on handling of money that has been routed to Fiscal section and back to the bureau. (This process may prove to be of value to Financial Responsibility).

Resolution: The FR mail routing procedure will be analyzed by Bureau Chief for possible streamlining.

Restraining Force #3: Poor distribution of mail in bureau.
  a. Poor review of mail.

Resolution: All of the above resolutions will solve this restraining force also.

Resolution: Color code "reply back" envelopes for each bureau. This will assist in mail delivery in each bureau.

We will review this suggestion in more depth.

Resolution: Review the possibility of increasing the size of the lettering "REPLY TO" on forms or letters from the department and division so that the public will be sure to see the special reference and know where to reply to.

CAUSE #5: LEVEL OF PHONE SYSTEM IS TOO LOW.

Restraining Force #1: No direct phone lines to courts (Broward, Dade, Palm Beach).
  a. State phone book does not provide SUN-COM for Broward County.
  b. Security numbers required to access Broward County Clerk's office.

Resolution: UTC Specialist will make a personal contact with the Clerk of Court's office in Broward, Dade, and Palm Beach County to secure a contact person and phone number. These numbers will be secured as soon as UTC Specialist can get by their offices.

Restraining Force #2: No standard systems for log out.
> a. Special assignments, schools, staff meetings.

Resolution: Bureau Chief of Driver Improvement will establish a uniform log out system for the telephone network for all review officers. This will be accomplished by March 15.

Restraining Force #3: No corrective action against duty shirkers.

Resolution: First-line supervisors in all bureaus will be instructed to administer closer supervision and fair supervision of employees.

Resolution: Management training courses for first-line supervisors will be conducted as soon as possible in the "Basic Principles of Supervision."

Restraining Force #4: Measuring number of calls is wrong (evaluations).

Resolution: The quality of work done by the review officers in Driver Improvement and Financial Responsibility will be evaluated in addition to the quantity.

Quality service/quality work will be the watchword for the division and quality will consist a large portion of an employee's evaluation. Quality of calls will be averaged and realistic standards set. This criteria will begin immediately.

Restraining Force #5: Monitoring of calls.

Resolution: Review officers in Driver Improvement and Financial Responsibility will be informed and instructed on the capabilities of the new telephone system and its purpose and the purpose of a supervisor monitoring telephone calls from time to time.

Resolution: Supervisors will also use the management by walking around. (MBWA) it too is a good technique.

This technique will begin immediately by all supervisors within the Division of Driver Licenses.

CAUSE #6: THE LEVEL OF USE OF FUNDS IS TOO LOW.

Restraining Force #1: Improper use of funds.
   a. Unnecessary office equipment.
   b. Unnecessary travel expense.
   c. Creating unnecessary positions.
   d. End of year spending.

The suggestion by Quality Action Team was to use the funds for upgrades, pay raises, and bonuses.

Resolution: The Division of Driver Licenses has 1,663 employees within the division which have been authorized by the legislature. These 1,663 employees are divided among all five (5) bureaus and the division director's staff.

Funds by category are for the following:

1. Salaries and benefits to pay 1,663 employees monthly salaries, retirement benefits, social security benefits, and insurance benefits. If a person is promoted, the additional salary comes out of this same fund. Upgrades and overtime work will come out of this fund also.

2. Other Personal Services (OPS) covers any contractual services such as janitorial and cleaning service for all of our field offices, special contracts for counseling services to the division, maintenance contracts for duplicating machines, and extra OPS people to help with the backlog of work, etc.

3. Expense funds pay for travel expenses of our employees who must travel as part of their duties. Paint jobs, renovation of offices, roof repairs, repairs to vehicles such as body work and paint jobs to the driver license vehicle fleet statewide and gas and oil to run these cars daily.

   Training of division employees also comes out of the expense fund. One of the largest and most expensive items in this category is monthly rent for the 78 leased driver license offices statewide. Also, utilities for our offices are paid out of this one fund.

Some other items that this expense fund covers are printing of our letter forms; suspension, revocation and FR suspension forms; all DL renewal forms; driver license handbooks, motorcycle handbooks, information brochures; printing of over 1,000,000 uniform citations for all police departments statewide; and uniforms for 1,000 driver license examiners.

A division our size is expensive and it takes quite a bit of money to keep us operating.

4. Operating capital outlay covers the purchase of large pieces of equipment we need to perform our duties such as typewriters, printers, duplicating machines, vehicles, carpet, and any item that costs over $200. Remember that one car will probably cost $10,000, so this fund is watched very closely as it can be depleted very quickly.

5. Purchase of driver license funds are only spent to pay our present color photo contractor (N.B.S.) 43 cents for each license issued. This covers film, laminates, cameras, developing of 35 mm film, and service from NBS to our 160 driver license offices statewide. We issued over three million licenses plus replacement licenses and duplicate licenses last year.

6. Data processing services fund is the driver license portion to support the department's data processing system. It is a large budget and one that must last the entire year.

7. Insurance information program was a one-shot fund for this year to inform the public of the new financial responsibility reform act and new law that becomes effective this year.

There is a state law that prohibits us or any other state department to go into deficit spending. We must spread the total funding over the entire year and make sure that on June 30, we have paid all the salaries, benefits, rent, utilities, gas, oil, tires, and bought the right equipment for our driver license employees to get their job done in a proper manner.

We try to anticipate the budget spending to allow for emergencies that might arise and hold back enough money for that until the very last month or two of the fiscal year. For example, this year we have had two field offices flooded out, one major fire that destroyed an office and a couple of state vehicle crashes that totaled out the cars. These cars had to be replaced at ten thousand dollars each.

We try to be as free with our appropriated funds as possible, but sometimes we must turn down a request for spending. However, as you look around, we do have excellent equipment to work with. One prime example is all of the new data processing equipment being installed now which will make our jobs easier.

The suggestion for pay raises and or bonuses cannot be granted to division employees as this nor any state department is not authorized to grant pay raises at will.

The legislature each year grants the pay raises, if any, to all state employees and they then allocate enough salary money to cover that item in the budget.

The category items listed here must be spent for those items mentioned only, and we cannot spend money from the expense fund, for example, to buy cars, trucks, or typewriters. Budget categories are watched by the state comptroller office and they regulate that spending very strictly.

The suggestion to upgrade positions is a good one and we do have that right. We exercise that option only when the position warrants an upgrade. We as a division must abide by *all* of the Department of Administration rules and regulations governing that option. We *cannot* just do an upgrade at will.

We are powerless to upgrade all positions in the Division of Driver Licenses at the end of a budget year just because there is money left in the budget. That *cannot* be done.

We only purchase equipment for our employees to use or work with that has been requested by the supervisor and bureau chief, and we hope there is not any excessive equipment laying around not being utilized.

Resolution: Division of Driver License funds will be spent wisely and expeditiously.

CAUSE #7: LEVEL OF HARD TIMING THE PUBLIC IS TOO HIGH.

Restraining Forces #1: Being rude.
        #2: Not listening.

Resolution: All bureau training managers will conduct in-service training programs for all employees that answer the phone and contact the public on "Telephone Techniques." Also, use "Telephone Doctor" training. Stress courteous service to the public in all training programs with our employees.

Restraining Force #3: Not providing enough information or wrong information.
        a. Insufficient information.
        b. Partial information.

Resolution: All bureaus will instruct all employees who answer the telephone from the public that when transferring the call to another section, they must do the following:

1. Identify yourself to the person you have transferred the call to.
2. Give a short overview of the person's (public's) problem or his or her needs.
3. Tell the public (the person who called in) that you are unable to provide the correct information and you must transfer them to so and so.
4. When the call has been transferred and the second employee has been given the overview of the call, please tell the public (person being transferred): "Your call has been transferred to me and my name is so and so. May I help you?"

We must get back into the mode of providing quality service to the public.

Proper telephone etiquette will be practiced within the Division of Driver Licenses beginning immediately.

Resolution: In-service training will begin as soon as possible for employees in all sections on job duties, job assignments, etc., with the objective in mind to develop employees into well-trained driver license employees. People with sufficient knowledge will be able to provide quality service to the public.

Resolution: FR training manual and training guidelines are presently being reviewed for possible updating and revisions. Training will follow.

Resolution: Allow DI Reviewing Officers to clear suspensions after research with Clerk of Courts office. This will be analyzed as soon as possible, and Bureau Chief will make recommendations to the Division Director for implementation.

Resolution: Bureau Chief has re-emphasized to all of his review officers that SR 21 information *will be taken* via phone call. This is effective immediately.

Restraining Force #4: Sending the public to driver license offices unnecessarily.

    a. Vice Versa - driver licenses offices tell the public to call GHQ instead of helping them while they are already there.

Resolution: All employees within the Division of Driver Licenses will be reinstructed and reinformed of our dedication to quality service to the public. Service is all we have to offer to the public. If we will strive to assist a person in need while we have them on the phone, instead of transferring them to someone else or sending them by a field office, and if the field office handles the people while they are in the office, we will take a giant step toward that quality service.

cc: Quality Team I
    Quality Action Team I

SECTION TWO

Quality Service Improvement—Group II

Bureau of Records

Quality Resolution Team

Quality Review Team

Group II—Quality Service Improvement
Bureau of Records

Cause #1—The Level of Supervision Is Too Low

Restraining force	Driving forces
(1) No pat on the back/no encouragement.	(1) Say thanks for a job well done/encourage.
(2) Credit not given to the right people.	(2) Recognize the individual's accomplishment in writing.
(3) Supervisor fearful of grievances.	(3) Supervisors need more training on enforcing rules and regulations to relieve the worry of potential grievances.
(4) Letting someone else take up the slack.	(4) Supervisors need to work more closely with employees who are putting in a full eight hours of work so he/she will not be so resentful.

(5) Confusion regarding standards (statutes and laws).

(5) Employee should be involved in the performance appraisal evaluation. Items on evaluation that do not apply to their job. Also advise the employee how he/she can achieve an exceeds rating.

(6) Inconsistency in allowing days off.

(6) Cross-training from each section to allow for days off by reassigning personnel to help out on phones.

(7) Tracking errors instead of achievements.

(7) More emphasis on positive and not negative. Employee and supervisor agree on negative information going into personnel files before placement.

(8) Late instructions (not timely).

(8) Inform employees immediately when changes are made to prevent error.

(9) Supervisors do not listen.

(9) Supervisors listen and have open discussions without repercussions.

(10) Inconsistent direction/instruction.

(10) Specific formats and instructions. Update procedures manuals.

(11) Bawling out entire group, not individual.

(11) Always discuss individual errors with person involved, not entire section as a whole.

(12) Rivalry between supervisors/sections.

(12) More cooperation among supervisors to work as a team. Supervisors correct errors within section and not depend on another section to have correction completed.

Cause #2—Level of Training Is Too Low

Restraining force

(1) Given a little packet of instruction and you are on your own.

(2) Inconsistent in training (trainer vs. supv.)

(3) Too much involvement of employees.

(4) Supv. too busy to help new employee.

(5) Not getting written instruction on a timely basis.

(6) Bad environment for training.

(7) Training manuals are not kept up-to-date.

(8) Lack of cross-training.

Driving forces

(1) Need verbal instructions with better interpretation.

(2) A designated trainer.

(3) A designated trainer.

(4) Training new employees should be top priority.

(5) Pamphlets and instructions should be given to ensure that each employee understands.

(6) Place for basic instruction with no interruptions.

(7) Update manuals.

(8) Decide who needs training and send them.

Cause #3—Level of Communications Is Too Low

Restraining force

(1) Lack of instruction.

(2) Bad attitude of supv. in answering.

(3) Employee fear.

Driving forces

(1) Open discussion of problems, etc.

(2) Listen to problems.

(3) Although you may feel intimidated, ask questions anyway.

(4) Lack of understanding.   (4) (Same as above.)

(5) Not listening to employee   (5) (Same as above.)
suggestions.

Cause #4—Level of Communications Is Too Low

Restraining force   **Driving forces**

(1) Negative criticism.   (1) Give positive criticism.

(2) Self-centeredness (employee   (2) Be considerate of others
& supv.)   (everyone).

(3) Passing the buck (employee   (3) Everybody do their own
& supv.)   share. If you do not know
                                         how to handle something,
                                         learn.

(4) Not accepting responsibili-   (4) No recommendation given.
ties (employee & supv.).

(5) Negative attitudes   (5) No recommendation given.
(employees & supv.).

(6) Lack of pre-planning.   (6) Plan for and notify
                                         employees ahead of time.

Cause #5—The Level of Inadequate Job Title or Job Description Is Too High

Restraining force   **Driving forces**

(1) Title does not fit job   (1) Create new job title.
description.

(2) Same title but different job   (2) Update job descriptions to
descriptions.   match responsibility.

(3) Pay too low for job   (3) No recommendation given.
description.

Cause #6—The Level of Not Finding the Source of Errors Is Too High

Restraining force

Driving forces

(1) Not finding the source of the mistake.
  (a) Tickets—not enough research on the part of coders to find the correct record.
  (b) D-6 suspensions being placed on wrong records.

(1) Find the source of the error and correct it.

(2) Accepting mistakes as the norm instead of correcting the process.
  (a) More dummy files opposed to numerous corrections.

(2) Repeated mistakes should be researched to correct process.

TO: Director
            Division of Driver Licenses

FROM: Assistant Director
            Division of Driver Licenses

SUBJECT: Quality Resolution Team (QRT) Report for Group II

The Quality Resolution Team for Group II has discussed all of the suggestions from the Quality Action Team #2 for the improvement of the quality of service to the public from the Division of Driver Licenses.
Following are the resolutions:

CAUSE #1: LEVEL OF POOR SUPERVISION IS TOO HIGH.

Restraining Forces #1: No pat on the back/no encouragement.
             #2: Credit not given to the right person.
             #4: Letting someone else take up the slack.

Resolution: First and second level supervisors will receive extra supervisory training on "The Basic Principles of Supervisory Management." DHSMV Training Manager will be consulted by all bureau chiefs for assistance in setting up this training. Training will begin as soon as possible.

Resolution: To ensure that employees receive proper recognition and credit for a job well done, supervisors are encouraged to give credit and a pat on the back to deserving employees. Supervisors shall answer in writing all letters of appreciation from the public to an employee of good service. A copy of both letters will go in the employee's personnel file. Letters of appreciation will even include small "Thank you for a job well done" notes or cards. All bureau chiefs will begin this practice immediately, March 1.

Restraining Force #3: Supervisors fearful of grievances.

Resolution: Effective March 1 all first-line supervisors in all bureaus will be included in all bureau staff meetings.

Resolution: Supervisor levels 1, 2, and 3 will receive more training on personnel policies such as leave and attendance, standards of disciplinary actions, labor union contract, and rules and regulations in general. This will reduce the fear of employees filing grievances.

Each bureau chief will make contact with DHSMV Training Manager to set up training agenda.

Restraining Force #5: Confusion Regarding Work Standards and Job Tasks.

Resolution: Each bureau chief will see that all supervisors receive refresher training on conducting evaluations of employees.

All bureau chiefs will review the evaluation forms to ensure that the proper job tasks are evaluated, the evaluations are not on too many tasks, and also that the assignments are reasonable.

Supervisors will be trained and instructed to work with and advise employees on how they can achieve an exceeds evaluation. DHSMV Training Manager will be consulted by our bureau chiefs for this special training, and the retraining and review process will begin as soon as possible.

Restraining Force #6: Inconsistency in allowing days off.

Resolution: To compensate for too many people being off duty at the same time in the same section, supervisors are cautioned to evaluate their work priorities to ensure proper coverage.

The most important resolution to this problem will be to cross-train employees from each section to cover for shortage of workers in other sections where the workload is critical, i.e., correspondence section cross-trains with the telephone section.

Resolution: Cross-training in homogeneous sections will begin in all bureaus by April 1.

Restraining Force #7: (Included with restraining force #1.)

Restraining Forces #8: Late instruction (not timely).
           #9: Supervisors do not listen.
          #10: Inconsistent direction/instruction.

Resolution: All bureaus within the Division of Driver Licenses will have their first-line supervisors begin holding 30-minute employee meetings once a week. We suggest the meetings be held each Monday morning as the first order of business that day. The meetings to begin March 13.

Restraining Force #11: Bawling out the entire group, rather than one individual.

Resolution: First and second level supervisors will receive extra supervisory training on the "Basic Principles of Supervision." (See resolution to cause #1.)

Restraining Force #12: Rivalry between supervisors and sections.

Resolution: DL Administrators will retrain supervisors under their jurisdiction to make sure the individual jobs are known.

CAUSE #2: LEVEL OF TRAINING IS TOO LOW.

Restraining Forces #1: Employees are given a little packet of instruction, and you are on your own.
          #2: Inconsistent training.
          #3: Too much involvement of employees.
          #4. Supervisor too busy to help new employee.

Resolution: All five bureau chiefs within the Division of Driver Licenses will designate an employee to be the trainer to train all new employees within the various sections.

The designated trainer's position description will be amended to include training duties.

DHSMV Training Manager will be contacted to provide "Train the Trainer" programs for these trainers.

Restraining Force #5: Not getting written instructions on a timely basis.

Resolution: The first-line supervisors will get out the latest infor-mation to all employees at the weekly 30-minute meetings. This will establish an excellent communication link with all employees and give everyone the opportunity to discuss all latest changes.

Restraining Force #6: Bad environment for training.

Resolution: The designated trainer will be authorized to use the department's classroom, auditorium, and conference room on the fourth floor, and other quiet rooms for training. All supervisors will assist with this effort.

Resolution: All bureaus will establish "New Employee Orientation" programs within each bureau to introduce the new employees to the department, division, and specific bureaus. This will give the new employee the overall picture and establish our goals and objectives with that employee. Programs will begin immediately.

Restraining Force #7: Training manuals are not kept up to date.

Resolution: Section supervisors will review the manuals and take corrective action to make sure they are updated. The designated trainers should assist in this project.

Restraining Force #8: Lack of cross-training.

Resolution: Cross-training will begin in all bureaus by April 1. See same resolution under cause #1.

CAUSE #3: LEVEL OF COMMUNICATION IS TOO LOW.

Restraining Forces #1: Lack of instruction.
　　　　　　　　#2: Bad attitude of supervisor in giving answers.
　　　　　　　　#3: Employee fear.
　　　　　　　　#4: Lack of understanding.
　　　　　　　　#5: Not listening to employee suggestions.

Resolution: Every Monday morning, conduct a 30-minute employee meeting. This meeting is to be conducted by the first-line supervisor and will provide a forum for open discussion of problems from the employees and to listen to the suggestions on how to improve the quality of service. The supervisor will use this time to discuss latest information and changes within the bureau. These sessions will begin March 13.

See same resolution under cause #2.

CAUSE #4: LEVEL OF COMMUNICATION IS TOO LOW.

Restraining Forces #1: Negative criticism.
        #2: Self-centeredness (employee and supervisor).

Resolution: Train all levels of supervisors within each bureau in the "One Minute Manager" techniques. Training to begin as soon as possible.

Restraining Force #3: Pass the buck (employee and supervisor).

Resolution: This is a symptom of not knowing the job. Retrain employees and supervisors in their jobs. Training to begin in each bureau as soon as possible.

Restraining Forces #4: Not accepting responsibilities.
        #5: Negative attitudes.
        #6: Lack of preplanning.

Resolution: Train supervisors and employees in the Investment in Excellence program. Training to begin as soon as possible but not later than May 1. This will be an ongoing training program and long range.

CAUSE #5: THE LEVEL OF INADEQUATE JOB TITLE ON JOB DESCRIPTION IS TOO HIGH.

Restraining Forces #1: Title does not fit job description.
        #2: Same title but different job description.

Resolution: Bureau Chiefs will review position descriptions to ensure that job titles are appropriate and are consistent with actual duties. If duties are not consistent with position descriptions, the latter shall be amended accordingly. If job titles do not appear appropriate, chiefs may recommend the use of "working" titles since we have no authority to change career service job titles.

Restraining Force #3: Pay too low for job description.

Resolution: The Department of Administration assigns all job classes to specific pay grades after analysis of responsibilities. The assignment considers many factors and is intended to fairly compensate employees for the duties generally performed in each class. Actual pay is the result of a lengthy process which includes collective bargaining and legislative action. DHSMV is powerless to alter pay schedules or to increase any salary without specific authority. In this matter, bureau chiefs will continually review to make certain position descriptions reflect actual duties performed.

CAUSE #6: THE LEVEL OF NOT FINDING THE SOURCE OF ERRORS IS TOO HIGH.

Restraining Force #1: Not finding the source of the mistake.
      a. Tickets—not enough research on the part of coders to find the correct record.
      b. D-6 suspensions being placed on wrong records.

Resolution: A new policy has been placed into effect in the video lookup section which is: The lookup section will not force driver license numbers on tickets or D-6 notices. A person's full name and date of birth must match exactly on both the ticket or D-6 notice with the driver record on file before the number is placed on the lookup document.

If there is any doubt of the name or there is not an exact match, don't put it on the record. This will eliminate placing D-6 suspensions and traffic violations on the wrong person's record. This policy is effective immediately.

Restraining Force #2: Accepting mistakes as the norm instead of correcting the process.
      a. More dummy files opposed to numerous corrections.

Resolution: The above new policy for the video lookup section will eliminate many errors. Continued training for employees in all bureaus on Quality Control and Quality Improvement will stamp out the acceptance of mistakes as the norm.

cc: Quality Resolution Team
    Quality Action Team

SECTION THREE

Quality Service Improvement—Group III
Bureau of Uniform Traffic Citations

Quality Resolution Team

Quality Review Team

Group III—Quality Service Improvement
Uniform Traffic Citation

Cause #1—The Level of Favoritism Is Too High

Restraining force	Driving forces
(1) Employees being evaluated on items that do not apply to their job.	(1) Employee should be involved in the performance appraisal evaluation. Evaluate employees according to work. Also advise employee how he/she can achieve an exceeds rating.
(2) Hiring practices.	(2) Hire the most qualified person.
(3) Hiring outside the office rather than someone within the office who might already know the job.	(3) Promote within the section as these employees are more qualified since they already know much of the job.
(4) Title does not fit job description.	(4) Match the job title with the work employee does.

(5) Employees believe it's who you know and not what you know that determines who gets hired, promoted, etc.

(5) Treat everyone equal.

(6) Supervisors are not consistent in how they discipline one employee vs. another.

(6) Be consistent regarding discipline.

(7) Quotas are not established in a fair manner.

(7) Establish fair quotas for all.

(8) There is no incentive for someone to go over their quota.

(8) Base evaluation in part on the amount of work done. Compliment or give compensation when someone goes over their quota.

(9) Credit not given to the right people. Do not think the work they do is appreciated.

(9) Say thanks for a job well done.

Cause #2—The Level of Supervisors Not Knowing Their Work Is Too High

Restraining force

Driving forces

(1) Hiring supervisors out of section.

(1) Promote from within office for supervisor positions.

(2) Clerks/clerk specialists having to train supervisors.

(2) Give adequate notice to train next employee.

(3) Passing the buck.

(3) Go up the line of command.

(4) Too much work load on one person—no way to account for.

(4) Be responsible for own work.

Cause #3—The Level of Morale Is Too Low

Restraining force

Driving forces

(1) Not enough variety in work.

(1) Have more cross-training.

(2) "Bawl" out everyone instead of the individual.

(2) Talk individually to employee and not in a group.

(3) Dirty offices.

(3) Improve janitorial services.

(4) Problems with heat and air conditioning make it uncomfortable to work.

(4) Have maintenance work on this.

(5) Stress caused by all of the above.

(5) Correct the above.

Cause #4—The Level of Personnel Is Too Low (Lack of Personnel)

Restraining force

Driving forces

(1) Backlog.

(1) Allow employees to work overtime. Each office do own work.

(2) Working hours—only allowed to use flex time within the work day.

(2) Allow flex time to be used within the week rather than just the day.

(3) Keypunch.

(3) Keypunchers correct own errors. Keep work in the building.

(4) Untrained personnel. One employee is taught one way and another is taught to do it a totally different way.

(4) Make sure all employees are trained consistently.

Cause #5—The Level of Training Is Too Low

Restraining force

Driving forces

(1) Lack of information from supervisors. Not given needed information (changes, etc.) on a timely basis.

(1) Distribute information in a timely manner.

(2) Not sure what to do, so set it aside. Lack of instruction.

(2) Supervisor and employee work to assure problem work is not set aside.

(3) Not enough time for training—wait until last minute.

(3) Allow enough time for training. Plan time for training.

(4) Wrong people doing the training.

(4) Most qualified should do training.

(5) Bad environment for training—improper training area.

(5) Establish a certain area to be used for training.

Cause #6—The Level of Communication Is Too Low

Restraining force

Driving forces

(1) Inconsistent instructions. Given a packet of instructions and you are on your own.

(1) Be consistent with instructions.

(2) Not updating changes.

(2) Update all changes as soon as possible.

(3) Back from courts (send disposition copies back to court for correction—come back still incomplete).

(3) Improve communication between headquarters and courts.

(4) Lack of communication between supervisors.

(4) Improve communication between supervisors.

Cause #7—The Level of Storage Problems Is Too High

Restraining force

(1) Delayed retention causing old files to stack up.

(2) Not enough filing space.

(3) Holding unnecessary tickets.

(4) Storage of unnecessary "junk" (chairs, tickets, void tickets).

Driving forces

(1) Speed up retention.

(2) Create larger storage area.

(3) Destroy unnecessary tickets. Convert tickets to microfilm.

(4) Auction off unnecessary junk.

Cause #8—The Level of Traffic Citation Problems Is Too High

Restraining force

(1) Illegible handwriting and incomplete information on tickets.

(2) Statute numbers wrong— not enough knowledge regarding correct numbers.

(3) Unfair quotas.

(4) Back from courts.

(5) Back from keypunch.

(6) Having to patch torn citations.

Driving forces

(1) Print legibly and give complete information on tickets.

(2) Learn the correct statute numbers. Update everyone when there has been a change in statute numbers.

(3) Use the same quotas within a group.

(4) Better communication with and training of court clerks.

(5) Provide terminals for the employees to directly enter the information instead of going through keypunch. (Upgrade the positions in the process.) Stop sending the work outside country/building.

(6) Find a solution to the problem of torn citations.

TO: Director
             Division of Driver Licenses

FROM: Assistant Director
             Division of Driver Licenses

SUBJECT: Quality Resolution Team (QRT) Report for Group III

The Quality Resolution Team for Group III has thoroughly discussed all of the suggestions from Quality Action Team #III for the improvement of the quality of service to the public from the Division of Driver Licenses.
Following are the resolutions:

CAUSE #1: LEVEL OF FAVORITISM IS TOO HIGH.

Restraining Force #1: Employees being evaluated on items that do not apply to their job.

Resolution: All DL Bureau Chiefs will review all job descriptions to make sure they match the job tasks and make corrections if needed.

Resolution: Retrain first, second, and third level supervisors on employee evaluations.

Resolution: Supervisor should evaluate employees on job tasks that are done only. Supervisor will be trained and instructed to work with and advise employees how they can achieve an exceeds evaluation.

DHSMV Training Manager will be consulted by our bureau chiefs for this special training. The process will begin as soon as possible.

Restraining Force #2: Hiring Practices.

Resolution: All bureaus within the Division of Driver Licenses hire people to fill vacant positions according to department personnel guidelines. We use the interview module for that position which assesses the knowledge, skills, and abilities of each individual interviewed. The most qualified person is then recommended for the job by the supervisor holding the interview.

The entire interview package of all the people is delivered to the next level manager and then the bureau chief for review. The bureau chief then gives the complete package to the division director who makes the final selection on who will be hired for the job.

Other forces that must be considered in the selection process are demotions and reassignment requests. The union contract and the state of Florida rules require that persons receiving demotions into that specific job opening be given first choice and reassignment requests next. We cannot deviate from this requirement.

Restraining Force #3: Hiring outside the office rather than promoting someone within the office who might already know the job.

Resolution: The previous resolution also explains the promotional selection process. The most qualified person is selected regardless of their location.

Restraining Force #4: Title does not fit the job description.

Resolution: Bureau chiefs will review the position descriptions and make corrections where necessary.

Employees may be asked to assume different duties from time to time, but no employee should work out of class more than 30 days.

Restraining Force #5: Employees believe it's who you know and not what you know that determines who gets hired and promoted.

Resolution: The same resolution as in force #2. We promote the most qualified person based on the interview module and that person's knowledge, skills, and abilities.

Restraining Force #6: Supervisors are not consistent in how they discipline one employee vs. another.

Resolution: All first-line supervisors will be instructed in the correct disciplinary procedures by their immediate supervisor.

All first- and second-line supervisors within each bureau will attend DHSMV disciplinary action training classes as soon as possible. DHSMV Training Coordinator will be consulted by our bureau chiefs as to the next available training programs.

Restraining Force #7: Quotas are not established in a fair manner.

Resolution: Bureau chiefs will reevaluate quotas to make sure they are fair and that the quotas are achievable. This should be resolved by April 1.

After quotas are reevaluated, the first line supervisor should discuss them with his or her employees.

Restraining Force #8: There is no incentive for someone to go over their quota.

Resolution: The first-line supervisor should attend supervisory training programs in the "Basic Principles of Supervision" and thus learn the skills of motivating employees. One of the basic elements is giving compliments to employees for a job well done. This training to be made available as soon as possible.

Supervisors should work with employees to help them achieve an exceeds evaluation.

Employees who receive an overall exceeds performance rating become eligible to receive an incentive pay increase. An employee may achieve an exceeds evaluation when their work performance is at a level that far exceeds the normal work standards and the employee has contributed significantly to the overall accomplishments of the goals and objectives of the section, bureau, or division.

Restraining Force #9: Credit not given to the right people. Employees do not think the work they do is appreciated.

Resolution: Effective immediately, all bureaus will begin management training programs for first and second level supervisors.

In thinking about training, we *must* train at all levels. We must institute a vigorous program of education and retraining within the Division of Driver Licenses. Quality improvement will come as a result of people at all levels knowing their jobs and wanting to do a better job.

Through training, supervisors will find out that motivating employees begins with letting the employees know their job is appreciated and how important each employee is to the division. After all, there would be no service if it were not for the expert employees of our division.

It is imperative that supervisors give credit where credit is due and to commend employees for excellent service.

CAUSE #2: LEVEL OF SUPERVISORS NOT KNOWING THEIR WORK IS TOO HIGH.

Restraining Force #1: Hiring supervisors out of section.

Resolution: Please see resolution under cause #1—restraining force #2.

We attempt to select the most qualified person to fill the vacant supervisory job regardless of their prior duty assignment, and sometimes a person from outside the work section will be selected as supervisor. Of course it stands to reason that the newly selected supervisor will need to work diligently to learn the job at hand and to provide excellent supervision to the "expert" employees doing the day-to-day job.

The Division of Driver Licenses will train new supervisors in the "Basic Principles of Supervision" just as soon as possible after the new supervisor is selected.

Quoting from *The Deming Management Method* by Mary Walton, "Leadership is the job of management. It is the responsibility of management to discover the barriers that prevent workers from taking pride in what they do."

Restraining Force #2: Clerks/clerk specialists having to train supervisors.

Resolution: It would be ideal to overlap an incoming supervisor with the outgoing one to learn the job, but Department of Administration rules will not allow this practice. Therefore, we expect the new supervisor to receive the bulk of their training from the assistant section supervisor. This new training on the job by the assistant section supervisor will be augmented by the new supervisor working for a period of time with the employees actually doing the job. This hands-on job training is effective and offers a good blend of training for the new person.

Restraining Force #3: Passing the buck.

Resolution: When a supervisor "passes the buck" by not giving an answer or a solution to a problem, it indicates that the job is not known thoroughly. The supervisors will be instructed to seek assistance from the next higher level of supervisor. Answers shall be given to employees as soon as possible.

Restraining Force #4: Too much workload on one person. No way to account for work.

Resolution: We realize that the workload in the Division of Driver Licenses is heavy, and the work done by our employees is appreciated. We do provide excellent service in most cases. We do request additional employees each fiscal year from the legislature, and we have again this year. Whether or not we will be granted this request is still unknown at this time.

Resolution: In the Bureau of Uniform Traffic Citations, employees account for their work by making special notations on the reverse side of their daily *activity* report of extra work duties or tasks they do. The employees also list the time spent on these extra duty assignments. All employees are encouraged to keep accurate track of the extra duties and time, as we intend to give the person credit for this extra work. This will assist the first line supervisors in evaluating the employees for exceeds standards but also in assigning other duties as workload demands. Each employee must keep up with their accurate accounting of work performed.

CAUSE #3: LEVEL OF MORALE IS TOO LOW.

Restraining Force #1: Not enough variety in work.

Resolution: Cross-training in homogeneous sections will begin by April 1. This resolution applies to *all bureaus.*

Note: The Bureau of Uniform Traffic Citations will be an excellent area to cross-train employees. So much of the work is homogeneous, and it will help to break up the monotony of doing the same thing hour after hour.

Cross-training will also give depth to the employees' knowledge and an excellent resource to draw from if need arises to get out a specific job in a short order (you will be able to use these already trained employees to get the job done).

Restraining Force #2: Bawl out everyone instead of the individual.

Resolution: Agree. If an individual has made the error then that person should be counseled with—not "bawl" out the entire group.

Resolution: First and second level supervisors will receive extra supervisory training on the "Basic Principles of Supervision."

In this management training the supervisor is trained on the techniques of motivating, dealing, working, and leading employees.

Restraining Forces #3: Dirty offices.
     #4: Problems with heat and air conditioning make it uncomfortable to work.

Resolution: We will write a memo and make personal contact with Office Operations Supervisor with the Division of Administrative Services of the problem areas. We will ask that the janitor clean the offices more thoroughly and the maintenance engineer balance out the air conditioning and heating in the offices.

Restraining Force #5: Stress caused by all previous restraining forces.

Resolution: The preceding forces will be corrected and thus reduce employee stress.

CAUSE #4: LEVEL OF PERSONNEL IS TOO LOW.

Restraining Force #1: Backlog.

Resolution: Overtime will be allowed when salary money is available. However, working overtime to correct a backlog is only a temporary fix.

Resolution: Cross-training employees from other like sections to fill in these critical backlog sections to get the job done will also help.

Cross-training will begin April 1.

Special note: For the past several years, the Division of Driver Licenses' budget request to the legislature has included the request for additional positions for the Bureau of Uniform Traffic Citations, but we have not been granted our request.

We will again ask for more employees from the 1989 session of the legislature.

Restraining Force #2: Working hours—only allowed to use Flex time within the workday.

Resolution: All bureaus will assess the Flex time schedule in their bureaus, and they will allow Flex time within the work week. Employees will be allowed to work the 40 hour work week within department guidelines for Flex time. This will begin by March 13.

Restraining Force #3: Keypunch errors.

Resolution: Uniform Traffic Citation blue tickets are keypunched in Bradenton and have many errors. The supervisor of the blue ticket area will keep a list of the errors and work with the bureau chief on the number and type of keypunch errors.

Mrs. Simpson will then work with the Data Center to reach a solution in order to correct the error problems. This corrective action is going on now.

Some of the errors are also coming in from Barbados. It seems that Barbados is not familiar with the codes, and thus they are rejecting the tickets. This correction is being done now.

Resolution: Our coders will be instructed to write code numbers very clearly in order for the keypunch operators to read them.

Restraining Force #4: Untrained personnel. One person is taught one way and another is taught to do it a totally different way.

Resolution: Establish designated trainers for each section. This will ensure that all employees are taught the same way.

Resolution: The 30-minute employee meetings each Monday morning will help reduce the lack of communication and give employees and supervisors the forum for feedback.

CAUSE #5: LEVEL OF TRAINING IS TOO LOW.

Restraining Force #1: Lack of information from supervisors. Not given needed information (changes, etc.) on a timely basis.

Resolution: All bureau chiefs within the Division of Driver Licenses will have their first-line supervisors begin holding *30-minute* employee meetings *once* a week. We suggest the meetings be held each Monday morning as the first order of business. The meetings to begin by March 13.

This will enable the supervisors to distribute bulletins, changes, etc., on a timely basis. The meetings will provide employees the opportunity to communicate with one another and their supervisor.

Restraining Force #2: Not sure what to do, so set it aside. Lack of instruction.

Resolution: All first-line supervisors will be instructed to seek proper answers and information from their own supervisor if they do not know the answers.

Resolution: The 30-minute employee meetings each Monday morning will help the first-line supervisors' knowledge grow in all levels of his or her job.

Restraining Force #3: Not enough time for training—wait until the last minute.

Resolution: Establish designated trainers in each section to conduct on-the-job training for employees.

Resolution: A bureau trainer will also be designated to coordinate and conduct training sessions. It will be the trainer's responsibility to plan for the training and coordinate same.

Restraining Force #4: Wrong people doing the training.

Resolution: When designating persons to do the training, the supervisors will select *the* most qualified person to do the job.

Restraining Force #5: Bad environment for training—improper training area.

Resolution: Designated trainers have access to the department's training facilities (classroom, auditorium, and conference rooms). These can be reserved for training if needed. Most of the on-the-job training, however, will be done on site.

The Bureau Chief will assist in securing training rooms for our trainers.

CAUSE #6: LEVEL OF COMMUNICATION IS TOO LOW.

Restraining Forces #1: Inconsistent instructions. Given packet of instructions and you are on your own.
#2: Not updating changes.

Resolution: The 30-minute employee meetings that will be conducted each Monday morning by the first line supervisor will help to eliminate Restraining Forces #1 and #2.

The appointment of designated trainers will also be consistent with our other resolution to adequately train employees.

Resolution: All bureaus will conduct new employee orientation sessions for all new employees.

Restraining Force #3: Back from courts (send disposition copies back to court for correction—come back still incomplete).

Resolution: After the dispositions have come back from the courts and they are still uncorrected, we issue them (uncorrected disposition) to the UTC Specialist. The UTC Specialist will make a personal visit to the Clerk of Court offices to have correction made.

Restraining Force #4: Lack of communication between supervisors.

Resolution: All bureaus will have once a month staff meeting and the first-line supervisors will be included in these staff meetings.

This will improve communications between supervisors.

CAUSE #7: LEVEL OF STORAGE PROBLEMS TOO HIGH.

Restraining Forces #1: Delayed destruction causing old files to stack up.
#2: Not enough filing space.

Resolution: The destruction schedule for the old blue tickets has been refiled with State Archives requesting authorization to destroy three-month-old tickets. When the authorization is given the large batch of three-month-old tickets will be destroyed thus allowing more storage space.

Restraining Force #3: Holding unnecessary tickets.

Resolution: Our retention schedule is three months for old blue tickets, and we must secure permission from State Archives for authority to destroy. We do request permission in a timely manner.

Resolution: We are unable to microfilm old tickets unless they are retained in storage five years or more. State Archives has informed us that it is not cost effective to microfilm for a shorter period of time.

Our new retention schedule that just came out this month is: traffic infraction tickets—three years from conviction date; DUI, etc.—75 years (we microfilm these).

Restraining Force #4: Storage of unnecessary "junk" chairs, tickets, void tickets.

Resolution: The "junk" chairs are not junk; they are good chairs that are extra. These chairs are kept in reserve for summer time OPS positions, etc.

Resolution: The old void tickets must be kept until authorization has been received to destroy. The department will look into the suggestion that they be shredded rather than transported to the dump. Shredding might save time.

CAUSE #8: LEVEL OF TRAFFIC CITATION PROBLEMS IS TOO HIGH.

Restraining Forces #1: Illegible handwriting by police officers and incomplete information on tickets.
#2: Statute numbers wrong—not enough knowledge regarding correct numbers.

Resolution: This may be a restraining force that we must learn to work with. There are over 400 law enforcement agencies with several thousand police officers, deputy sheriffs, and state troopers writing these tickets. Unfortunately, the handwriting of many of them is less than desirable.

We have our UTC Specialists instruct at police academies statewide on the art of completing the UTC, and we do advise them of the special need to write clearly.

Statute numbers are issued to all agencies by our division for the police officers' use, and we do inform the agencies of all law changes after each legislative session.

Restraining Force #3: Unfair Quotas.

Resolution: The work standards or quotas have been reevaluated to determine if there are unfair quotas.

Bureau Chief of Uniform Traffic Citations has determined that the quotas are fair and all employees in the citation coding section are currently achieving standards.

Restraining Force #4: Back from Courts.

Resolution: If there are errors on the dispositions, we send them back to the Clerk of Court for correction. If the errors have not been corrected when the Clerk of Court returns them, we issue the disposition to the UTC Specialist to take to the court for correction. UTC Bureau Chief will have the UTC Specialist check the disposition to make sure proper correction was made by the Clerk of Court.

There are 67 Clerks of Court and only 4 UTC Specialists.

Restraining Force #5: Back from keypunch.

Resolution: (See the same resolution to Restraining Force #3 under Cause #4).

Restraining Force #6: Having to patch torn citations.

Resolution: When the corner is torn off of the ticket, it ruins the ticket number, which has to be keypunched.

The uniform tickets now have been changed and the number repositioned on the ticket so that it will be unnecessary to patch numbers back on torn citations in the future.

cc: Quality Resolution Team
    Quality Action Team

SECTION FOUR

Quality Service Improvement—Group IV

Driver Improvement Regions

Quality Resolution Team

Quality Review Team

Group IV—Quality Service Improvement
Driver Improvement Field

Cause #1—The Level of Morale Is Too Low

Restraining force

Driving forces

(1) False promises.
    (a) Promised pay grade
        increase, response "not
        this year" or "not in
        the budget."

(1) Do not make promises that
    you cannot keep.

(2) Upgrade the position as
    promised over two years ago.

(2) Frustration in not providing
the kind of service that can
be provided.

(1) Check causes 2 through 6 to
make changes.

(3) Lack of recognition.

(1) Need a strong voice in
    legislature for DL.

(2) Need recognition in other
    forms.
    (a) Certificates, bonds, pay
        incentives, etc.

(3) Revamp merit system.
    (a) Not based on ability,
        needs to be more
        equitable.

(4) Cause 2 through 6.

It was felt that any improvement in causes 2 through 6 would benefit the morale.

(5) Ineffective backing of employee by supv.
(a) Assumed guilty until proven innocent.

(1) More education for management on how to manage people in the 1990s.
(a) Humanize.
(b) Increase team work.

(6) Inappropriate pay level for position.

(1) Pay for the knowledge and experience that the job requires.
(a) Compare with other states.

Cause #2—The Level of Cooperation Between BFO/BDI Too Low

Restraining force

(1) Duties and responsibilities not clear between bureaus.
(a) Not working together.

(2) Feelings of animosity between bureaus.

Driving forces

(1) Clarify duties.

(2) BDI/BFO supervisors meet regularly.

(3) BDI/BFO attend each other's training meetings.

(1) More communication.

Cause #3—The Level of Communication Is Too Low

Restraining force

(1) Poor communication between coworkers.

(2) Lack of meetings between BFO & BDI.

Driving forces

(1) Inter-office meetings held regularly.

(1) In-service meetings mandatory, combining BFO/BDI.

(3) Communication between workers and mngt.
  (a) Management is slow to respond to suggestions.

(4) Poor communication between BFO & BDI.

(1) Management action and unsolved problems.

(2) Employees rate supervisor.

(1) See 2 and 3 and Cause 2 (poor cooperation).

Cause #4—The Level of Training Is Too Low

Restraining force

Driving forces

(1) Training not given before implementation of procedures.
  (a) Laws implemented before training received.

(1) Training prior to implementation.

(2) Not enough on-the-job training.

(1) Initiate an ongoing on-the-job training.

(2) Qualify trainers.

(3) Not enough qualified trainers.
  (a) "Over the head" instructions.

(1) Certify trainers.

(2) Have enough BDI specialists to train.

(4) Not enough cross-training.

(5) No follow-up review after training.

(1) Implement an intra-office training.

(1) Periodically review by supervisors.

Cause #5—The Level of Indifference Is Too High

Restraining force	Driving forces
(1) Poor attitudes and morale.	(1) Supervisor or chain of command should find out root of problem, keep "Confidential." (a) Because of fear, use an intermediary to relay problem.
(2) Think the boss does not care.	THIS WOULD AFFECT RESTRAINING FORCES 2, 3, AND 4.
(3) Unresolved personal problems.	(1) Promote communications between employee and employer.
(4) Boss covers self.	(a) Always be open (chain of command). (b) One-on-one resolution as soon as possible. (c) Human relation classes (utilize what they learn). (d) Knowledge of employee assistance program.
(5) Poor pay.	(1) Pay raises, incentives.
(6) Attitude of supervisor, how they treat people.	(1) Communication with supervisor. (a) If not satisfied, go through chain of command with discretion.
(7) No backing from the boss.	(1) Communications. (Employees are afraid to break the chain of command should they not receive a satisfactory answer.)

Cause #6—The Level of Uniformity Is Too Low

Restraining force	Driving forces
(1) Procedures vary from offices.	(1) Comply with examiner manual procedures.
(2) Priorities vary from office to office, supervisor to supervisor.	(1) Comply with examiner manual procedures. (a) Supervisors need to establish priority list for BDI personnel, such as, medicals, investigations, etc.
(3) Too much deviation from examiner manual. (a) Instructions from GHQ to field.	(1) Comply with existing manual requirements. (1) Present proposed forms to regionals, and work to standardize form statewide. (a) Example: medical release forms for doctor's signature.
(4) Locally initiated forms vary.	

TO: Director
            Division of Driver Licenses

FROM: Assistant Director
            Division of Driver Licenses

SUBJECT: Quality Resolution Team (QRT) Report for Group IV

The Quality Resolution Team for Group IV has thoroughly discussed all of the suggestions from Quality Action Team #IV for the improvement of the quality of service to the public from the Division of Driver Licenses.

Following are the resolutions:

CAUSE #1: LEVEL OF MORALE IS TOO LOW.

Restraining Force #1: False promises
                    a. Promised pay grade increase, response "not this year" or "not in the budget."

Resolution: The QRT recommends that *an attempt* be made to reclassify the Driver Improvement Investigators and Hearing Officers into the same pay grade and retitle that position "Driver Improvement Officer."

Resolution: Supervisors will communicate to all employees in a more effective manner and make sure that the employees are *not* promised reclassifications and pay raises.

Resolution: Supervisors will inform all employees that pay raises are negotiated between the AFSCME labor union and the Department of Administration (DOA). Our Department of Highway Safety and Motor Vehicles has *no control over raises*. This is done through negotiations and then the legislature has its say on the matter. We suggest you talk to your representative and let your voice be heard.

Restraining Force #2: Frustration in not providing the kind of service that can be provided.

Resolution: Please see resolutions to Causes #2–6 (following).

Restraining Force #3: Lack of recognition.

Resolution: All Bureau Chiefs will retrain all supervisors in the "One Minute Manager" training program and have supervisors look for the good that employees do.

Resolution: Supervisors will ensure that employees receive proper recognition and credit for a job well done.

Resolution: Supervisors shall instruct all employees on the entire program of the Merit System. Employees have a need to know.

Resolution: Supervisors will instruct all employees of DHSMV Management Policy #45 "Agency Awards Program" and how the awards are achieved.

Quoting from the policy, "The DHSMV Policy is to recognize through the establishment of the Agency Awards Program *all* members of this department (either individual or group) who perform in a manner which *exceeds* what is normally expected and make a significant, extraordinary contribution to the Department. It shall also be the policy of this agency to reward those individuals who make suggestions that are implemented through the issuance of a cash or honor award in accordance with Section 110.1245, Florida Statutes."

Following are the agency awards:

1. Executive Directors Award (awarded annually)
   This is a cash award of $500 and a plaque.

2. Deputy Executive Directors Award (awarded annually)
   This is a cash award of $200 and a certificate or plaque.

3. Division Directors Award (awarded annually)
   This is a cash award of $200 and a certificate or plaque.

4. Award for Special Achievement (awarded at any time)
   This is a cash award of up to $200 and a certificate.

5. Distinguished Achievement in EEO Award (awarded annually)
   This is an honor award of a plaque.

6. Public Service Award (awarded at any time)
   This is a cash award of up to $100 and a certificate or a pin.

7. Heroism Award (awarded at any time)
   This is a cash award of up to $100 and a certificate.

8. Individual Safety Award (awarded at any time)
   This is a cash award of up to $100 and a certificate.

9. Special Division Awards (granted quarterly)
   Division of Driver Licenses awards the "Golden Sun Award."

All employees of our Department are eligible to be nominated for all of these awards. Get your nominations in as soon as possible.

Restraining Force #4: All of the causes under #2–6.

Resolution: See all resolutions under causes #2–6.

Restraining Force #5: Ineffective backing of employees by supervisors.
   a. Assumed guilty until proven innocent.

Resolution: Supervisors need more management training on how to manage employees, how to motivate, and how to be a good leader.

Driver Improvement Training Manager will coordinate the management training as soon as possible.

Restraining Force #6: Inappropriate pay level for position (Driver Improvement Investigator).

Resolution: See Resolution #1.

Resolution: *Attempt* to establish a position of Driver License Specialist for each Driver Improvement field region.

CAUSE #2: LEVEL OF COOPERATION BETWEEN BUREAU OF
FIELD OPERATIONS AND BUREAU OF DRIVER
IMPROVEMENT IS TOO LOW.

Restraining Force #1: Duties and responsibilities not clear between bureaus.
a. Not working together.

Resolution: Begin conducting in-service training sessions as soon as possible, and include in the agenda the duties of examiners, investigators, and hearing officers. Be sure to keep all employees informed of latest changes in the jobs as they occur.

Resolution: Conduct supervisor meetings by combining BFO and BDI supervisors on a regular basis.

Resolution: Allow BDI—BFO employees to attend each other's training sessions.

Resolution: Cross-train employees in BDI/BFO. Allow and encourage BFO examiners to accompany BDI investigators and/or hearing officers in performance of their duties. Allow and encourage BDI employees to conduct driver license examinations and road tests. This will have an effect to join the two bureaus in a tighter bond.

Restraining Force #2: Feelings of animosity between bureaus.

Resolution: The resolutions under Restraining Force #1 will help cement our relationship with BFO/BDI.

Resolution: Each employee should be encouraged to establish better communications with each other and exhibit a willingness to assist one another on the job. The public will benefit as the quality of service improves.

CAUSE #3: LEVEL OF COMMUNICATION IS TOO LOW.

Restraining Force #1: Poor communication between coworkers.

Resolution: First-line supervisor to conduct regularly scheduled employee meetings at GHQ in Tallahassee. The bureaus are conducting 30-minute employee meetings each Monday morning. Due to the public lining up for service at the field offices at 7:00 A.M. in both BFO and BDI, we suggest bi-weekly employee meetings and monthly supervisor meetings.

Resolution: Invite BFO/BDI supervisors to each other's meetings.

Restraining Force #2: Lack of meetings between BFO/BDI.

Resolution: See resolution above. These meetings will increase communications between bureaus.

Restraining Force #3: Communications between workers and management.
a. Management is slow to respond to suggestions.

Resolution: The bi-weekly employee meeting that the first-line supervisor conducts will decrease the response time back to the employees on suggestions. These meetings will give employees an excellent forum for communications with their supervisor.

Restraining Force #4: Poor communication between Bureau of Field Operations and Bureau of Driver Improvement.

Resolution: Cross-train employees in each bureau. See Resolution #1 under Cause #2.

Resolution: Conduct bi-weekly employee meetings, conduct in-service training sessions and invite BFO/BDI employees—supervisors to attend. See Resolution #1 under Cause #2.

CAUSE #4: LEVEL OF TRAINING IS TOO LOW.

Restraining Force #1: Training not given before implementation of procedures.
a. Laws implemented before training received.

Resolution: The Bureau of Driver Improvement will establish in-service training in all field regions. Designated trainers will be instructed to assist with field training. These trainers will receive "Train the Trainer" instructions as soon as possible.

Restraining Force #2: Not enough on-the-job training.

Resolution: Same resolution as under Resolution #1 above. (Establish in-service training schedules in BDI as soon as possible.)

Restraining Force #3: Not enough qualified trainers.
a. "Over the head" instructors.

Resolution: Designated trainers will be selected in each field region within BDI and they will receive "Train the Trainer" instructions. (See Resolution #1 above.)

Restraining Force #4: Not enough cross-training.

Resolution: Establish cross-training in all areas of activities. (See Resolution #1 under Cause #2 above.)

Resolution: F.R. trainers will be available for field training sessions. Please have the training sessions large enough to make it cost effective for the trainer to go out from Tallahassee. These F.R. instructors are available *now* for your sessions.

Restraining Force #5: No follow-up review after training.

Resolution: Instruct all supervisors to review all training received.

CAUSE #5: LEVEL OF INDIFFERENCE IS TOO HIGH.

Restraining Force #1: Poor attitudes and morale.

Resolution: The previous resolutions to conduct monthly supervisors meetings, bi-weekly employee meetings, and in-service training programs for supervisors and employees will help to change attitudes and morale for the better.

Knowledge will help us do our job better. Quality service to the public will be the outcome.

Resolution: By communicating at these meetings, we can drive out the fear that might exist. When an employee is afraid of the job, afraid of a supervisor, or afraid of the unknown, quality service suffers. Employees should not be afraid to ask for additional instructions or to call attention to things that might interfere with quality service. We must all improve.

Dr. Deming says "Fear will disappear as management improves, and as employees develop confidence in management."

Restraining Forces #2: Employees think that the boss does not care.
   #3: Unresolved personal problems.
   #4: Boss covers himself.

Resolution: Earlier resolutions set up meetings with employees and first-line supervisors and in-service training for employees and supervisors. Also special management training programs will be conducted for supervisors. These resolutions will drive out all three of the above restraining forces.

The primary job of the supervisor is to lead and to help people to do their jobs better. Proper training will ensure that the supervisor is empathetic.

Resolution: Supervisors will inform all employees of the Department's Employee Assistance Program and help employees secure the help when needed.

Restraining Force #5: Poor Pay.

Resolution: See resolution under Cause #1.

Restraining Force #6: Attitude of supervisors, how they treat people.

Resolution: All supervisors in Driver Improvement will receive in-depth management training. This in-depth management training does emphasize human relations.

Restraining Force #7: No backing from the boss. Employees are *afraid* to break the chain of command should they not receive a satisfactory answer.

Resolution: Employees should not be afraid to express ideas, nor be afraid to ask questions of their supervisors. As stated previously, employees are encouraged to make suggestions.—*Management will listen.* Quoting from Dr. Deming again, "Fear takes a horrible toll. Fear is all around, robbing people of their pride, hurting them, robbing them of a chance to contribute to the company. It is unbelievable what happens when you unloose fear."

We must drive out fear from the Division of Driver Licenses.

We believe the regularly scheduled employee meetings will set the stage for better understanding between supervisor and employee.

CAUSE #6: LEVEL OF UNIFORMITY IS TOO LOW.

Restraining Forces #1: Procedures vary from offices.
        #2: Priorities vary from office to office, supervisor to supervisor.

Resolution: Employees will receive in-service training on the need to comply with established policies as outlined in the examiners manual and in the Driver Improvement Manual. It is important that uniform procedures be followed.

Resolution: Supervisor shall also receive in-service training on the need to comply with established procedures and priorities from GHQ.

Restraining Force #3: Too much deviation from examiner manual.
        a. Instructions from GHQ to the field.

Resolution: Bureau of Driver Improvement Regional Field Administrators will be instructed to run all offices as much alike as possible. Establish uniformity in all offices. Regional Administrators are encouraged to make suggestions for changes or revampments where needed.

Resolution: Bureau of Field Operation examining offices will be instructed to assist the public in Driver Improvement matters while they have them in their offices rather than refer the public to the Bureau of Driver Improvement office.

Quality service to the public is our watchword.

Resolution: In-service training for BFO examiners will include Bureau of Driver Improvement hearings, medical case information, suspensions, and revocations information. Likewise, Bureau of Driver Improvement employees will receive in-service training in examining duties. Armed with this knowledge, we can provide better service to the public. Training will begin as soon as possible.

Restraining Force #4: Locally initiated forms vary.

Resolution: All offices should present proposed forms to their regional offices and work to standardize forms statewide. This will begin April 1, 1989.

cc: Quality Resolution Team
    Quality Action Team

SECTION FIVE

Quality Service Improvement—Group V
Driver License Specialists

Quality Resolution Team

Quality Review Team

**Group V—Quality Service Improvement
DL Specialists—Field Operations**

Cause #1—The Level of Morale Is Too Low

Restraining force	Driving forces
(1) Structure problem.	
(a) No respect.	(a) Give encouragement (pat on back).
(b) No recognition.	(b) Good for supervisor to give recognition to boost morale.
(c) Suppressed workers.	(c) Give employee a chance to do something on his/her own.
(d) Low pay—examiners are a special classification, yet are classified and paid under clerical positions.	(d) More pay in job class. Longevity pay increases.
(e) Too many computer-related failures.	(e) Management action on computer problems.
(f) Lack of team work.	(f) Team effort toward becoming an effective unit.
(g) Lack of promotions.	(g) Reclassifications of positions.

(2) Chain of command.

   (a) Stops at regional.
   (b) Not effective.
   (c) Fail to communicate.
   (d) Fear of reprisal.

(3) Too much paperwork.

   (a) Too many reports due at one time.
   (b) Checklist (cover yourself).
   (c) Lack of uniformity between bureaus.

(4) Positions not being filled in a timely manner.
   (a) Not being advertised in a timely manner.
   (b) Positions not getting advertised as anticipated.
   (c) Difference between interview date and employment date needs to be closer.

(2) Higher management take action on each of the problems.

(3) Review first of month reports. Do we really need them all? What are they used for?
   (a) Stagger the reporting times.
   (b) Trust. Reduce checklist.
   (c) Share information between bureaus.

(4) Knowledge of proper procedures.

Cause #2—Level of Communication Is Too Low

Restraining force

(1) Lack of communication between Driver Improvement and Field Operations.

(2) Supervisor to work communication too low.

Driving forces

(1) Bureaus of Driver Improvement and Field Operations have joint meetings.

(2) Require more one-on-one meetings between supervisor and worker.

(3) Headquarters to regional and regional to supervisor communication too low.

(3) Include key people in regional meetings, i.e., examiners, DL specialist, DL supervisors.

(4) Outside of the structure.

(4) Need to be put inside the chain of command.

(5) Lack of coordination.
   (a) In training.

   (a) In-service training for supervisors.

   (b) Teamwork.

   (b) Chiefs/Assistant Chief need to make sure training procedures are adopted—need to enforce implementation. Need cooperation of *all* in accomplishing tasks.

   (c) Getting work to us.

   (c) Need changes sent in writing immediately to field personnel.

(6) Not being notified of redesign of computer changes.
   (a) Unable to give input to redesign.

   (a) Use worker input.

Cause #3—Level of Resistance to Change Is Too High

Restraining force

Driving forces

(1) Failure to adopt new procedures. Doing "one way" for years.
   (a) Supervisor gets in the way.

(a) Reinforcement from chain of command.

   (a) Chief's Assistant Chief needs to make sure training procedures are adopted; need to enforce implementation.

   (b) Supervisors (some regionals) not supportive of training.

   (b) Training needs to be made a priority.

(2) Lack of uniformity. Not willing to be flexible.

(2) In-service training for supervisors.
  (a) Give supervisors a refresher on information new employees receive.
  (b) Notify changes in writing before implementation.
  (c) Uniformity of procedures in field/GHQ.

Cause #4—Level of Continuous Training Is Too Low

Restraining force

Driving forces

(1) Not enough time for training.

(1) Upper management arrange time for training.
  (a) Management reinforcement.
  (b) Make training a priority.

(2) Lack of training for supervisor, regional, and DL specialist.

(2) Plan training needs and implement.
  (a) Specialists get together quarterly to exchange ideas and promote uniformity.
  (b) Have DL specialist plan some of training needs.
  (c) Alternate training person.

(3) Lack of tools; i.e., training module, portable TV monitors, updated training materials.

(3) Update equipment if needed.

(4) Lack of training classrooms. Current facilities are inadequate for training purposes.

(4) Allot funds for classroom— enlarge or recondition current facilities.
  (a) Set aside area of current facility to be used for training purposes.

(5) Not enough help to cover offices during training. Must pull people out to train.

(5) Utilize employees from other regions or other bureaus.

Cause #5—Level of Funds Is Too Low

Restraining force

(1) No voice in legislature.

   (a) Not enough legislative contact on local levels.
   (b) At what level must work load get before it's noticed?

(2) Lack of knowledge of how legislature and department work together.

(3) No knowledge of priorities of fund spending.
   (a) What is available?
   (b) How do we get it?
   (c) How are funds used?

(4) No knowledge of turnaround on obsolete equipment. How old must equipment be to get new?

Driving forces

(1) Need advanced knowledge of budget request by department. Share the knowledge.

(2) Share the knowledge.

(3) Share the knowledge.

(4) Share the knowledge.

Cause #6—Level of Firefighting Is Too High

Restraining force

(1) Poor planning.
   (a) Computer programming.
   (b) Implementation of changes.

Driving forces

(1) Proper planning.
   (a) Pretesting of equipment.
   (b) Headquarters needs to keep supply of forms and equipment on hand at all times.

(c) Untimely messages.

(c) Know the effects of change prior to implementation.

(2) Needs are not being prioritized.

(2) Prioritize needs. Training #1.

(3) Manpower is not used effectively.
(a) No alternates.

(3) Do not disrupt training.

(a) Use alternates for appropriate problem areas.

(4) Lack of alternatives.

(a) Must firefight.

(4) Whenever possible give choices.
(a) Know your options and alternatives.

TO: Director
            Division of Driver Licenses

FROM: Assistant Director
            Division of Driver Licenses

SUBJECT: Quality Resolution Team (QRT) Report for Group V

The Quality Resolution Team for Group V has thoroughly discussed all of the suggestions from Quality Action Team #V for the improvement of the quality of service to the public from the Division of Driver Licenses.
Following are the resolutions:

CAUSE #1: LEVEL OF MORALE IS TOO LOW.

Restraining Force #1: Structure problem.
            a. No respect.
            b. No recognition.

Resolution: DL Specialists are not in the chain of command and thus they are granted no respect or recognition from office supervisors or examiners. A request will be made to the Division Director to put the DL Specialist in the chain of command. This will give them authority to supervise, make management decisions, and be more effective to the Regional Administrator.

Resolution: The Regional Administrators as immediate supervisors for the DL Specialists shall begin giving commendations such as a pat on the back for a job well done when deserved. As effective managers, this needs to be done.

Restraining Force #1C: Suppressed worker.

Resolution: Conduct Quality Action Teams in all regions and apply the cause and effect, force field analysis technique on the problem. All Quality Action Teams to begin as soon as possible.

Resolution: The regularly scheduled meetings with the employees by the first-line supervisor will reduce the level of suppression to the workers. These employee meetings will give the employees the opportunity to express ideas, suggestions, and ask questions.

Restraining Force #1D: Low pay—Examiners are a special classification, yet are classified and paid under
clerical positions.

Resolution: *All Bureau Chiefs* will inform *all* supervisors to conduct
special informative sessions with their employees that
pay raises are negotiated between the AFSCME labor
union and the Department of Administration (DOA). Our
Department of Highway Safety and Motor Vehicles has
no control over raises. This is done through negotiations
and then the legislature has its say on the matter. We
suggest to all employees that you talk to your labor
union representative and let your voice be heard.

Resolution: The federal government has established eight (8) EEO
categories, and from these categories, the Department
of Administration places each job classification into one
of the categories. Driver license examiners have been
placed in group six (6) which is in the office and clerical
category. These eight categories are:

1. *Officials and Administrators:* Occupation in which employees set
   broad policies, exercise overall responsibility for execution of these
   policies, direct individual departments or special phases of the
   agency's operations, or provide specialized consultation on a
   regional, district or area basis. Includes: department heads, bureau
   chiefs, division chiefs, directors, deputy directors, controllers,
   examiners, wardens, superintendents, sheriffs, police and fire
   chiefs, inspectors, and kindred workers.

2. *Professionals:* Occupations which require specialized and theore-
   tical knowledge which is usually acquired through college training
   or through work experience and other training which provides
   comparable knowledge. Includes: personnel and labor relations
   workers, social workers, doctors, psychologists, registered nurses,
   economists, dietitians, lawyers, systems analysts, accountants,
   engineers, employment and vocational rehabilitation counselors,
   teachers or instructors, police and fire captains, lieutenants, and
   kindred workers.

3. *Technicians:* Occupations which require a combination of basic
   scientific or technical knowledge and manual skill which can be
   obtained through specialized post-secondary school education or
   through equivalent on-the-job training. Includes: computer programmers and operators, draftsmen, surveyors, licensed practical
   nurses, photographers, radio operators, technical illustrators,
   highway technicians, technicians (medical, dental, electronic,

physical sciences), assessors, inspectors, police and fire sergeants, and kindred workers.

4. *Protective Service Workers:* Occupations in which workers are entrusted with public safety, security and protection from destructive forces. Includes: police patrol officers, fire fighters, guards, deputy sheriffs, bailiffs, correctional officers, marshals, harbor patrol officers, and kindred workers.

5. *Para-Professionals:* Occupations in which workers perform some of the duties of a professional technician in a supportive role, which usually requires less formal training and/or experience normally required for professional or technical status. Such positions may fall within an identified "New Careers" concept. Includes: library assistants, research assistants, medical aides, child support workers, police auxiliary, welfare aides, recreation assistants, homemaker aids, home health aids, and kindred workers.

6. *Office and Clerical:* Occupations in which workers are responsible for internal and external communications, recording and retrieval of data and/or information and other paperwork required in an office. Includes: bookkeepers, messengers, office machine operators, clerk typists, stenographers, court transcribers, hearing reports statistical clerks, dispatchers, license distributors, payroll clerks, and kindred workers.

7. *Skilled Craft Workers:* Occupations in which workers perform jobs which require special manual skill and a thorough and comprehensive knowledge of the process involved in the work which is acquired through on-the-job training and experience or through apprenticeship or other formal training programs. Includes: mechanics, repair persons, electricians, heavy equipment operators, stationary engineers, skilled machining occupation, carpenters, compositors, typesetters, and kindred workers.

8. *Service and Maintenance:* Occupations in which workers perform duties which result in or contribute to the comfort, convenience, hygiene or safety of the general public or which contribute to the upkeep and care of building facilities or grounds of public property. Workers in this group may operate machinery. Includes: chauffeurs, laundry and dry cleaning operatives, truck drivers, bus drivers, garage laborers, custodial personnel, gardeners and groundskeepers, refuse collectors, and construction laborers.

Restraining Force #1E: Too many computer-related failures.

Resolution: The switch over of computer programs on February 13 was massive and devastating to say the least. The Data Center worked on the failures as rapidly as possible, and they have just about completed debugging the system. The big changeover to the driver license new design will begin in April-May. We have selected our driver license office at St. Petersburg South as the first office to be switched over. We will use that office as the training site for DL Specialists and supervisors to become familiar with the new field programs and to ensure there will be no failures in the programs.

We will expand the system from that office only when we are sure the system works, and then only turn on one driver license office at a time.

Restraining Force #1F: Lack of teamwork.

Resolution: The regularly scheduled supervisor and employee meetings will enhance teamwork. We believe that open communications will increase the level of morale, thus add to the team spirit in the office. The end result will improve the quality of service.

Restraining Force #1G: Lack of promotions.

Resolution: The Department of Highway Safety and Motor Vehicles is powerless to add positions to the list of open positions for promotions. The number of full-time employee positions is authorized by the legislature, and we do fill the vacant positions as soon as possible.

Restraining Force #2: Chain of command.
           a. Stops at the regional level.
           b. Not effective.
           c. Fail to communicate.

Resolution: See Resolution #1. Same applies here.

Resolution: The DL Specialists were selected and promoted to that position for their knowledge, skills, and ability. They know as much about the field driver license functions as anyone in driver licensing. They are the *experts!* They should be consulted by local DL supervisors for answers for problems of any type. Supervisors should be instructed to go through the DL Specialists for answers rather than call Tallahassee. This procedure will let the specialist know what the training needs are and where the lack of knowledge is.

Resolution: All Regional Administrators can communicate more effectively with their supervisors by taking minutes of the supervisor meetings and circulating the minutes. They will also send a copy of the minutes to the Bureau Chief and Assistant Bureau Chief.

Restraining Force #2D: Fear of reprisal.

Resolution: The Division Director of Driver Licenses *will not allow reprisals* within our division from any level of supervisors.

When an employee is afraid of the job, afraid of a supervisor, or afraid of the unknown, quality of service suffers.

Dr. Deming says in his book *Out of the Crisis,* "No one can put in his best performance unless he feels secure. Secure means without fear, not afraid to express ideas, not afraid to ask questions. Fear takes on many faces. A common denominator of fear in any form, anywhere, *is* loss from impaired performance and padded figures.

"Some actual expressions of fear follow:
"My boss believes in fear. How can he manage his people if they don't hold him in awe? Management is punitive.

"The system that I work in will not permit me to expand my ability.

"I'd like to understand better the reasons for some of the company's procedures, but I don't dare to ask about them.

"We mistrust the management. We can't believe their answers when we ask why we do it this way."

We must drive out fear within the Division of Driver Licenses.

Resolution: Our Division Director encourages all employees to communicate freely with their supervisors, to express ideas for changes, and give us your suggestions for improvement of the quality of service to the public. You are the experts and we need your input.

Restraining Force #3: Too much paperwork.
> a. Too many reports due at the same time.

Resolution: Bureau Chief will review *all* reports for need and their due date. He will try to stagger report due dates thus reduce the first of month work load.

> b. Checklist to cover yourself.

Resolution: Supervisors and employees through communication and cooperation will build a trust and thus reduce the need to maintain checklists to cover yourself. Trust is built on an individual basis and must be earned.

> c. Lack of uniformity between bureaus.

Resolution: Bureaus will conduct in-service training sessions to instruct employees on the DHSMV Management Policy Manual, and not only in Examiner Manual. Supervisors will train in all department procedures such as employee benefits, employee assistant program, vehicle use policy, wearing the uniform properly, etc. Bureau of Field Operations and Bureau of Driver Improvement will notify each other of pending meetings and extend invitations to each other to attend.

Restraining Force #4: Vacant positions not being filled in a timely manner.

Resolution: Supervisors will be retrained on how to conduct interviews and fill out interview modules. Modules must be accurately completed before an applicant can be selected.

Resolution: Regional Administrators will make requests of DHSMV personnel to advertise vacant positions in a timely manner.

Resolution: All bureaus will utilize the technique of *"anticipated vacancy"* and thus obtain an early advertisement on that position.

Restraining Force #5: Difference between interview date and employee date needs to be closer.

Resolution: Bureau Chief will work with Bureau Chief of Human Resource and Development (HRD) to speed up that time frame.

Resolution: Bureau Chief will check with personnel to request them to send each Regional Administrator a few extra "employee packets." This will enable the new employees to have this useful information as soon as possible. At present, the packets are coming in late and employees need as much time as possible to select insurance, health, dental, etc.

CAUSE #2: LEVEL OF COMMUNICATION TOO LOW.

Restraining Force #1: Lack of communication between Driver Improvement and Field Operations.

Resolution: Both bureaus will hold joint meetings of supervisors, employees and in-service training sessions. This will begin statewide immediately.

Restraining Force #2: Supervisor to worker communications too low.

Resolution: The Field Bureau will begin conducting monthly employee meetings immediately. These employee meetings will be conducted by office supervisors. Employees are encouraged to talk to their supervisors at these meetings to express ideas and ask questions.

Restraining Force #3: Headquarters to regional and regional to office supervisor communication too low.

Resolution: Include key people in regional meetings: DL Specialists, supervisors, and/or examiners will be invited and included in future statewide regional meetings.

Restraining Force #4: Structure of regional boundaries and territories is restrictive.

Resolution: All Regional Administrators will cooperate with each other to allow the drawing from each other's regions for assistance in training or examiners on the counter. This applies to BFO and BDI both.

Restraining Force #5: Lack of coordination.
               a. In training.
               b. In teamwork.
               c. In getting word to us.

Resolution: BFO to conduct in-service training programs for supervisors. They need training as much or more than the rest of the employees.

Resolution: Bureau Chief will establish the quarterly regional meetings as far in advance (yearly if possible) as possible. This will enable the DL Specialist to set up a solid training program schedule and agenda.

Resolution: Bureau Chief and Assistant Bureau Chiefs will insist that training schedules and agendas are established in *all* regions and enforce implementation of them. Reporting of training activities by DL Specialists will be required.

Resolution: The regularly scheduled supervisor and employee meetings will open up the lines of communications and help to get the word out to all people in the field.

Resolution: BFO will make a concerted effort to disseminate pertinent information in a more timely manner as employees need to get changes of policies and procedures as soon as possible.

Restraining Force #6: Not being notified of redesign of computer changes.
               a. Unable to give input to redesign.

Resolution: BFO will use worker input into the redesign training and dissemination of information.

Resolution: An information seminar will be conducted in Tallahassee the week of April 24 for all Regional Administrators and DL Specialists on the redesign program.

CAUSE #3: LEVEL OF RESISTANCE TO CHANGE IS TOO HIGH.

Restraining Force #1: Failure to adopt new procedures. Doing it "one way" for years.
  a. Supervisors get in the way. "I don't care what they taught you in training class or Tallahassee. You will do it *my way* in *my* office."
  b. Supervisors and some regionals are not supportive of training.

Resolution: All Bureau Chiefs *will* give training top priority. All Regional Administrators in BFO will give training top billing in all regions. Changing of attitudes and accepting changes begins with training and passing on information of policy changes and law changes. It is unbelievable that managers cannot see the tremendous value of training. Quality service depends on highly trained employees.

Resolution: DL Supervisors will make employees available for training.

Resolution: Training programs will be supported by all Regional Administrators. This is a *must.*

Restraining Force #2: Lack of uniformity. Not willing to be flexible.

Resolution: In-service training will be conducted for supervisors. The training agenda will include a refresher course on information that new employees receive.

Resolution: To establish uniformity, *all* changes will be noticed in writing before implementation.

Resolution: GHQ will attempt to establish uniformity of procedures statewide.

Resolution: It is evident that all supervisors do not carry the ball when examiners have been trained. They go back to doing things their own way and not use new knowledge gained in training sessions. Regional Administrators will monitor this situation and not allow it to happen.

CAUSE #4: LEVEL OF CONTINUOUS TRAINING IS TOO LOW.

Restraining Force #1: Not enough time for training.

Resolution: Training *is important.* Training will be given top priority in *all* regions. All Regional Administrators *will* support training.

Resolution: Assistant Bureau Chiefs *will* monitor monthly training reports as to consistency and regularity of training in each region.

Restraining Force #2: Lack of training for supervisors, regionals, and DL Specialists.

Resolution: In-service training programs will be conducted for supervisors.

Resolution: BFO will see that management training programs will be conducted for regionals and supervisors.

Resolution: BFO will conduct a special training school for DL Specialists to assist them in developing their skill in training.

Resolution: BFO will allow DL Specialists to conduct statewide meetings for the purpose of planning for future training programs.

Resolution: Regional Administrator will appoint an alternate training person in each region to assist in training.

Restraining Force #3: Lack of tools.
        a. Training modules.
        b. Portable TV monitors.
        c. No updated training materials.

Resolution: BFO will have the training manager begin developing more training modules.

Resolution: Considerations will be given to purchasing of more training equipment as the budget allows. BFO will set priorities on operating capital outlay items and request purchase of training equipment accordingly.

Restraining Force #4: Lack of training classrooms. Current facilities are inadequate for training purposes.

Resolution: Classroom space will be included in new leases as they become due in each region.

Restraining Force #5: Not enough help to cover offices during training.

Resolution: Utilize a task force of examiners to cover for examiners who are away from the counter while in training.

Resolution: BFO Chief allow other examiners from other regions to be pulled into neighboring regions to cover during training sessions.

CAUSE #5: LEVEL OF FUNDS IS TOO LOW.

Restraining Force #1: More effective voice in the legislature.
a. Not enough legislative contact on local level.

Resolution: Encourage employees to contact their local legislative delegation to explain the needs. Example—pay raises, staff, etc., and ask for their support.

Resolution: BFO will see that budget information for the division is handed out to Regional Administrators with specific instructions for them to pass on to office supervisors.

b. At what level must work load get before it's noticed?

Resolution: A monthly activity report is compiled each month for each office in the field and for each region. Regional Administrators will monitor the work load and reassign examiners according to work load.

Resolution: Extra positions for GHQ and the field are requested of the legislature each session to keep up with the growth of the population in the state.

Restraining Force #2: Lack of knowledge of how the legislature and the department work together.

Resolution: This information will be shared with employees in supervisors' meetings.

Resolution: Legislative information will be compiled and sent out to all regions.

Restraining Force #3: No knowledge of priorities of fund spending.
   a. What is available (funds)?
   b. How do we get it?
   c. How are funds used?

Resolution: The Division of Driver Licenses has 1,663 employees within the division which have been authorized by the legislature. These 1,663 employees are divided among all five (5) bureaus and the division director's staff.

Funds by category are for the following:

1. Salaries and benefits to pay 1,663 employees monthly salaries, retirement benefits, social security benefits, and insurance benefits. If a person is promoted, the additional salary comes out of this same fund. Upgrades and overtime work will come out of this fund also.

2. Other Personal Services (OPS) covers any contractual services such as janitorial and cleaning service for all of our field offices, special contracts for counseling services to the division, maintenance contracts for duplicating machines, and extra OPS people to help with the backlog of work, etc.

3. Expense funds pay for travel expenses of our employees who must travel as part of their duties. Paint jobs, renovation of offices, roof repairs, repairs to vehicles such as body work and paint jobs to the driver license vehicle fleet statewide and gas and oil to run these cars daily.

   Training materials such as books, forms, etc., and equipment that costs less than $200 and training of division employees comes out of this expense fund. One of the largest and most expensive items in this category is monthly rent for the 78 leased driver license offices statewide. Also, utilities for our offices are paid out of this one fund.

   Some other items that this expense fund covers are printing of our letter forms; suspension, revocation and FR suspension forms; all DL renewal forms; driver license handbooks, motorcycle handbooks, information brochures; printing of over 1,000,000 uniform citations for all police departments statewide; uniforms for 1,000 driver license examiners, and postage for mailing all revocation and suspension notices and for mailing of the thousands of renewal notices each month.

A division our size is expensive and it takes quite a bit of money to keep us operating.

4. Operating capital outlay covers the purchase of large pieces of equipment that we need to perform our duties, such as typewriters, printers, duplicating machines, vehicles, carpet, and any item that costs over $200. Remember that one car will probably cost $10,000, so this fund is watched very closely as it can be depleted very quickly. Training equipment that costs more than $200 per item would come out of the OCO fund.

5. Purchase of driver license funds are only spent to pay our present color photo contractor (NBS) 43 cents for each license issued. This covers film, laminates, cameras, developing of 35 mm film, and service from NBS to our 160 driver license offices statewide. We issued over three million licenses plus replacement licenses and duplicate licenses last year.

6. Data processing services fund is the driver license portion to support the department's data processing system. As you can see it is a large budget and one that must last the entire year.

7. Insurance information program was a one shot fund for this year to inform the public of the new financial responsibility reform act and new law that becomes effective this year.

There is a state law that prohibits us or any other state department to go into deficit spending. We must spread the total funding over the entire year and make sure that on June 30 we have paid all the salaries, benefits, rent, utilities, gas, oil, tires, and bought the right equipment for our driver license employees to get their job done in a proper manner.

We try to anticipate the budget spending to allow for emergencies that might arise and hold back enough money for that until the very last month or two of the fiscal year. For example, this year we have had two field offices flooded out, one major fire that destroyed an office and a couple of state vehicle crashes that totaled out the cars. These cars had to be replaced at $10,000 each.

We try to be as free with our appropriated funds as possible, but sometimes we must turn down a request for spending. However, as you look around, we do have excellent equipment to work with. One prime example is all of the new data processing equipment being installed now which will make our jobs easier.

The legislature each year grants the pay raises, if any, to all state employees and they then allocate enough salary money to cover that item in the budget.

The category items listed here must be spent for those items mentioned only, and we cannot spend money from the expense fund, for example, to buy cars, trucks, or typewriters. Budget categories are watched by the state comptroller office and they regulate that spending very strictly.

The suggestion to upgrade positions is a good one and we do have that right. We exercise that option only when the position warrants an upgrade. We as a division must abide by all of the Department of Administration rules and regulations governing that option. We cannot just do an upgrade at will.

We are powerless to upgrade all positions in the Division of Driver Licenses at the end of a budget year just because there is money left in the budget. That cannot be done.

We only purchase equipment for our employees to use or work with that has been requested by the supervisor and Bureau Chief, and we hope there is not any excessive equipment laying around not being utilized.

Resolution: Division of Driver License funds will be spent wisely and expeditiously.

Restraining Force #4: No knowledge of turnaround on obsolete equipment.
      a. How old must equipment be to get new?

Resolution: Regional Administrators have the complete information on disposing of surplus equipment. They will share this with all supervisors.

Resolution: Regional Administrators only need to request a purchase order to replace old worn-out equipment. If funds are available then new equipment will be purchased.

Resolution: Budget information will be shared with the Regional Administrators on a timely basis. They in turn will share this information with *all* supervisors.

CAUSE #6: LEVEL OF FIREFIGHTING IS TOO HIGH.

Restraining Force #1: Poor planning.
                    a. Poor computer planning.

Resolution: Planning is important to the division in achieving its missions. The Regional Administrators *all* have developed a five-year plan for each region. This plan is updated each year.

Resolution: GHQ will endeavor to notify field forces of pending changes as soon as possible. GHQ will give advanced notice with as much lead time as possible of changes.

Resolution: The new computer redesign will be tested thoroughly before it is implemented statewide. The South St. Petersburg Driver License Office will be used as the pretest site and as a classroom to train DL Specialists and supervisors on the new design.

Restraining Force #2: Needs are not being prioritized.

Resolution: The Regional Administrators, DL Specialists, and supervisors will work together in prioritizing regional needs. These work type meetings are a must.

Resolution: Training will be given a high priority in each region.

Restraining Force #3: Manpower is not used effectively.
                    a. No alternates.
                    b. Canceled training classes.

Resolution: Training classes will not be disrupted except in extreme emergencies. An alternate trainer will be appointed and utilized to fill in for the DL Specialist in each region.

Restraining Force #4: Lack of alternatives.

Resolution: Meetings between the Regional Administrators and DL Specialists are a must. Planning the strategies of work products for each region, for each office and even for each employee within the regions is a must. It falls on the shoulders of the Regional Administrators to implement a sound, well-rounded training program. Training programs need not only be in the area of the 80 hours for *new* employees but should include management classes for supervisors, and without a doubt, the seasoned examiners have to be included.

A well-planned training program that has been implemented to a fine tune will provide knowledge, skills, and abilities to our employees and thus produce quality service to the public.

cc: Quality Resolution Team V
    Quality Action Team V

SECTION SIX

Quality Service Improvement—Group VI

Driver License Specialists

Quality Resolution Team

Quality Review Team

Group VI—Quality Service Improvement
Field Operations Field

Cause #1—The Level of Communication Is Too Low.

Restraining force

(1) Unwillingness to communicate, i.e., office supervisor to employee.
  (a) Employees not given information on status of positions applied for, i.e., position re-advertised and no notice or reason is given to applicants. Afraid to communicate— job scared. Supervisors afraid to communicate with employees in fear that employees will know more than themselves or subordinates will promote over them.

Driving forces

(a) Inform the boss (i.e., Reg. Admin.) that subordinate not communicating.

(b) Make supervisor accountable for communication material (i.e., signoff sheet).

(2) Employees receiving conflicting information.
  (a) Receive conflicting information and different interpretations of information. This causes employees to follow different procedures and handle cases inconsistently from region to region, office to office and have insufficient knowledge of job.
  (b) Examiner's Manual receives changes in some areas of the manual but not every area that the subject to be changed is addressed.
  (c) Headquarters ambiguity.

  (a) Put qualified people in key positions.

  (b) Have qualified people conduct training.

(3) Constant unnecessary changes. There are many unnecessary changes in policies and/or procedures that cause confusion and disorganization.

  (a) Research the impact of change before change is made. Include field personnel in these change effects and have them review policy/procedure changes before implementation.

(4) Bulletins/TC messages don't get to employees.
  (a) Inconsistent distribution of bulletins, memos, messages.
  (b) No follow-up procedure to assure distribution.
  (c) Numbered messages.
  (d) Poor planning (timing).

  (a) Have a standard operating procedure for any communication materials, i.e., TC message, memos.

  Have 2: A = TC # message.
  B = # memo.

(5) Telephone system inadequate/outdated.

  (a) Upgrade phone system, i.e., caller push a number for a certain service (#2 for appointment).

(6) Information not sent out. Errors/omissions.
  (a) Some verbal information is received by some in the field reference a problem, but is not distributed statewide. Most of this type of information is received in general conversation.

  (a) Have experts proofread materials for understanding.
  (b) Appoint one person in each bureau to meet regularly to exchange and disseminate information.

(7) Little or no communication between bureaus.
  (a) Changes are not passed from one to another when they affect all in the field.
  (b) Time allotment problems with hiring procedures.

  (a) Appoint one person in each bureau to meet regularly to exchange and disseminate information.

Cause #2—The Level of Responsibility Is Too High

Restraining force

Driving forces

(1) Too much work and too little time.
  (a) Lack of direction.
  (b) Must try to accomplish task within 40 hours because DL Specialists are included class employees and cannot accumulate comp time; can't be paid for overtime because of availability of funds.

  (a) Give DL Specialist authority to delegate.

(2) Too much paperwork.
  (a) There are some meaningless reports that are done by some DL Specialists and not others.

  (a) Review reports and eliminate meaningless paperwork.

(b) Much of the paperwork from BFR in the field is redundant and could be streamlined.

(c) Redundant paperwork.

(3) Lack of manpower.

    (a) Speed up hiring process.

(a) This causes moral/stress problems and creates/promotes high turnover rate of employees.

(4) DL Specialist must be experts in all aspects of driver licensing.

    (a) Create new position, i.e., Asst. Regional Administrator or Training Officer.

(a) Must be able to fill in for regional administrator, supervisor, examiner, conduct training, computer work, supplies, maintain offices, i.e., plumbing repairs, air conditioning repairs.

    (b) Reevaluate DL Specialist position.

(b) Too many job standards on appraisals.

(c) Performance appraisals don't match job description.

(5) No real authority.

    (a) Put DL Specialist in chain of command.

(a) Can identify problems but can't do anything about them. Job responsibilities warrant authority.

(b) Lack of cooperation from some supervisors because they feel DL Specialists have no authority to request their assistance or cooperation.

Cause #3—The Level of Morale Is Too Low

Restraining force

Driving forces

(1) Bad attitude.
  (a) Poor supervision.
  (b) Insufficient equipment for training.
  (c) Bad working environment.
  (d) Rate of pay being too low.

  (a) Train supervisors and get positive feedback.
  (b) Use "One-Minute Manager" training.
  (c) Provide proper equipment/supplies.

(2) Overworked.
  (a) Too much responsibility.
  (b) Lack of manpower due to abundance of work.
  (c) Excessive absenteeism.
  (d) Too much work for positions; high volume of work.

  (a) Specialize job duties.
  (b) BDI handle suspensions.
  (c) More help/more offices.
  (d) Control absenteeism.

(3) Poor supervision.
  (a) Dead meat. Some employees not doing their share of work load.
  (b) Lack of training. This contributes to high turnover. Some offices say they have no time for training because offices too busy.
  (c) Supervisors not informed on what is happening in region/division.

  (a) Observe work counters and rewrite job descriptions.
  (b) Examine alternate methods of using manpower.
  (c) Get rid of dead meat employees.

(4) Lack of communication.
  (a) Bad attitudes.
  (b) Poor supervision.
  (c) Bad work environment.

  (a) Train supervisors.
  (b) Promote positive feedback.
  (c) Promote "One-Minute Manager" training.
  (d) Provide proper equipment/supplies.

(5) Poor work environment.
  (a) Old building needs improvement or remodeling. Doors falling off of some offices, etc.

  (a) Get new buildings or remodel old ones.

(6) Lack of training.
  (a) Lack of communication, i.e., promote training, explaining advantages of training, etc.
  (b) No classrooms, supplies.

  (a) Train supervisors.

Cause #4—The Level of Training Is Too Low

Restraining force

Driving forces

(1) Lack of time.
  (a) Too many to train caused by too many responsibilities.
  (b) Frequent changes of policies or procedures.

  (a) Allow more time for training.
  (b) Have a regional training officer.
  (c) Promote refresher training.

(2) Little or no training room.
  (a) Not a management priority.

  (a) Make this a management priority.

(3) Insufficient equipment.

  (a) Allow more money for training.

(4) Lack of uniformity.
  (a) At all levels causes many problems, causes confusion, i.e., DL-16 not taught to all examiners.
  (b) Regional Administrators/supervisors do not support training procedures.
  (c) Secretaries were trained on office automation system to meet GHQ needs not field needs.

  (a) Promote cross-training. Train examiners and clerks for all DL duties in office, i.e., DL16, monthly activity reports, out-of-state licenses. Train DL Specialists on leases, contracts.
  (b) In-depth training on office automation to all secretaries and DL Specialists.
  (c) Follow-up training on training received.

(5) Refresher training.
    (a) 12 hours of in-service
       training for examiners
       by supervisors not being
       kept up.
    (b) Regional Administrator/
       supervisors not getting
       refresher training.

(a) Have a regional training
    officer.

Cause #5—The Level of Quality Control Is Too Low

Restraining force

(1) Lack of uniformity.
    (a) Procedures done
       differently from region
       to region, office to office,
       examiner to examiner.
    (b) Lack of communication.
    (c) No follow-up to oversee
       and check for
       standardization from
       office to office.

(2) No one responsible for
    oversight of quality control.
    (a) No time to check offices
       for standardization.
    (b) No quality control for
       GHQ or GHQ over
       regions.

(3) No standards of quality.
    (a) No standard of quality
       for applicant processing;
       this causes high error
       ratio.
    (b) Not issuing a quality
       product.
    (d) Forms/letters are written
       illegibly and cannot be
       understood.

Driving forces

(a) Enforce mandated
    procedures.
(b) Create Assistant
    Regional Administrator
    position to follow up on
    quality.
(c) Have a GHQ position to
    monitor quality control.

(a) Create Assistant
    Regional Administrator
    position.

(a) Establish standard of
    quality and enforce it.
(b) Additional training.
(c) Follow-up for legibility of
    forms.
(d) Have supervisor spot-
    check quality of product.
(e) Quality control should
    be of higher priority—
    supervisor on up.

(4) Visitation to local office by Regional Administrators does not involve quality control.

(a) Regional Administrator visits should include concern for quality control.

Cause #6—The Level of Computer Problems Is Too High.

Restraining force

Driving forces

(1) Excessive downtime.
  (a) No advance notice when computer is going down.
  (b) Insufficient spare parts.
  (c) Low priority given to downtime.

(a) Make computer #1 priority when down.

(2) Insufficient equipment.
  (a) Unable to transfer equipment from office to office. Equipment sitting idle when could be used in other offices.

(a) Change procedures for transferring property where needed.

(3) Haphazard implementation of new programs.
  (a) Short notice on changes.
  (b) Not enough research of new programs, procedure changes, etc.

(a) Better planning; more research. Prevent short notice of changes.

(4) Lack of training on office automation system.

(a) Designate a person to train on the office automation system in field usage.

(b) Train secretaries and DL Specialists on how to use the OAS.

(5) Lack of communication.
  (a) Not sharing information on problems and solutions.

(a) Share information on problems and solutions.

(6) Supplier problems.
  (a) Excessive waiting time for technicians.

(a) Monitor/enforce contract.

TO: Director
             Division of Driver Licenses

FROM: Assistant Director
             Division of Driver Licenses

SUBJECT: Quality Resolution Team (QRT) Report for Group VI

   The Quality Resolution Team for Group VI has thoroughly discussed all of the suggestions from Quality Action Team #VI for the improvement of the quality of service to the public from the Division of Driver Licenses.
   Following are the resolutions:

CAUSE #1: LEVEL OF COMMUNICATION IS TOO LOW.

Restraining Force #1: Unwillingness to communicate; i.e., office supervisor to employee.

Resolution: Monthly employee meetings will be conducted at *all* driver license offices statewide. These meetings will be conducted by the local office supervisor. These meetings will begin immediately.

Resolution: Establish a team of examiners (task force) in each region to report to an assigned office to relieve the local examiners from their work stations in order for them to attend the monthly employee meetings.

Resolution: All supervisors will have *all* employees initial messages, policy changes, t.c. messages, etc., to verify they have read and understood.

Resolution: Secure permission from the Division Director to close every office down statewide for two hours per month at the same time, thus enabling the supervisors to conduct in-service training and employee meetings. Example: Every second Wednesday of each month, offices are closed from 7:00 A.M. until 9:00 A.M. for meetings, planning sessions, and in-service training. The offices would then open at 9:00 A.M. for public service.

a. Employees not given information on status of positions applied for; i.e., the vacant position is readvertised and no notice or reason is given to applicants.

Resolution: The Division Director *has* instituted a policy for all bureaus within the division to send a letter to all unsuccessful applicants advising them that someone else was selected for the position. The program is *now* in effect.

b. Afraid to communicate—job scared. Supervisors are afraid to communicate with employees in fear that employees will know more than themselves or subordinates will promote over them.

Resolution: The monthly employee meetings will overcome the fear that supervisor might have of communicating with employees. We must establish an open communications link throughout the entire division. In Dr. Edward Deming's book *Out of the Crisis,* he talks about this very topic "Fear!"

Quoting from him, "No one can put in his best performance unless he feels secure. Secure means without fear, not afraid to express ideas, not afraid to ask questions. Fear takes on many faces. A common denomination of fear in any form, anywhere, is loss from impaired performance and padded figures.

"There is widespread resistance of knowledge.—Pride may play a part in resistance to knowledge. New knowledge brought into the company might disclose some of our failings. A better outlook is of course to embrace new knowledge because it might help us to do a better job.

"Some actual expressions of fear follow:

"I could do my job better if I understood what happens next.

"I am afraid to put forth an idea. I'd be guilty of treason if I did.

"I am afraid that my next annual rating may not recommend me for a raise.

"I am afraid that I may not always have an answer when my boss asks something.

"I am afraid to contribute my best efforts to a partner or to a team because someone else, because of my contribution, may get a higher rating than I get.

"I am afraid to admit a mistake. My boss believes in fear. How can he manage his people if they don't hold him in awe? Management is punitive.

"The system that I work in will not permit me to expand my ability.

"I'd like to understand better the reasons for some of the company's procedures, but I don't dare to ask about them.

"We mistrust the management. We can't believe their answers when we ask why we do it this way. The management have a reason but tell us something else."

Resolution: We will drive out fear from the Division of Driver Licenses. Communication and training will help us to achieve the quality service we are striving for. We need highly trained employees within the division, thus the strong emphasis placed on training and for each bureau chief and regional administrator to demand a well-rounded training program.

Restraining Force #2: Employees receiving conflicting information.
a. Receive conflicting information and different interpretations of information. This causes employees to follow different procedures and handle cases inconsistently from region to region, office to office, and have insufficient knowledge of job.

Resolution: Uniformity in interpreting policies and procedures is very important and must be as close to uniform as possible statewide. Through several resolutions so far with in-service training programs, employee meetings, supervisor meetings, open communications meetings, and management training programs, we believe regions will become closer to uniformity than in the past.

Resolution: Regional Administrators, DL Specialists, and office supervisors should have *no fear* to ask questions to clear up any misunderstanding of information.

Resolution: The DL Specialists are the trainers for the region, and they will conduct training sessions when necessary. Their instructions and teachings of policies or of the material at hand will be enforced by the Regional Administrators.

Resolution: Effective immediately, each DL Specialist will have the full weight and support of the Regional Administrator behind them in their training and instructions throughout the region.

Resolution: The DL Specialists are expected to monitor procedural compliance and make corrections or recommendations as appropriate. In the event of disagreements between DL Specialists and examiners or office supervisors regarding procedural matters, the considered opinion of the DL Specialist shall prevail.

b. The *Examiner's Manual* receives changes in some areas of the manual but not every area that the subject to be changed is addressed.

Resolution: The *Examiner's Manual* is now in office automation, and an automatic index by topic will be included to ensure that all changes are corrected on all pages.

Resolution: A concerted effort will be made to correct all phases of the *Examiner's Manual* when a change is made. Please notify the Bureau of Field Operations when errors are located.

c. Headquarters ambiguity.

Resolution: If there is a question of a message, the DL Supervisor is to contact the DL Specialist or Regional Administrator for positive interpretation and clarification. GHQ encourages clarifying questions.

Restraining Force #3: Constant unnecessary changes. There are many unnecessary changes in policies and/or procedures that cause confusion and disorganization.

Resolution: The Bureau of Field Operations will research the impact of changes before change is made. Bureau Chief will include field personnel in the changes that affect that area and have them (the field) review proposed policy/ procedure changes prior to implementation.

Restraining Force #4: Bulletins/T.C. messages don't get to employees.
    a. Inconsistent distribution of bulletins, memos, and messages.
    b. No follow-up procedure to assure distribution.
    c. Numbered messages.
    d. Poor planning (timing of sending messages out)

Resolution: The Bureau of Field Operations *has* implemented a numbering system for statewide telecommunications messages and memos. This system was effective February 27, after the Quality Action Team report.

Resolution: Employees will begin to initial all messages to indicate they have received, read, and understand the message. This practice to begin immediately.

Resolution: Regional Administrators and DL Specialists will spot-check for latest messages received by examiners. The DL Specialists are expected to monitor procedural compliance and make corrections or recommendations as appropriate. Follow-up is a must to assure distribution of messages and implementation.

Resolution: GHQ will strive to have consistent distribution of bulletins, memos, and messages and make sure proper people have copies supplied. The above resolution also applies here. The Regional Administrator shall ensure that all supervisors and examiners receive appropriate copies of all messages.

Resolution: Many times there is not enough advance notice on changes for GHQ to give must lead time. We will give all due consideration on proper timing and allow as much lead time as possible prior to implementation of a new procedure.

Resolution: Messages that are sent out via T.C. on Friday are imperative in many cases as it would be Wednesday of the following week before *all* offices and examiners could be notified of impending changes. You must remember that express renewal offices are closed Sunday, Monday, and Tuesday.

Restraining Force #5: Telephone system inadequate and outdated.

Resolution: Recommendation to upgrade the phone system; i.e., caller key in certain number for specialized service, example: push #2 for appointments, etc. This has potential and is an ideal program. Funding must be secured from the legislature. The system will be included in our long-range plan.

Restraining Force #6: Information not sent out. Errors/omissions.
a. Some verbal information is received by some people in the field about a particular, but that information is not distributed statewide. Most of this time information is received in general conversation.

Resolution: When a Regional Administrator, DL Specialist, or office supervisor becomes aware of verbal instruction that has been picked up in a general conversation, the BFO chief encourages that person to check with their supervisor for verification and request a message of clarification be sent out for all offices to benefit of the information.

Resolution: Sometimes the type of information that is picked up via general conversation is wrong and not official. It needs to be verified and if it is valid then it needs to be distributed statewide.

Resolution: Messages of instruction, policies, and procedures will be proofread for understanding before being distributed to the field.

Restraining Force #7: Little or no communication between bureaus.
a. Changes are not passed from one bureau to another when they affect all in the field.

Resolution: All Bureau Chiefs are informed that their policy changes may affect other bureaus and their operation; therefore, all changes will be discussed with each of the other bureaus. This practice will begin immediately.

Resolution: Bureau Chiefs in all bureaus will be responsible to see that information is exchanged, discussed, and distributed to each of the other bureaus. Good cooperation and communications is a must.

CAUSE #2: LEVEL OF RESPONSIBILITY IS TOO HIGH.

Restraining Force #1: Too much work and too little time.
a. Lack of direction.
b. Must try to accomplish task within 40 hours because DL Specialists are included class employees and cannot accumulate comp time; can't be paid for overtime because of funding.

Resolution: The DL Specialists have the authority to delegate special work projects after communicating needs with their Regional Administrator and establishing priorities of job assignments.

Resolution: The Regional Administrator and DL Specialists will meet on a regular basis to communicate with each other their immediate work plans and long-range work plans and share with each other division activities. As immediate supervisors, the Regional Administrators will provide direction to the DL Specialists.

Restraining Force #2: Too much paperwork.
a. There are some meaningless reports that are done by some DL Specialists and not others.
b. Much of the paperwork regarding Bureau of Financial Responsibility in the field is redundant and could be streamlined.
c. Redundant paperwork.

Resolution: DL Specialists will discontinue summary evaluations of people coming off of probation. These were evaluation #1 and #2 of the probation employees on their weak areas.

Resolution: DL Specialists will make suggestions to their Regional Administrators to which forms can be combined into one form or as few as possible and eliminate all unused or unnecessary forms.

Resolution: Encourage employees to make suggestions on Bureau of Financial Responsibility paperwork that is unnecessary or redundant. The DL Specialists will collect the suggestions and transmit to Bureau of Field Operations along with their recommendations.

Resolution: The new computer DL Redesign will reduce paperwork and thus eliminate redundant paperwork.

Restraining Force #3: Lack of manpower.
　　　　　　　　　　a. This causes moral/stress problems and creates/promotes high turnover rate of employees.
　　　　　　　　　　b. Time allotment problems with hiring procedures.

Resolution: BFO Chief will contact DHSMV Bureau of Human Resource Management and Development (Personnel) and work out a system to allow us more time on personnel action deadline.

Resolution: Use the technique of "anticipated" vacancy on advertising of positions.

Resolution: BFO Chief will also work with DHSMV Bureau of Human Resource Management and Development to cut down on the time it takes to process paperwork through General Headquarters.

Resolution: Manpower allocation is made by the legislature each year. We have asked for additional employees again this year, and we will make every effort to convince the legislature of the pressing need for them.

Restraining Force #4: DL Specialists must be experts in all aspects of driver licensing.

a. Must be able to fill in for Regional Administrators, supervisors, examiners, conduct training, computer work, supplies, maintain offices; i.e., plumbing repairs, air conditioning repair.
b. Too many job standards on appraisals.
c. Performance appraisals don't match job description.

Resolution: Review the recommendation to create a position of Assistant Regional Administrator with the Division Director.

Resolution: Review the possibility of establishing a position of Training Officer in each region.

Resolution: Bureau Chief *has* appointed a task force to review the performance appraisals and description to ensure they match. Thus the DL Specialists will be evaluated fairly.

Restraining Force #5: No real authority.
a. Can identify problems but can't do anything about them. Job responsibilities warrant authority.
b. Lack of cooperation from some supervisors because they feel DL Specialists have no authority to request their assistance or cooperation.

Resolution: Request authority of the Division Director to put DL Specialists in the chain of command.

Resolution: Effective immediately, the DL Specialists will have the full weight and support of the Regional Administrators behind them in their training and instructions throughout the region.

CAUSE #3: LEVEL OF MORALE IS TOO LOW.

Restraining Force #1: Bad attitude.
a. Poor supervision.
b. Insufficient equipment for training.
c. Bad work environment.
d. Rate of pay too low.

Resolution: Conduct management training sessions for *all* bureaus.

Resolution: Request Regional Administrators to submit purchase order requests for training materials needed, and funds will be allocated on priority basis.

Resolution: Include a training room in the next leased office space that will come up in your region.

Resolution: The Division of Driver Licenses can do nothing about the rate of pay for employees. Pay raises are negotiated between the AFSCME labor union and the Department of Administration. Our department has no control over pay. This is done through negotiations and then the legislature has its say on the matter. We suggest you talk to your union representative and let your voice be heard.

Restraining Force #2: Overworked.
      a. Too much responsibility.
      b. Lack of manpower due to abundance of work.
      c. Excessive absenteeism.
      d. Too much work for positions; high volume of work.

Resolution: To reduce the overworked condition, we have requested ten (10) new offices, staffed by 70 examiners, in this year's budget which is now at the legislature for their consideration.

Resolution: We have also requested ten Examiners II's for our roving teams in the rural areas of Florida.

Resolution: To help control excessive absenteeism, all Bureau Chiefs have been instructed on the art of tracking an employee's absenteeism problem and how to administer disciplinary action.

Resolution: DL Specialists should show all employees the training film on excessive absenteeism. The supervisors should be in attendance at the training program to support the training action.

Restraining Force #3: Poor supervision.
      a. Dead meat. Some employees not doing their share of work load.

Resolution: All levels of supervisors are to emphasize to employees that simply because an employee has 15 or 20 years service with the Division of Driver Licenses, this does not give them the right to sit around and retire on the job. All levels of employees, from examiners up through supervisors, must work to get the job done and provide quality service to the public. Regional Administrators will see that the "dead meat" employees are counseled with and motivated to get the job done.

> b. Lack of training. This contributes to high turnover. Some offices say they have no time for training because offices are too busy.

Resolution: Training is most important to the Division of Driver Licenses! We need training of our employees, supervisors, and managers. We cannot just set someone down in front of a computer, vision machine, or typewriter and tell them to go to work and be sure to do a good job without proper training. Quality service depends on the skills of our employees. Training *will be supported* by all Regional Administrators and supervisors.

> c. Supervisors not informed on what is happening in region/division.

Resolution: All Regional Administrators will make more frequent office visits and use the time there to communicate with the office supervisor and employees. BFO Chief will supply each Regional Administrator with an itemized checklist that will be used on the office visits.

Resolution: Regional Administrators and office supervisors will observe the work counters and examiners on duty to ensure that quality service is being performed. Observation for adequate resources will also be made.

Resolution: The job description and evaluation of employees will be reviewed for possible revisions. There may be too many evaluation tasks to be evaluated on.

Resolution: BFO Chief will instruct all regionals to implement an "exchange" program of supervisors to visit and work in other driver license offices statewide. This will achieve excellent cross-training of supervisors.

Resolution: The Bureau of Field Operations will begin Quality Action Team and Quality Action Teams in all regions statewide. The Bureau of Driver Improvement shall also begin conducting QAT and QRT statewide.

Restraining Force #4: Lack of communication.
a. Bad attitudes.
b. Poor supervision.
c. Bad work environment.

Resolution: Training of supervisors in the proper techniques of supervision is a must. All bureaus within the Division of Driver Licenses will begin conducting supervisory training for all levels of supervisors.

The state university system in Florida should be contacted by each DL Specialist to secure instructors for supervisory classes and begin immediately conducting these classes. We have funds available for training fees, tuition fees, and textbooks.

Resolution: Training of supervisors will change their attitudes for the better and improve the quality of supervision. All supervisors shall be instructed in the "One-Minute Manager" technique also.

Resolution: The lack of communication will be driven out when regularly scheduled employee meetings are conducted. In a previous resolution, it was resolved to have the Bureau of Field Operations to schedule these employee meetings.

Meetings will also be conducted for supervisors. The communications link will open up to all in the division.

Resolution: Regional Administrators and office supervisors are hereby requested to send in a purchase order request for repairs, paint jobs, remodeling construction of offices, steam cleaning of offices (outside and carpet cleaning), landscaping, and any other to eliminate the bad or poor work environment that our employees work in.

There should not be any office out in the field statewide that is suffering from need of repairs. All requests will be given consideration. We want *all* driver license offices to be in top quality condition.

Resolution: The Regional Administrators will use the checklist that BFO Chief will be providing to them to inspect the buildings to assist in keeping the facilities in top shape. Office supervisors will assist in this endeavor by communicating with the Regional Administrators, and the employees will communicate with the office supervisor of *any* needs at that office.

There should never be any reason why employees must work in a bad environment or work with lack of equipment or supplies.

Restraining Force #5: Poor work environment.
   a. Old buildings need improvement or remodeling. Doors falling off of some offices, etc.

Resolution: Please see resolution above. We need to have the purchase order request coming in to correct deficiencies.

There is no excuse to have a driver license office in the above described condition.

Resolution: The DL Specialists will also be on the alert for needed repairs to offices and report needs to the Regional Administrators.

Restraining Force #6: Lack of training.
   a. Lack of communication, i.e., promote training, explaining advantages of training, etc.

Resolution: See resolution under Restraining Force #4 reference training—same applies here—supervisors, managers, and employees will be trained in all areas of their responsibilities.
   b. No classrooms—supplies.

Resolution: Classrooms will be included in the next new lease that comes up for bid in the region that needs one. DL Specialists will communicate training needs to the Regional Administrator.

Resolution: Training supplies will be furnished to trainers upon request for same. Send in your purchase order requests through the Regional Administrators.

CAUSE #4: LEVEL OF TRAINING IS TOO LOW.

Restraining Force #1: Lack of time.
    a. Too many to train caused by too many responsibilities.
    b. Frequent changes of policies or procedures.

Resolution: Regional Administrators and DL Specialists will allow more time in the work schedule to. train.

Resolution: DL Specialist training will be given top priority. Training is a must to help employees provide quality service.

Resolution: Regional Administrators to select an alternate training officer in each region to assist the DL Specialist on an as need basis.

Resolution: Regional Administrators will promote refresher training programs and reinforce the in-service training policy that is now in effect. This 12-hour in-service training requirement for all examiners is a must. BFO Chief will review training schedule to ensure this is being done.

Restraining Force #2: Little or no training room.
    a. Not a management priority.

Resolution: Training is a management priority. The Director of the Division of Driver Licenses has given his full support to quality training of all employees within this division. Employees who have not received quality training cannot provide quality service.

Restraining Force #3: Insufficient equipment.

Resolution: Training funds are included in our budget as expenses and OCO. Please submit purchase order requests for your needs.

Restraining Force #4: Lack of uniformity.
    a. At all levels, causes many problems, causes confusion, i.e., DL-16 not taught to all examiners.

Resolution: Promote cross-training in all regions statewide. Train examiners and clerks for all driver license duties in an office, i.e., how to complete the DL-16, monthly activity reports, and out-of-state license reports. Train DL

Specialists on leases and contracts. Cross training will begin immediately in all regions.

Resolution: GHQ to select a trainer to train in office automation and set up classes for all division secretaries as soon as possible.

Note: A trainer has been selected to train in office automation at the Neil Kirkman Building. The office automation training will begin on May 10.

Resolution: The Regional Administrator's secretaries will train the DL Specialists in office automation use, and the Regional Administrators' secretaries will also supply the needed secretarial support to the DL Specialists.

"Teamwork will work."

b. Regional Administrators and office supervisors do not support training procedures.

Resolution: Previous resolutions have addressed this problem, and there should be no doubt in anyone's mind that training is a must. Bureau Chief will impart to all Regional Administrators and supervisors the importance of training. Training will be supported.

c. Secretaries were trained on office automation system to meet GHQ needs—not field needs.

Resolution: Office automation training at GHQ will begin on May 10, 1989. All GHQ secretaries and field secretaries will be trained. During this training, we expect all training needs of the secretaries to be expressed and covered.

Restraining Force #5: Refresher training.
a. Twelve hours of in-service training for examiners by supervisors not being kept up.

Resolution: Regional Administrators statewide will reinforce the Bureau of Field Operation's policy of "Each DL Examiner shall complete 12 hours of in-service training each year. This training will be conducted by the office supervisors. The Bureau of Field Operations staff in Tallahassee will monitor the training and require it to be accomplished.

b. Regional Administrator/supervisors not getting refresher training.

Resolution: The Regional Administrators and office supervisors will be required to attend the management training courses of "Basic Principles of Supervisory Management" and the "One-Minute Management" courses. The DL Specialists will schedule these courses as soon as possible.

CAUSE #5: LEVEL OF QUALITY CONTROL IS TOO LOW.

Restraining Force #1: Lack of uniformity.
   a. Procedures done differently from region to region, office to office, and examiner to examiner.

Resolution: The Regional Administrators will enforce Bureau of Field Operations and Division of Driver License policies to the letter. We need to be uniform in all regions and offices statewide.

Resolution: The DL Specialists will assist the Regional Administrator in seeing that the entire region is operating uniformly according to statewide policy. This will include wearing of the uniforms, completion of DL-16's, DL-34 forms, etc.

The Regional Administrators and DL Specialists will use the checklist that BFO Chief is to develop in assisting them with seeing that all offices are operated uniformly.

Resolution: The previous resolution reference cross-training of supervisors will also assist in seeing that a uniform operation is instituted.

b. Lack of communication.

Resolution: The previous resolutions calling for regularly scheduled supervisor and employee meetings will enhance the level of communications and uniform operation.

   c. No follow-up to oversee and check for standardization from office to office.
   d. No quality control for GHQ or GHQ over region.

Resolution: The Division Director will be requested to take into consideration the creation of a position of Assistant Regional Administrator to assist in monitoring quality control and help with administrative duties. This position would also assist Regional Administrators in uniform operation of that region.

Resolution: The Division of Driver Licenses added a new position on April 1, of Management Review Specialist that will also assist in monitoring driver license policies statewide.

Resolution: Bureau Chief will reemphasize the Assistant Chiefs to also monitor division policies and procedures for quality and uniformity.

Restraining Force #3: No standard of quality.
  a. No standard of quality for applicant processing. This causes high error ratio.
  b. Not issuing a quality product.
  c. Forms/letters are written illegibly and cannot be understood.

Resolution: Our division trainers will instruct all employees that our standard of quality is 100 percent *error-free* work. The emphasis will be placed on quality instead of quantity. No standard that allows any errors could be considered as acceptable by the division. We must strive for quality service. All future training will emphasize error-free product.

Resolution: Each office supervisor will spotcheck examiner's work product for quality.

Restraining Force #4: Visitation to local office by Regional Administrator does not involve quality control.

Resolution: Regional Administrators' visits to field offices shall include spotchecks for quality of product, i.e., photo on license issued, DL-16, DL-34 reports, etc.

The checklist that BFO Chief will develop and provide shall require quality of product observations.

CAUSE #6: LEVEL OF COMPUTER PROBLEMS IS TOO HIGH.

Restraining Force #1: Excessive downtime.
     a. No advance notice when computer is going down.
     b. Insufficient spare parts.
     c. Low priority given to downtime.

Resolution: GHQ has made the computer and/or the lack of computer service a top priority since the big changeover began.

Our Division Director has been personally involved with troubleshooting the computer problems by requiring a daily report from BFO Chief's office of the problems experienced in *all* of the field offices. This report is compiled daily and given to Division Director from the telephone calls received from the field offices. The trouble spots are then reviewed with Division Director of Administrative Services in order that prompt corrections are made.

Resolution: The Division of Driver Licenses is the largest customer of the Data Center, and we do demand quality work from them. We will not relent until all the problems on the new system have been corrected.

Restraining Force #2: Insufficient equipment.
     a. Unable to transfer computer equipment from office to office. Equipment sitting idle when it could be used in other offices.

Resolution: Transfer of computer equipment *is* allowed. The Regional Administrators have the knowledge to accomplish this transfer of property, and if they are unsure of how to do the transfer, assistance from Assistant Bureau Chiefs is available. It is an excellent idea to reassign excess equipment and thus get maximum use from our resources.

Restraining Force #3: Haphazard implementation of new programs.
     a. Short notice on changes.
     b. Not enough research of new programs, procedure changes, etc.

Resolution: The driver license office located in South St. Petersburg has been designated as the first office to be converted to the new computer DL design. This will begin July 1.

That office will be used as the test site for all the new programs. We will make sure that all of the bugs are worked out prior to switching over any other offices.

We will progress *slowly* throughout the state from office to office making sure that all systems and programs are running smoothly. We expect it may take six months or more to turn the entire state over to the new system. Every effort will be made to have a 100 percent flawless system when our examiners begin working with it.

Resolution: BFO Chief will make every effort to have his staff up to speed on the new design. Assistant Bureau Chief and her staff have been working with the Data Center for approximately two years plus on the new design planning and researching every conceivable need of Division of Driver Licenses to have included in the programs.

Regional Administrators and DL Specialists will be supplied with adequate information and briefings as the countdown progresses.

We resolve not to spring surprises on the field, but if a problem pops up, corrective action must be taken as soon as possible.

Restraining Force #4: Lack of training on office automation.

Resolution: The Division Director's staff will begin conducting office automation training for Division of Driver Licenses secretaries on May 10 in Tallahassee.

We anticipate the office automation training will also include DL Specialists when time permits.

Restraining Force #5: Lack of communication with the Data Center.
   a. Not sharing information on problems and
      solutions.

Resolution: Bureau Chief will assign Assistant Chief and DL Specialist the task of updating and compiling computer trouble calls from the field into the Data Center and passing this information out to all field offices.

This trouble report will be done on a timely basis. We do need to share computer problems and solutions statewide.

Restraining Force #6: Supplier Problems.
 a. Excessive waiting time for technicians.

Resolution: When field offices experience this type of problem with supplier, the field office supervisors should notify Bureau of Field Operations Assistant Chief or DL Specialist of the problem. One or the other will include the problem in their daily transfer to the Division Director, for disposition.

Division Director will make every effort to see that the supplier fulfills their end of the contract.

We demand quality service from them.

This concludes the final report from the Quality Resolution Teams of the original six (6) Quality Action Teams as facilitated by Mr. Don Stratton in his program *An Approach to Quality Improvement that Works.*

This has been a very rewarding experience for me and our staff. I'm sure that these six action teams are just the beginning of many more that will follow.

Our major objective with this program is quality service improvement, and we have met that objective with these first six team efforts.

cc: Quality Action Team VI
 Quality Resolution Team VI

REFERENCES

1. Peters, Tom. *Thriving on Chaos.* New York; Alfred A. Knopf, 1987, p. 286.

2. Deming, W. Edwards. *Out of the Crisis.* Massachusetts Institute of Technology, 1982, p. 310.

3. Ishikawa, Kaoru. *Guide to Quality Control.* Tokyo: Asian Productivity Organization, 1983, pp. 18–26.

4. Lewin, Kurt. *Field Theory and Social Science.* Ed. D. Cartwright. Westport, Conn: Greenwood Press, 1975, p. 3.

5. NBC White Paper—If Japan Can—Why Can't We? 1980.

6. The Deming Library of Tapes. Films, Inc., 1987. CC-M Productions.

7. MacCoby, Michael. *The Leader.* New York: Simon and Schuster, 1981, p. 52.

8. Peters, Tom and Robert H. Waterman, Jr. *In Search of Excellence.* New York: Harper and Row, 1982, p. 1.

9. Naisbitt, John and Patricia Aburdene. *Re-Inventing the Corporation.* New York: Warner Books, 1985, p. 2.

10. Scherkenbach, William W. *The Deming Route to Quality and Productivity.* Washington, DC: CEE Press, ASQC Quality Press, 1986, pp. 100–101.

11. Imai, Masaaki. *Kaizen: The Key to Japan's Competitive Success.* New York: Random House Business Division, 1986, p. 18.

12. McGregor, Douglas. *The Human Side of Enterprise.* New York: McGraw-Hill Book Co., Inc., 1960, pp. 33–34.

13. Bradford, Leland P. *Making Meetings Work: A Guide for Leaders and Group Members.* LaJolla, Calif.: University Associate, 1976, pp. 42–50.

14. Juran, J.M. "The Quality Trilogy." *Quality Progress* 19, No. 8 (August 1986): pp. 19–24.

15. Houghton, James R. "A Message from the Chair of National Quality Month." *Quality Progress* 20, No. 10 (October 1987): p. 19.

16. *Road Map for Change/The Deming Approach.* Encyclopaedia Brittanica Educational Corporation of Chicago, Part I, 1984.

17. The Deming Series of Lectures. Sponsored by Western Electric Company Merrimac Valley Works. Cape Cod, October 1983.

INDEX